NEW Close-up English in Use

B2

David McKeegan

Additional material: Helen Kidd

NATIONAL GEOGRAPHIC
LEARNING

Australia • Brazil • Canada • Mexico • Singapore • United Kingdom • United States

Contents

Unit	Grammar	Vocabulary and Use of English
13 pages 90–95	the passive	phrasal verbs; prepositions; collocations and expressions; words easily confused; word formation; sentence transformation
14 pages 96–100	causatives	phrasal verbs; prepositions; collocations and expressions; words easily confused; word formation; sentence transformation
15 pages 101–106	conditionals	phrasal verbs; prepositions; collocations and expressions; words easily confused; word formation; sentence transformation
16 pages 107–111	mixed conditionals; conditionals without *if*	phrasal verbs; prepositions; collocations and expressions; words easily confused; word formation; sentence transformation
Review 4 pages 112–116	B2 Practice: First (Parts 1–4) B2 Practice: ECCE (Grammar and Vocabulary)	
17 pages 117–121	relative clauses	phrasal verbs; prepositions; collocations and expressions; words easily confused; word formation; sentence transformation
18 pages 122–126	reduced relative clauses; participle clauses	phrasal verbs; prepositions; collocations and expressions; words easily confused; word formation; sentence transformation
19 pages 127–133	reported speech	phrasal verbs; prepositions; collocations and expressions; words easily confused; word formation; sentence transformation
20 pages 134–138	reporting verbs	phrasal verbs; prepositions; collocations and expressions; words easily confused; word formation; sentence transformation
Review 5 pages 139–143	B2 Practice: First (Parts 1–4) B2 Practice: ECCE (Grammar and Vocabulary)	
21 pages 144–149	comparative and superlative structures; *so, such, too, enough*	phrasal verbs; prepositions; collocations and expressions; words easily confused; word formation; sentence transformation
22 pages 150–155	gradable and ungradable adjectives; adjectives and adverbs	phrasal verbs; prepositions; collocations and expressions; words easily confused; word formation; sentence transformation
23 pages 156–161	wishes; other ways of talking about unreal situations	phrasal verbs; prepositions; collocations and expressions; words easily confused; word formation; sentence transformation
24 pages 162–166	negative inversion	phrasal verbs; prepositions; collocations and expressions; words easily confused; word formation; sentence transformation
Review 6 pages 167–171	B2 Practice: First (Parts 1–4) B2 Practice: ECCE (Grammar and Vocabulary)	

Unit 1

Awareness

1 **Which of these sentences are correct (C) and incorrect (I)?**

1 Are you knowing my friend Sam? _I_
2 Sally loves reading bestsellers. _C_
3 I'm thinking about going to university. _C_
4 You're seeming unhappy. What's wrong? _I_
5 We live in the countryside. _C_

6 I'm not understanding this documentary. _I_
7 What do you think about at the moment? _I_
8 The train leaves at 9.20. _C_
9 The teacher is always shouting at us. _C_
10 Oh dear! It rains very heavily now. _I_

How many did you get right? ☐

Grammar

Present simple

Affirmative	Negative	Questions
I / We / You / They **work**. He / She / It **works**.	I / We / You / They **don't** work. He / She / It **doesn't** work.	**Do** I / we / you / they **work**? **Does** he / she / it **work**?
Short answers		
Yes, I / we / you / they **do**. **Yes**, he / she / it **does**.	**No**, I / we / you / they **don't**. **No**, he / she / it **doesn't**.	

We use the present simple for:

• facts or general truths.
*The sun **sets** in the west.*

• routines or habits (often with adverbs of frequency).
*Charlotte **rides** her bike to school every day.*

• permanent states.
*Her family **lives** in Germany.*

• timetabled events in the future.
*The train to London **leaves** at 10.30 on Sunday.*

• narratives (a story, a joke, a plot, sports commentaries, etc.).
*Two men **walk** into a restaurant ...*

Note

Some common time expressions that are often used with the present simple are:
every day / week / month / summer, every other day, once a week, twice a month, at the weekend, in January, in the morning / afternoon / evening, at night, on Tuesdays, on Friday mornings, etc.
*John **goes** to the gym **twice a week**.*

Remember

We often use adverbs of frequency with the present simple. They tell us how often something happens. They come before the main verb, but after the verb *be*.
*My basketball team **rarely loses**.*
*Janet **is often** late for her music lessons.*

Some common adverbs of frequency are: *always, usually, often, sometimes, rarely / hardly ever / seldom, never.*

Present continuous

Affirmative	Negative	Questions
I **am ('m)** work**ing**. He / She / It **is ('s)** work**ing**. We / You / They **are ('re)** work**ing**.	I **am ('m) not** work**ing**. He / She / It **is not (isn't)** work**ing**. We / You / They **are not (aren't)** work**ing**.	**Am** I work**ing**? **Is** he / she / it work**ing**? **Are** we / you / they work**ing**?
Short answers		
Yes, I **am**. **Yes**, he / she / it **is**. **Yes**, we / you / they **are**.	**No**, I**'m not**. **No**, he / she / it **isn't**. **No**, we / you / they **aren't**.	

Spelling: ride → rid**ing**, travel → trave**lling**, study → study**ing**

We use the present continuous for:

- actions that are in progress at the time of speaking.
Irene is playing football at the moment.
- actions that are in progress around the time of speaking, but not right now.
I'm looking for a new house.
- situations that are temporary.
The kids are staying with their uncle until Saturday.
- an annoying habit (often with *always, continually, constantly* and *forever*).
Our maths teacher is always forgetting to mark our homework.
- what is happening in a picture.
Two boys are climbing a tree.
- plans and arrangements for the future.
I'm going to the bank this afternoon.
- situations that are changing or developing in the present.
Computers are getting faster and faster.

> **Note**
>
> Some common time expressions that are often used with the present continuous are: *at the moment, now, for the time being, this morning / afternoon / evening / week / month / year, today,* etc.
> *Tonya is having a bath at the moment.*

Stative verbs

Some verbs are not usually used in continuous tenses. They are called *stative verbs* because they describe states and not actions. The most common are:

- verbs of emotion: *hate, like, love, need, prefer, want.*
I don't like greedy people.
- verbs of senses: *feel, hear, see, smell, sound, taste.*
You sound upset, Kevin.
- verbs which express a state of mind: *believe, doubt, forget, imagine, know, remember, seem, suppose, think, understand.*
I don't understand Spanish.
- verbs of possession: *belong to, have, own, possess.*
Simon owns three laptops.
- other verbs: *be, consist, contain, cost, include, mean.*
Does the price of the room include breakfast?

Some verbs can be both stative verbs and action verbs, but with a different meaning. The most common are:

be	*Michael is very kind to his baby sister.* (usual behaviour) *The children are being very well-behaved.* (at the moment; not their normal behaviour)
expect	*I expect you want to eat now.* (expect = think or believe) *We're expecting a delivery this morning.* (expect = wait for)
have	*Imogen has a lot of clothes.* (have = own / possess) *I'm having trouble with my maths homework.* (have = experience)
look	*You look happy. What happened?* (look = seem) *I'm looking for my glasses.* (look = search)
taste	*This coffee tastes strange!* (taste = have a particular flavour) *I'm tasting the sauce in case it needs more sugar.* (taste = test the flavour)
think	*Do you think this is a good film?* (think = have an opinion) *Mary is thinking of changing jobs.* (think = consider)
see	*I'm sorry, but I don't see the point of this.* (see = understand) *We're seeing Charlie on Thursday.* (see = meet)
smell	*Mmm! Dinner smells great!* (smell = have a particular smell) *I'm smelling the meat because I think it is old.* (smell = action of smelling)
weigh	*I weigh 90 kilos.* (weigh = have a particular weight) *I'm weighing myself in the bathroom.* (weigh = measure the weight)

1

Grammar exercises

2 Choose the correct option to complete the sentences.

1 He *tastes* / is tasting the soup at the moment to see if it needs more salt.

2 They *are visiting* / visit their grandparents every Sunday.

3 What do you think / *are you thinking* the best way to overcome stress is?

4 Please be quiet. I am trying / *try* to concentrate.

5 I can't come with you to the exhibition because I am seeing / *see* an old friend.

6 He is thinking / *thinks* of buying a house in the country.

7 This perfume smells / *is smelling* awful.

8 Jack always *is wearing* / wears a helmet when he rides.

9 That isn't true. I *am not believing* / don't believe it.

10 Martha *stays* / is staying with Julia for the time being.

3 Complete the sentences with the present simple or present continuous form of the verbs.

1 Mrs Owen _____*receives*_____ (receive) a letter from her son every month. He _____*'s studying*_____ (study) abroad and _____*never forgets*_____ (never / forget) to write to her.

2 When people _____*talk*_____ (talk) loudly on the phone, I _____*feel*_____ (feel) annoyed.

3 Sam _____*finds*_____ (find) it difficult to remember new words after studying them. He _____*doesn't seem*_____ (not / seem) to be able to learn them.

4 She _____*'s watching*_____ (watch) TV at the moment. She _____*watches*_____ (watch) TV every night to relax before she _____*goes*_____ (go) to bed.

5 Kate can't come to the phone because she _____*'s washing*_____ (wash) her hair. She _____*washes*_____ (wash) her hair every day.

6 _____*Do you always lock*_____ (you / always / lock) your windows before you leave?

7 Look! It _____*'s snowing*_____ (snow). It _____*rarely snows*_____ (rarely / snow) at this time of year.

8 Dan _____*is seeing*_____ (see) a doctor about his headaches tomorrow morning.

4 Complete the questions with the present simple or present continuous.

1 **A:** Where _____*do you usually go at the weekend*_____ ?
   B: I usually go to the recording studio at the weekend.

2 **A:** What time _____*do you go to the gym (every day)*_____ ?
   B: I go to the gym at five o'clock every day.

3 **A:** Where _____*does your sister work*_____ ?
   B: My sister works in London.

4 **A:** What _____*are you doing*_____ on Saturday night?
   B: I'm attending a lecture on climate change.

5 **A:** _____*Are you coming*_____ with us to the party on Sunday?
   B: No, I'm not. I think I will stay at home.

6 **A:** Why _____*are you wearing*_____ that woolly hat?
   B: It was a present from my aunt, and I'm meeting her in five minutes.

7 **A:** _____*Do you always wear*_____ a heavy coat?
   B: No, I don't. I only wear a heavy coat when it is cold outside.

8 **A:** What _____*are you doing*_____ right now?
   B: I'm rewriting my history essay.

5 Rewrite the sentences using the question form. Then complete the short answers.

1 My parents eat out during the week.
A: *Do your parents eat out during the week* ?
B: No, *they don't* .

2 We are going to a concert today.
A: *Are you going to a concert today* ?
B: No, *we aren't* .

3 Sue is sitting her exams in June.
A: *Is Sue sitting her exams in June* ?
B: Yes, *she is* .

4 It snows in the Sahara Desert.
A: *Does it snow in the Sahara Desert* ?
B: No, *it doesn't* .

5 Paul likes chocolate pancakes.
A: *Does Paul like chocolate pancakes* ?
B: Yes, *he does* .

6 She comes home from work at 7 p.m.
A: *Does she come home from work at 7 p.m.* ?
B: No, *she doesn't* .

6 Correct the sentences where necessary. Tick those which do not need correcting.

1 Does Emily cycles to work every day?
Does Emily cycle to work every day?

2 My father always telling us not to eat junk food.
My father is always telling us not to eat junk food.

3 What time do the last train leave?
What time does the last train leave?

4 She is seeing the dentist at 4 p.m. today.
✓

5 Nobody thinks that John will pass the exam.
✓

6 My brother don't have a job right now.
My brother doesn't have a job right now.

7 My friend isn't liking her new running shoes.
My friend doesn't like her new running shoes.

8 Maria thinks of doing a bungee jump.
Maria is thinking of doing a bungee jump.

7 Complete the sentences with one word in each gap.

1 Why *are* you always borrowing my laptop?
2 We *are* going to the baseball game next week.
3 Kick off for the match *is* at 12.30.
4 My little brother *is* getting taller every month.
5 I'm *not* leaving until this problem is solved.
6 *Is* that boy laughing or crying?
7 *Do* you appreciate how hard I have been working?
8 That *does* not surprise me at all!

1

Vocabulary

8 Match the phrasal verbs (1–8) with their meanings (a–h).

1 cheer up / cheer (somebody) up   `f`   **a** make someone sad

2 chill out   `c`   **b** stop liking

3 fall out   `g`   **c** relax

4 get (somebody) down   `a`   **d** be friendly with someone

5 go off (something / somebody)   `b`   **e** not meet someone you've arranged to meet

6 hit it off   `d`   **f** feel happier, or make someone feel happier

7 put up with   `h`   **g** have an argument and stop being friends

8 stand (somebody) up   `e`   **h** tolerate

9 Complete the sentences with the correct form of the phrasal verbs from Exercise 8.

1 I used to like them, but I _____*went off*_____ them after their last song.

2 I've had a hard day at work, so I just want to _____*chill out*_____ in front of the TV this evening.

3 Jake waited half an hour for Emma, but she _____*stood*_____ him _____*up*_____ . He was angry and upset.

4 Mark and Sue _____*fell out*_____ last month, and now they aren't speaking to each other.

5 The new teacher will not _____*put up with*_____ bad behaviour in her class.

6 Sonja looks very sad. Let's try to _____*cheer*_____ her _____*up*_____ .

7 Simon and Ben _____*hit*_____ it _____*off*_____ the first time they met because they like the same music.

8 This wet weather is _____*getting*_____ me _____*down*_____ . I want to go to the beach!

10 Choose the correct option to complete the sentences.

1 Failing the test is nothing to be ashamed (of)/ with.

2 This kind of music really gets (on)/ up my nerves.

3 Deep under / (down), she knew that she had made a mistake.

4 She used to be a keen hockey player, but last year she broke her leg at / (in) two places.

5 I was with / (under) the impression that you didn't approve of violent films.

6 My cousin Sarah has to be (at)/ to the airport at five o'clock.

Collocations and expressions

11 Choose the correct option to complete the sentences.

1 Greg's mother thinks his friends are a wrong / (bad) influence on him.

2 John's first girlfriend (broke)/ cracked his heart when she left him.

3 I can't (face)/ head doing any more work today. I'm going home.

4 He was afraid to go on stage because he didn't want to (make)/ show a fool of himself.

5 You should know more / (better) than to try and cheat in an exam!

6 Please (convey)/ express my apologies to your mum.

Words easily confused

12 Complete the sentences with the correct form of these words. Use each word at least once.

1 | say | speak | talk | tell

a He _____said_____ he was going out, but he didn't _____tell_____ me where.

b Actions _____speak_____ louder than words.

c You're _____talking_____ nonsense again. Stop _____telling_____ lies and start _____telling_____ the truth.

d What language were they _____speaking_____? I can't _____tell_____ the difference between German and Dutch.

e Sue _____told_____ us some marvellous stories during her stay.

2 | journey | travel | trip | voyage

a He's away on a business _____trip_____ at the moment.

b Going on a long sea _____voyage_____ was dangerous at one time.

c The _____journey_____ will be shorter once they've completed the tunnel.

d _____Travel_____ is said to broaden the mind.

3 | cost | price | value | worth

a The _____cost_____ of living has risen again.

b It's _____worth_____ far more than I paid for it.

c We can't afford a new washing machine at that _____price_____.

d These rare stamps are of great _____value_____.

4 | blame | error | fault | mistake | wrong

a They sent me two copies of the book in _____error_____.

b It is often quite difficult to tell the difference between right and _____wrong_____.

c According to her mother, she could do no _____wrong_____.

d Try not to make so many _____mistakes_____.

e You can't put the _____blame_____ on me this time.

f I invited her by _____mistake_____.

g Employing him was a(n) _____error_____ of judgement.

h It's not my _____fault_____ you lost your wallet.

Word formation   noun → adjective

13 Use the word in capitals to form a word that fits in the gap.

1 I was _____amazed_____ when I won the competition. I couldn't believe it!   AMAZEMENT

2 Tom felt _____guilty_____ about breaking his brother's headphones.   GUILT

3 The players were _____overjoyed_____ when they won the match.   JOY

4 My brother is quite _____sensitive_____. He gets upset easily, but he knows when other people are upset, too.   SENSE

5 Laura is a very _____confident_____ speaker. She enjoys giving presentations.   CONFIDENCE

6 Matt is a _____sympathetic_____ friend. He always listens to my problems.   SYMPATHY

7 Emily is working hard at the moment. She's _____desperate_____ for a holiday.   DESPAIR

8 We were so _____relieved_____ that no one was hurt in the accident.   RELIEF

9 I felt so _____embarrassed_____ when everyone was looking at me.   EMBARRASSMENT

10 My little sister gets very _____frustrated_____ when she doesn't get what she wants.   FRUSTRATION

Sentence transformation

14 Complete the second sentence so that it has a similar meaning to the first sentence, using the word given. Do not change the word given. You must use between two and five words.

1 My brother has the annoying habit of borrowing my socks.

FOREVER

My brother _____ *is forever borrowing* _____ my socks.

2 We used to like this café, but then it changed owners.

WENT

We _____ *went off this café* _____ when it changed owners.

3 The temperature is rising every day.

GETTING

It _____ *'s / is getting hotter* _____ every day.

4 Sam doesn't want to go out tonight. He's too tired.

FACE

Sam _____ *can't / cannot face going out* _____ tonight. He's too tired.

5 I thought you enjoyed going for long walks.

UNDER

I _____ *was under the impression* _____ that you enjoyed going for long walks.

6 The departure time for the Manchester train is 12.45.

AT

The Manchester train _____ *leaves / departs at* _____ 12.45.

7 It's not your friend's fault that you forgot your homework.

BLAME

You can't put _____ *the blame on your friend* _____ for forgetting your homework.

8 I'm not going to tolerate this ridiculous behaviour any longer.

PUT

I'm not going to _____ *put up with* _____ this ridiculous behaviour any longer.

Unit 2

Awareness

1 **Which of these sentences are correct (C) and incorrect (I)?**

1 He's tired because he's work all day.   _I_
2 I haven't saw that play yet.   _I_
3 Where have you been all afternoon?   _C_
4 Have you ever been bursting into tears in class?   _I_
5 Stan has competed in a lot of bicycle races.   _C_
6 This is the first time I haven't been passing a maths test!   _I_
7 We've been trying to contact you all morning.   _C_
8 The prisoner has escaped!   _C_
9 Sara hasn't been eating octopus ever before.   _I_
10 Your eyes are red. Have you cried?   _I_

How many did you get right? ☐

Grammar

Present perfect simple

Affirmative	Negative	Questions
I / We / You / They **have ('ve) eaten.** He / She / It **has ('s) eaten.**	I / We / You / They **have not (haven't) eaten.** He / She / It **has not (hasn't) eaten.**	**Have** I / we / you / they **eaten?** **Has** he / she / it **eaten?**
Short answers		
Yes, I / we / you / they **have.** **Yes**, he / she / it **has.**	**No**, I / we / you / they **haven't.** **No**, he / she / it **hasn't.**	

Spelling: walk → walk**ed**, love → lov**ed**, travel → trave**lled**, tidy → ti**died**, play → pl**ayed**

We use the present perfect simple:
- for something that started in the past and is still true now.
*We **have worked** here for ten years.*
- for something that happened in the past, but it's not important exactly when.
*Sara **has seen** all of the Marvel films*
- for something that happened in the past and has a direct result that affects the present.
*I'm very hungry because I **haven't eaten** for hours.*
- for an action that finished very recently.
*They **have just done** the dishes.*
- for experiences and achievements.
*He **has run** ten marathons.*
- for an action that has happened several times up to now.
*We**'ve asked** this question many times before.*
- with superlatives.
*It was the best book I **have** ever **read**.*

> **Note**
>
> Some verbs are irregular and do not follow these spelling rules. See a list of irregular verbs and their past participles on pages 172–173.

> **Note**
>
> Some common time expressions that are often used with the present perfect simple are: *already, before, ever, for (ages), just, lately / recently, never, still, yet*, etc.
> *Have you **ever** been to London?*

> **Remember**
>
> We use *have been* when someone has gone somewhere and has now returned. However, we use *have gone* when someone has gone somewhere and is still there.
> *My basketball team **rarely loses**.*
> *Jane **has been** to the gym and now she's at work.*
> *Jane **has gone** to the gym, so try calling her later.*

2

Present perfect continuous

Affirmative	Negative	Questions
I / We / You / They **have ('ve) been** play**ing**. He / She / It **has ('s) been** play**ing**.	I / We / You / They **have not (haven't) been** play**ing**. He / She / It **has not (hasn't) been** play**ing**.	**Have** I / we / you / they **been** play**ing**? **Has** he / she / it **been** play**ing**?
Short answers		
Yes, I / we / you / they **have**. **Yes**, he / she / it **has**.	**No**, I / we / you / they **haven't**. **No**, he / she / it **hasn't**.	

Spelling: make → mak**ing**, run → ru**nning**, stu**dy** → stu**dying**

We use the present perfect continuous:

- for actions that started in the past and are still in progress now or have happened repeatedly until now.
*Henry **has been living** in Spain for a long time.*
- for actions that happened repeatedly in the past and have finished recently, but that have results affecting the present.
*Jane has got fitter because she**'s been exercising** every day.*
- to state how long actions have been in progress.
*I**'ve been studying** Spanish literature for two years.*
- for a recent unfinished action.
*I**'ve been thinking** about you.*

> **Note**
>
> Some common time expressions that are often used with the present perfect continuous are: *all day / morning / night / week, for years / a long time / ages, just, lately / recently.*
> *We've been painting the garage **all day**.*

Present perfect simple or continuous

We use the present perfect simple to talk about something we have done or achieved, or an action that is complete. It is also used to say how many times something happened.
*Oliver **has lived** in three different countries.*

We use the present perfect continuous to talk about how long something has been happening. It is not important whether it has finished or not.
*Amy**'s been working** on her project all summer.*

Grammar exercises

2 **Choose the correct option to complete the sentences.**

1 I *haven't been* / *haven't been going* to a party yet this year.
2 It *has rained* / *has been raining* all day. It seems it will never stop!
3 People *have called* / *have been calling* all morning to say 'Happy Birthday' and they are still calling.
4 I *have tried* / *have been trying* to contact Peter, but his phone is always engaged.
5 She *has done* / *has been doing* a parachute jump before, but she doesn't think she can do it now.
6 They *have worked* / *have been working* in the garden all afternoon.
7 The doctor warned James about his poor health, so he *has stopped* / *has been stopping* eating unhealthy food.
8 We *have missed* / *have been missing* the bus, so we're walking to school.

3 Complete the sentences with the present perfect simple or present perfect continuous form of the verbs.

1 What's all this mess? What ___*have you been doing*___ (you / do) all morning?

2 ___*Have you finished*___ (you / finish) cooking your omelette yet?

3 How long ___*have they been studying*___ (they / study) Spanish?

4 Sorry I'm late. ___*Have you been waiting*___ (you / wait) long?

5 Ask John if ___*he has locked*___ (he / lock) the garage.

6 I ___*'ve read*___ (read) this book before.

7 ___*Has Katy decided*___ (Katy / decide) to apply for the job?

8 Who ___*has been using*___ (use) my laptop? They forgot to switch it off again!

4 Complete the questions.

1 **A:** How long ___*has he been standing outside*___ ?
  B: He's been standing outside for ten minutes.

2 **A:** What ___*have you done*___ ?
  B: I haven't done anything.

3 **A:** How long ___*have you known Elena*___ ?
  B: I've known Elena for four years.

4 **A:** What ___*have the boys been doing*___ all afternoon?
  B: The boys have been playing basketball all afternoon.

5 **A:** Where ___*have you hidden my glasses*___ ?
  B: I haven't hidden your glasses anywhere!

6 **A:** Why ___*have you been crying*___ ?
  B: I've been crying because I've just seen a very sad film.

7 **A:** ___*Have you been using / Have you used*___ my toothbrush?
  B: No, I haven't. I've got my own toothbrush!

8 **A:** How long ___*have you been waiting*___ ?
  B: I've been waiting about half an hour.

5 Correct the sentences where necessary. Tick those which do not need correcting.

1 Someone has been cooking in here. I can smell onions.
  ✓

2 The house has belonged to the family from 40 years.
  The house has belonged to the family for 40 years.

3 She just has left her office.
  She has just left her office.

4 I've already been writing five emails this morning.
  I've already written five emails this morning.

5 It's the first time she is playing tennis with us.
  It's the first time she has played tennis with us.

6 We've been tidying the cupboard, but we haven't finished yet.
  ✓

7 Dan has been missing the bus, so he'll be late.
  Dan has missed the bus, so he'll be late.

8 Her eyes are red because she has cried.
  Her eyes are red because she has been crying.

6 Complete the sentences with one word in each gap.

1 Our teacher has _____*been*_____ marking tests all morning.

2 Have you bought your ticket _____*yet / already*_____ ?

3 Amelia and Mark have been living together _____*for*_____ nearly three years.

4 This is the first time I have _____*ever*_____ eaten sushi.

5 I need to work tonight because I _____*still*_____ haven't finished my essay.

6 _____*How*_____ long have you been trying to access the internet?

7 Has he broken his new toy _____*already*_____ ? That was quick!

8 Who _____*has*_____ been stealing my cheese from the fridge?

Vocabulary

Phrasal verbs

7 Match the phrasal verbs (1–8) with their meanings (a–h).

1 bottle up   `b`   **a** suddenly become very afraid or upset

2 burn out   `h`   **b** hide strong emotions

3 calm down   `e`   **c** recover from an illness or an upsetting situation

4 chicken out   `g`   **d** quickly become attracted to somebody

5 fall for   `d`   **e** become less excited

6 finish with   `f`   **f** end a relationship

7 freak out   `a`   **g** become too afraid to do something

8 get over   `c`   **h** become too ill or tired to do any more work

8 Complete the sentences with the correct form of the phrasal verbs from Exercise 7.

1 She _____*fell for*_____ him as soon as she met him, and they got married six months later.

2 Steve _____*finished with*_____ his girlfriend last month because they kept arguing about money.

3 I was going to jump off the top diving board, but I _____*chickened out*_____ in the end – it was too high!

4 It is hard to know how Jen is feeling because she always _____*bottles up*_____ her emotions.

5 I didn't think Harry would mind me borrowing his bike, but he totally _____*freaked out*_____ because he thought it had been stolen.

6 _____*Calm down*_____ ! You shouldn't get so excited about things.

7 You need to take a holiday before you completely _____*burn out*_____ .

8 It took her a long time to _____*get over*_____ her illness.

Prepositions

9 Complete the sentences with these words. Use each word at least once.

for	into	on	to

1 I'm not responsible _____*for*_____ the behaviour of your children!

2 Dan wasn't sure how to respond _____*to*_____ his friend's suggestion.

3 You need to stop playing games and focus _____*on*_____ your exam preparation.

4 Emily was so happy when she heard the news that she burst _____*into*_____ tears.

5 It's hard to concentrate _____*on*_____ this reading task while the television is on.

6 Travelling together led _____*to*_____ Ben and Max's friendship becoming stronger.

Collocations and expressions

10 Choose the correct option to complete the sentences.

1 Emily was in *hurt* / *agony* when she injured her arm in a skiing accident.
2 The film was so exciting – we were on the *edge* / *corner* of our seats!
3 It really gets under my *skin* / *hair* when my sister plays loud music.
4 When Zak received his excellent exam results, he was *missed* / *lost* for words.
5 I'm sad to say that, with *regret* / *relief*, we can't come to your wedding because we will be on holiday.
6 His parents are divorced, but they are still on good *terms* / *friends* with each other.

Words easily confused

11 Complete the sentences with the correct form of these words. Use each word at least once.

1 **advise   insist   persuade   suggest**

   a Do you think you can _____*persuade*_____ her to lend you her car?
   b He always _____*insists*_____ on staying at the most expensive hotels.
   c Her personal trainer _____*advised*_____ her to do more exercise.
   d Lauren _____*suggested*_____ to us that we should leave on Friday night.

2 **client   customer   guest   patient**

   a The hotel _____*guests*_____ panicked when they heard the alarm go off.
   b There were only a few _____*patients*_____ waiting to see the doctor.
   c He's a well-known lawyer whose _____*clients*_____ include showbiz personalities.
   d In order to attract _____*customers*_____ , the shop owner reduced his prices.

3 **pass   spare   spend   waste**

   a How do you _____*spend*_____ your free time?
   b Don't _____*waste*_____ time! You've got a lot of work to do.
   c Can you _____*spare*_____ ten minutes to discuss the camping trip?
   d Time _____*passes*_____ quickly during the holidays.

4 **course   court   pitch   track**

   a It's one of the best golf _____*courses*_____ I've played on.
   b I'm afraid all the tennis _____*courts*_____ are booked.
   c The spectator who ran onto the _____*pitch*_____ was removed from the football stadium by police.
   d Athletes enjoy running on _____*tracks*_____ where the spectators are close to the action.

5 **burgle   cheat   rob   steal**

   a Her flat has been _____*burgled*_____ twice this year.
   b Nobody knows who _____*stole*_____ the laptop.
   c My business partner tried to _____*cheat*_____ me out of my share of the profits.
   d Banks in the USA are _____*robbed*_____ quite frequently.

2

adjective → noun

12 Use the word in capitals to form a word that fits in the gap.

1 Our primary concern is for the _____ *safety* _____ of the children at this school. **SAFE**

2 Don't lie to me. I want to hear the _____ *truth* _____ . **TRUE**

3 It's _____ *madness* _____ to go swimming in this weather. You'll freeze! **MAD**

4 Do you know the _____ *difference* _____ between an adverb and an adjective? **DIFFERENT**

5 Most students suffer from _____ *anxiety* _____ before an important exam. **ANXIOUS**

6 The _____ *popularity* _____ of mobile apps is increasing all the time. **POPULAR**

7 It takes a lot of _____ *strength* _____ to lift your own weight. **STRONG**

8 What's the _____ *distance* _____ between London and Manchester? **DISTANT**

9 There was a lot of _____ *tension* _____ in the room before the meeting started. **TENSE**

10 You will need to improve your _____ *fitness* _____ if you want to compete at this level. **FIT**

Sentence transformation

13 Complete the second sentence so that it has a similar meaning to the first sentence, using the word given. Do not change the word given. You must use between two and five words.

1 The children aren't here – they're in the park with their uncle.

HAVE

The children _____ *have gone to the park* _____ with their uncle.

2 They started studying two hours ago, and they're still studying now.

STUDYING

They _____ *'ve / have been studying for* _____ two hours.

3 I didn't know what to say about Maria's bad news.

LOST

I was _____ *lost for words* _____ about Maria's bad news.

4 The small child suddenly started to cry when he dropped his ice cream.

BURST

The small child _____ *burst into tears* _____ when he dropped his ice cream.

5 I'm glad that you two are friendly with each other.

TERMS

I'm glad that you two _____ *are on good terms* _____ with each other.

6 He was going to enter the race, but he got scared.

CHICKENED

He _____ *chickened out of* _____ entering the race.

7 She ended their relationship on his birthday.

FINISHED

She _____ *finished (her relationship) with* _____ him on his birthday.

8 After we gave him some food, the baby became quieter.

CALMED

The baby _____ *calmed down* _____ after we gave him some food.

Unit 3

Awareness

1 Which of these sentences are correct (C) and incorrect (I)?

1 We cancelled the party because Sami was ill. _C_
2 You didn't went home early, did you? _I_
3 Everyone agreed it was a great plan. _C_
4 What did you doing at eight o'clock last night? _I_
5 I would enjoy this cartoon when I was a child. _I_
6 My dad teached me how to make pancakes. _I_
7 I was working when I heard the celebration. _C_
8 Dan used to drive everywhere, but now he cycles. _C_
9 Did you used to fight with your brother? _I_
10 We were swimming in the lake last Sunday. _C_

How many did you get right? ☐

Grammar

Past simple

Affirmative	Negative	Questions
I / He / She / It / We / You / They walk**ed**.	I / He / She / It / We / You / They **didn't** walk.	**Did** I / he / she / it / we / you / they **walk**?
Short answers		
Yes, I / he / she / it / we / you / they **did**.	**No**, I / he / she / it / we / you / they **didn't**.	

Spelling: race → rac**ed**, control → contro**lled**, study → stu**died**, play → play**ed**

We use the past simple for:

• something that started and finished in the past.
*Archeologists **discovered** Tutankhamun in 1922.*

• past routines and habits (often with adverbs of frequency).
*We **often visited** the museum when we were children.*

• past states.
*We **loved** living in a different country.*

• actions that happened one after the other in the past, for example when telling a story.
*He **stood up**, **walked** to the window, and **shouted** into the night*

> **Note**
>
> Some verbs are irregular and do not follow these spelling rules. See a list of irregular verbs on pages 172–173.

> **Note**
>
> Some common time expressions that are often used with the past simple are: *yesterday, last night / week / month / summer, a week / month / year ago, twice a week, once a month, at the weekend, in March, in the morning / afternoon / evening, at night, on Thursdays, on Monday mornings, etc.*
> *I listened to some great new bands **at the weekend**.*

Past continuous

Affirmative	Negative	Questions
I / He / She / It **was** walk**ing**. We / You / They **were** walk**ing**.	I / He / She / It **was not (wasn't)** walk**ing**. We / You / They **were not (weren't)** walk**ing**.	**Was** I / he / she / it walk**ing**? **Were** we / you / they walk**ing**?
Short answers		
Yes, I / he / she / it **was**. **Yes**, we / you / they **were**.	**No**, I / he / she / it **wasn't**. **No**, we / you / they **weren't**.	

Spelling: shine → shin**ing**, control → contro**lling**, tidy → ti**dying**

3

We use the past continuous for:

- actions that were in progress at a specific time in the past.
*Susan **was walking** home at six o'clock this evening.*

- two or more actions that were in progress at the same time in the past.
*Martin **was reading** while Helen **was watching** TV.*

- giving background information in a story.
*It **was raining**, and a strong wind **was blowing**.*

- an action that was in progress in the past that was interrupted by another action.
*Daniel **was checking** the bill when the waiter **returned** to the table.*

- temporary situations in the past.
*We **were living** in the suburbs of Manchester at the time.*

used to and would

We use *used to* + infinitive for:

- actions that happened regularly in the past.
*I **used to collect** plastic dinosaurs.*

- states that existed for a long time in the past.
*Emily **used to like** gold jewellery, but now she prefers silver.*

We use *would* + infinitive for actions that happened regularly in the past. We don't use it for past states.
*During the summer holidays, we **would play** cricket every day until sunset.*

> **Note**
>
> Some common time expressions that are often used with the past continuous are: *while, as, all day / week / month / year, at ten o'clock last night, last Sunday / week / year, this morning*, etc.
> *They were learning about the Romans **this morning**.*

Grammar exercises

2 Complete the text with the past simple or past continuous form of the verbs.

I ¹ was _____was walking_____ (walk) along Regent Street when I ² _____realised_____ (realise) that a man ³ _____was following_____ (follow) me. I ⁴ _____turned_____ (turn) right and he ⁵ _____followed_____ (follow). Whenever I ⁶ _____stopped_____ (stop), he ⁷ _____did_____ (do) too. I ⁸ _____decided_____ (decide) to take the 717 bus. Just as it ⁹ _____was moving_____ (move) off, I ¹⁰ _____jumped_____ (jump) on. The man ¹¹ _____missed_____ (miss) the bus, but he ¹² _____got_____ (get) on another 717. He ¹³ _____didn't notice_____ (not / notice) me getting off or heading for the nearest police station.

3 Use the prompts to write sentences with the past simple, past continuous and *when* or *while*. Start with the words in bold.

1 **My mother** / watch the news / my father / cook
My mother was watching the news when / while my father was cooking.

2 **Kate** / do her homework / I / phone her
Kate was doing her homework when I phoned her.

3 **Pam** / paint her room / her friend / arrive
Pam was painting her room when her friend arrived.

4 **I** / read a comic / he / burst into the room
I was reading a comic when he burst into the room.

5 **A** lot of people / dance / Max and I / eat snacks
A lot of people were dancing when / while Max and I were eating snacks.

6 **We** / serve the food / it / start raining
We were serving the food when it started raining.

4 Complete the exchanges using the words in brackets.

1 **A:** Did he give the present to her? (him)   *Possible answers*
   B: *No, he didn't give the present to her. He gave the present to him.*

2 **A:** Did your mother know about it? (father)
   B: *No, my mother / she didn't know about it. My father knew about it.*

3 **A:** Was the dog barking at a cat? (the postman)
   B: *No, the dog / it wasn't barking at a cat. It was barking at the postman.*

4 **A:** Did she move here three years ago? (four years ago)
   B: *No, she didn't move here three years ago. She moved here four years ago.*

5 **A:** Were they celebrating a birthday? (wedding)
   B: *No, they weren't celebrating a birthday. They were celebrating a wedding.*

6 **A:** Did Dan cook you Italian food? (Japanese)
   B: *No, he / Dan didn't cook me / us Italian food. He cooked me / us Japanese food.*

7 **A:** Was she wearing a bracelet? (necklace)
   B: *No, she wasn't wearing a bracelet. She was wearing a necklace.*

8 **A:** Did the Aztecs come from Argentina? (Mexico)
   B: *No, the Aztecs / they didn't come from Argentina. They came from Mexico.*

5 Complete the questions.

1 **A:** _____ *Were you sleeping* _____ at nine o'clock last night?
   B: No, I wasn't sleeping. I was reading.

2 **A:** What _____ *were you doing* _____ at ten o'clock this morning?
   B: I was queuing outside the Anthropology Museum.

3 **A:** How long _____ *did you teach English in Spain* _____ ?
   B: I taught English in Spain for three years.

4 **A:** Where _____ *were they* _____ ?
   B: They were at the beach.

5 **A:** Why _____ *did you buy a new phone* _____ ?
   B: I bought a new phone because it has a better camera.

6 **A:** What *were you doing when the internet stopped working* ?
   B: I was buying tickets to a concert when the internet stopped working.

7 **A:** Why _____ *didn't you come to the festival* _____ ?
   B: I didn't come to the festival because I was at a wedding.

8 **A:** _____ *Were you cooking* _____ when I called you?
   B: No, I wasn't cooking. I was watching an interesting documentary.

6 Choose the correct option to complete the sentences.

1 He *used to* / *would* have long hair.
2 My father would *to take* / *take* us out for a meal on his birthday.
3 Did you use to *get* / *getting* a lot of pocket money?
4 They *would* / *were used to* send us a postcard every summer.
5 I *would* / *used to* understand German when I was a child.
6 When I was at primary school, I *would* / *use to* go to bed at eight o'clock.
7 My grandmother *would* / *used to* have enormous gold earrings.
8 Every year, Mum would *make* / *to make* birthday cakes in the shape of our age.

7 Complete the sentences with one word in each gap.

1 _____*Did*_____ you hear about the new exhibition at the art gallery?

2 The sun _____*was*_____ shining brightly when we woke up the next morning.

3 I was composing a song _____*while*_____ Jane was writing a poem.

4 Did you use _____*to*_____ enjoy dressing up as a pirate when you were younger?

5 I watched a documentary about clothes and culture, and _____*then*_____ I went to bed.

6 _____*Why*_____ didn't you go to school yesterday?

7 _____*How*_____ long have you been trying to book tickets online?

8 Where did Tina go _____*last*_____ night?

Vocabulary

Phrasal verbs

8 Match the phrasal verbs (1–8) with their meanings (a–h).

1	call round	*e*	**a**	telephone somebody again
2	call (somebody) back	*a*	**b**	discover by accident
3	call off	*g*	**c**	remember, think about the past
4	come across	*b*	**d**	become available to buy
5	come along	*f*	**e**	visit somebody's house
6	come out	*d*	**f**	go somewhere with somebody
7	date back	*h*	**g**	cancel an event
8	look back at	*c*	**h**	exist since a particular time in the past

9 Complete the sentences with the correct form of the phrasal verbs from Exercise 8.

1 We're going to the festival in the park. Why don't you _____*come along*_____ with us?

2 If I don't answer the first time, _____*call*_____ me _____*back*_____ in half an hour.

3 We're very excited that our first song is _____*coming out*_____ next week.

4 She was clearing out the attic when she _____*came across*_____ an old photo of her grandparents.

5 The tradition of decorating trees at Christmas _____*dates back*_____ to Germany in the 16th century.

6 I'll _____*call round*_____ to your house this evening.

7 You can learn a lot when you _____*look back at*_____ your mistakes.

8 The outdoor concert was _____*called off*_____ because of the rain.

Prepositions

10 Choose the correct option to complete the sentences.

1 We cannot lose this competition. We must win **at** / *by* / *in* all costs.

2 That was *at* / **by** / *in* far the dullest book I have ever read in my life.

3 *At* / *By* / **In** general, I think foreign travel makes people respect other cultures more.

4 I am writing to you *at* / *by* / **in** connection with my project on tribal costumes.

5 She knows the recipe *at* / **by** / *in* heart because she makes it so often.

6 We will have a car **at** / *by* / *in* our disposal for the duration of our stay.

Collocations and expressions

11 Choose the correct option to complete the sentences.

1 Mr Wilson has ⬚built / given a reputation as an expert in Native American history

2 Some traditional designs are protected. You can't ⬚use / know them without permission.

3 The festival of Halloween ⬚has / holds its roots in Celtic and Roman festivals.

4 The internet saved / ⬚played an important role in our research for this project.

5 Thankfully, the earthquake didn't ⬚do / have much damage to the museum.

6 The Romans did / ⬚built an empire that stretched from the Atlantic to the Middle East.

Words easily confused

12 Complete the sentences with the correct form of these words. Use each word at least once.

1 | **audience   crowd   gang   listener   member   spectator   viewer**

   a The police had difficulty in controlling the _____*crowd*_____ that had turned up to greet the singer at the airport.

   b _____*Viewers*_____ will be able to take part in the TV discussion programme.

   c Radio 1 _____*listeners*_____ should tune in at four o'clock for live coverage of the festival.

   d The _____*audience*_____ thoroughly enjoyed the play.

   e Fewer than 1,000 _____*spectators*_____ saw the game.

   f Every _____*member*_____ of the family brought food for Grandad's party.

   g After the robbery, the _____*gang*_____ escaped in a stolen car.

2 | **artificial   fake   false   imitation**

   a Jackets made of _____*artificial*_____ leather are much cheaper than those made of genuine leather.

   b There was no fire. It was a(n) _____*false*_____ alarm.

   c He lost his job when it was discovered that his diploma was a(n) _____*fake*_____ .

   d It wasn't a real Ming vase – it was just a cheap _____*imitation*_____ .

3 | **achieve   fulfil   manage   succeed**

   a She _____*achieved*_____ success very early in her career.

   b We _____*managed*_____ to complete the project in one week.

   c Robert never _____*fulfilled*_____ the promise he showed as a young pianist.

   d William _____*succeeded*_____ in discovering the truth.

4 | **bargain   chance   occasion   opportunity   situation**

   a The offer of a job abroad was a golden _____*opportunity*_____ for me to make a fresh start.

   b The scarf was a(n) _____*bargain*_____ at £10.

   c What are the _____*chances*_____ of you getting a job in the music industry?

   d It was a(n) _____*occasion*_____ on which all the family could celebrate.

   e We've got a problem to solve, so let's look at the _____*situation*_____ , shall we?

3

Word formation mixed

13 Use the word in capitals to form a word that fits in the gap.

1 What are the _____origins_____ of this celebration? **ORIGINAL**
2 It was a big wedding. There were 200 guests at the _____reception_____ . **RECEIVE**
3 The dancing and other _____festivities_____ continued until very late. **FESTIVE**
4 Almost every culture has _____traditions_____ based on food and eating. **TRADITIONAL**
5 The fireworks on New Year's Eve were an amazing _____spectacle_____ . **SPECTATE**
6 The festival can be very loud, so it isn't _____suitable_____ for young children. **SUIT**
7 The shirt is available in _____various_____ patterns and colours. **VARY**
8 Clothes and jewellery are _____significant_____ in many different cultures. **SIGNIFY**

Sentence transformation

14 Complete the second sentence so that it has a similar meaning to the first sentence, using the word given. Do not change the word given. You must use between two and five words.

1 I climbed trees when I was a young boy.
   USED
   When I was a young boy, _____I used to climb_____ trees.

2 I'll phone you again later, when I have more time.
   CALL
   I'll _____call you back (later)_____ when I have more time.

3 She cancelled her birthday party when she became ill.
   OFF
   When she became ill, she _____called off_____ her birthday party.

4 You must do everything you can to succeed tomorrow.
   COSTS
   You must succeed _____at all costs_____ tomorrow.

5 I've never seen a film that was nearly as exciting as that one.
   FAR
   That _____was by far_____ the most exciting film I've ever seen.

6 The festival always takes place on the last weekend of July.
   HELD
   The festival _____is always held_____ on the last weekend of July.

7 I found this by accident when I was cleaning your room.
   ACROSS
   I _____came across this_____ when I was cleaning your room.

8 This tradition started in the 17th century.
   DATES
   This tradition _____dates back_____ to the 17th century.

Awareness

1 Which of these sentences are correct (C) and incorrect (I)?

1 Our cat has disappeared last week. ____ I

2 Oh no! I've lost my mobile phone. ____ C

3 This band hasn't released a good song since 2018. ____ C

4 Nobody has ever spoke to me like that. ____ I

5 We haven't heard from Rob since ages. ____ I

6 I've known Charlie for seven years. ____ C

7 How long ago did you take up the piano? ____ C

8 I been on holiday to Morocco last summer. ____ I

9 He's use to travelling alone. ____ I

10 I've been getting used to the new computer system. ____ C

How many did you get right? ☐

Grammar

Past simple and present perfect

We use the past simple for actions that happened at a specified time in the past and we think of as finished.
I **read** an article about space travel last night.
She **worked** in a museum for two years. (She no longer works there.)

We use the present perfect for actions that happened at an unspecified time in the past and for actions or situations that began in the past and are still in progress or have an effect on the present.
Steven **has written** a poem for his girlfriend. (We don't know or don't say when.)
The children **have been** at the swimming pool all afternoon. (They are still at the swimming pool.)

be used to and get used to

We use *be used to* + verb + *-ing* form / noun to talk about actions and states which are usual or familiar.
Andy **is used to working** at night because he has been doing it for ages.

We use *get used to* + verb + *-ing* form / noun to talk about actions and states which are becoming more familiar.
The students **are getting used to the new head teacher's rules**.

> **Note**
>
> With *used to*, the verbs *be* and *get* change depending on the tense that is needed in the context.
> I **was used to** hot weather because I had been living in Egypt for many years.
> I **have been getting used to** going to bed early.

Grammar exercises

2 Choose the correct option to complete the sentences.

1 Martin *hasn't finished* / *didn't finish* writing his novel yet.

2 Mrs Black *has taught* / *taught* history last year.

3 Anna still *hasn't found* / *didn't find* her earring.

4 Archeologists *discovered* / *have discovered* the plates many years ago.

5 *I've been* / *I've gone* to the art exhibition. Look what I bought!

6 Our neighbours have moved. *They've been* / *They've gone* to live in Australia.

7 I'm not used to *tell* / *telling* other people what to do.

8 My brother *gets* / *is* used to doing his homework in the morning.

9 Have you *got* / *been* used to living in the city yet?

10 She has great difficulty in *being* / *getting* used to living alone.

3 Complete the sentences with these words. Use each word at least once.

| ago | already | ever | for | just | recently | still | yet |

1 I haven't finished decorating the house _____yet_____ .

2 I have _____just_____ bought these earrings. Do you like them?

3 I haven't seen John _____for_____ a while.

4 She started playing the violin three years _____ago_____ .

5 She _____still_____ hasn't finished cooking. The guests have already arrived!

6 We'll have to choose another film. I have _____already_____ seen this one.

7 Have you _____ever_____ visited an old castle?

8 I have been having terrible headaches _____recently_____ .

4 Correct the sentences where necessary. Tick those which do not need correcting.

1 It is been three years since I last went on holiday.

It has been three years since I last went on holiday.

2 Nobody has ever been here before.

✓

3 How long ago did you came to this city?

How long ago did you come to this city?

4 Laura has lost her passport last week.

Laura lost her passport last week.

5 We haven't heard from Simon for a long time.

✓

6 When have you sent the tickets? I haven't received them yet.

When did you send the tickets? I haven't received them yet.

7 I could get use to living in a luxury apartment.

I could get used to living in a luxury apartment.

8 They aren't used to eating out every night.

✓

5 Complete the sentences with the past simple or present perfect form of the verbs.

1 Since I _____left_____ (leave) school two years ago, I _____haven't seen_____ (not / see) Jenny.

2 I _____'ve never eaten_____ (never / eat) this kind of food before.

3 Sam _____hasn't been_____ (not / go) to a concert since he _____was_____ (be) 20.

4 **A:** __Have you ever flown__ (you / ever / fly) a helicopter?

B: Yes, I _____flew_____ (fly) a helicopter when I was in the air force.

5 Last week, Jim _____finished_____ (finish) one of the best pictures he _____'s ever painted_____ (ever / paint).

6 Katy _____went_____ (go) to live in the country six months ago and _____hasn't been_____ (not / be) back since then.

6 Complete the sentences with the correct form of *be used to* or *get used to*.

1 I find it difficult to _____get used to_____ driving on the left. I think it will take me some time.

2 Mark will never _____get used to_____ the cold winters in Canada after living in California.

3 The students _____are used to_____ studying hard as their teacher is very demanding.

4 I _____'m used to_____ having orange juice and eggs for breakfast.

5 You'll soon _____get used to_____ speaking Spanish every day when you move to Spain.

6 She _____isn't used to_____ (not) working so late into the night.

7 **Write questions for the answers.** *Possible answers*

1 **A:** *How long have you lived in this town* ?
  B: I've lived in this town for five years.

2 **A:** *When did Tom travel round Europe / What did Tom do two years ago* ?
  B: Tom travelled round Europe two years ago.

3 **A:** *Where did you camp / What did you do last night / When did you camp in the forest* ?
  B: We camped in the forest last night.

4 **A:** *Have you written a film review before* ?
  B: Yes, I have written a film review before.

5 **A:** *Did the teacher mark your / our test last night* ?
  B: Yes, the teacher marked our test last night.

6 **A:** *Has he spoken to her yet* ?
  B: No, he hasn't spoken to her yet.

7 **A:** *Is she used to swimming in cold water* ?
  B: Yes, she's used to swimming in cold water.

8 **A:** *Are you getting used to living in a hot climate* ?
  B: No, I'm not getting used to living in a hot climate.

Vocabulary

Phrasal verbs

8 **Match the phrasal verbs (1–8) with their meanings (a–h).**

1 call for — *c*   **a** ask
2 call on — *a*   **b** start to do something
3 come to — *g*   **c** require or demand
4 come up — *e*   **d** understand, feel the same as
5 go ahead — *b*   **e** be mentioned in a conversation
6 identify with — *d*   **f** persuade somebody to do something
7 spread out over — *h* **g** total, when added together
8 talk (somebody) into — *f* **h** happening over a long period of time

9 **Complete the sentences with the correct form of the phrasal verbs from Exercise 8.**

1 That meal was quite cheap. The bill _____*came to*_____ £35.50.
2 The issue of cultural identity _____*came up*_____ in the discussion about school uniform.
3 Having a shared interest, like music, can help you _____*identify with*_____ people from other cultures.
4 The organisers of the festival are planning to _____*go ahead*_____ , despite the wind and rain.
5 The audience _____*called on*_____ the author of the play to come on stage.
6 Zak's friends _____*talked*_____ him _____*into*_____ performing in the concert.
7 I can afford the trip because the payments are _____*spread out over*_____ six months.
8 Walking in the mountains _____*calls for*_____ a high level of fitness and warm, waterproof clothing!

4

Prepositions

10 Choose the correct option to complete the sentences.

1 He admitted that he was *at* / *in* / *by* fault, and apologised to the taxi driver.
2 The weather is getting warmer day *at* / *in* / *by* day.
3 I am very much *at* / *in* / *by* favour of students spending a year abroad.
4 She said that she found the novel 'unsatisfying' – *at* / *in* / *by* other words, she hated it.
5 The cost of air travel has increased *at* / *in* / *by* 20% in the past two years.
6 If your house is too close to the river, it is *at* / *in* / *by* risk of flooding.

Collocations and expressions

11 Choose the correct option to complete the sentences.

1 The carnival in Rio de Janeiro is widely *done* / *known* as one of the biggest festivals in the world.
2 We spent years *playing* / *building* a good relationship with our neighbours.
3 The festival is *held* / *had* every summer in a farmer's fields.
4 You'll *know* / *save* a lot of space if you give away some of the clothes you don't wear anymore.
5 I'm not sure how I'm going to deal with this situation – I'll just have to *use* / *play* it by ear.
6 The best man at my brother's wedding *gave* / *built* a very funny speech!

Words easily confused

12 Complete the sentences with the correct form of these words. Use each word at least once.

1 **beat   earn   gain   win**

   a I think we can _____ *beat* _____ his team in the final.
   b She _____ *won* _____ some money at the horse races.
   c The director is said to _____ *earn* _____ about £10,000 a month.
   d Who _____ *won* _____ the music competition last year?
   e Sally's mother says she's not losing a daughter, but _____ *gaining* _____ a son.

2 **forget   leave   lose   miss**

   a We'll be late if we _____ *miss* _____ the early train.
   b Have you _____ *left* _____ your book at home again?
   c Could I borrow a pencil? I've _____ *forgotten* _____ mine. It's in my other pencil case.
   d I can't find my sunglasses anywhere. I suppose I must have _____ *lost* _____ them.

3 **deny   refrain   refuse   reject   resist**

   a I _____ *refuse* _____ to help people who won't help themselves.
   b Although the cakes looked delicious, I _____ *resisted* _____ the temptation to eat one.
   c How can he _____ *deny* _____ losing the ring when he had it last?
   d All my job applications have been _____ *rejected* _____ .
   e Would visitors please _____ *refrain* _____ from touching the paintings?

4 **manner   path   route   way**

   a Do you know the _____ *way* _____ to the cathedral?
   b If we go by the shortest _____ *route* _____ , we'll get there by midday.
   c I enjoy walking along the _____ *path* _____ in Sherwood Forest.
   d She has such a charming _____ *manner* _____ .

5 | origin | source | stock | supply |

    a Nobody knows the _____ origin _____ of the word.

    b I'll check to see if we have those earrings in _____ stock _____ .

    c The rain and floods affected the country's food _____ supply _____ .

    d Explorers couldn't find the _____ source _____ of the river.

Word formation   noun → verb

13 Use the word in capitals to form a word that fits in the gap.

    1 All my dad's old CDs are _____ classified _____ according to musical type.   **CLASS**

    2 Can you _____ prove _____ that you were at the cinema last night?   **PROOF**

    3 Many medical conditions can be _____ relieved _____ by art or music, as well as medicines.   **RELIEF**

    4 We _____ encourage _____ students to make use of our excellent library.   **COURAGE**

    5 I hope you _____ succeed _____ in your ambition to become a professional dancer.   **SUCCESS**

    6 The newspaper was forced to _____ apologise _____ for printing incorrect information.   **APOLOGY**

    7 Don't let the dog out, or it will _____ terrorise _____ the children.   **TERROR**

    8 He doesn't like it if you _____ criticise _____ his work.   **CRITIC**

Sentence transformation

14 Complete the second sentence so that it has a similar meaning to the first sentence, using the word given. Do not change the word given. You must use between two and five words.

    1 She started to live here two years ago.

    FOR

    She _____ 's / has lived here for _____ two years.

    2 I haven't seen Tonya for three weeks.

    TIME

    The _____ last time I saw _____ Tonya was three weeks ago.

    3 He approves of children learning to play musical instruments.

    FAVOUR

    He _____ 's / is in favour of _____ children learning to play musical instruments.

    4 In the meeting, someone suggested having an art exhibition.

    UP

    The suggestion of an art exhibition _____ came up _____ in the meeting.

    5 There's a danger that you will injure yourself on this climb.

    RISK

    You are _____ at risk of injuring _____ yourself on this climb.

    6 The last time we performed was last July.

    SINCE

    We _____ haven't / have not performed since _____ last July.

    7 You were not to blame for the accident.

    FAULT

    You were _____ not at fault _____ for the accident.

    8 You need a lot of patience to do this task.

    CALLS

    This task _____ calls for a lot of / lots of _____ patience.

B2 Practice: First

Part 1

For questions 1–8, read the text below and decide which answer (A, B, C or D) best fits each gap. There is an example at the beginning (0).

Stockholm syndrome

Imagine the following (0) ___ . A gang of bank robbers cannot escape because police have surrounded the building. Automatically, the (1) ___ become hostages, while the criminals (2) ___ time deciding what to do. Outside the bank a crowd has gathered, with TV crews providing (3) ___ with live coverage of the incident. Back inside the building, a relationship is developing between the hostages and their captors. They start (4) ___ each other about themselves and the hostages begin to put the blame for the incident on the police and authorities.

You may think that this is a scene from a Hollywood movie, but you would be (5) ___ . The phenomenon is (6) ___ as 'Stockholm Syndrome' because it was first observed in Stockholm, Sweden. The hostages helped their captors solve any problems that (7) ___ up, and even protected their captors when they all left the building together. Nobody knows quite what (8) ___ this behaviour, but it seems that the value of communication cannot be overestimated.

0	A	condition	**(B)**	situation	C	happening	D	state
1	A	guests	**(B)**	customers	C	buyers	D	clients
2	A	pass	B	spare	C	do	**(D)**	spend
3	**(A)**	viewers	B	spectators	C	listeners	D	readers
4	A	talking	**(B)**	telling	C	speaking	D	saying
5	A	false	**(B)**	wrong	C	missing	D	off
6	A	called	B	described	**(C)**	known	D	named
7	**(A)**	came	B	held	C	stayed	D	moved
8	A	sets	B	brings	C	makes	**(D)**	causes

Part 2

For questions 9–16, read the text below and think of the word which best fits each gap. Use only one word in each gap. There is an example at the beginning (0).

Some spare-time activities

Spare-time activities basically fall into two categories: traditional (0) _____and_____ modern. Traditional activities include pastimes such (9) _____as_____ collecting and reading, while modern activities involve computer games, the internet and television.

Children often become interested in collecting when they come (10) _____across_____ something their parents or grandparents have collected. Although they might be keen (11) _____on_____ collecting when they first start, they very often become fed up with it when they reach their teens. Reading is a leisure activity that develops with parental encouragement. Unlike collecting, reading is a pastime that people hardly (12) _____ever_____ abandon.

Nowadays, it is not unusual to find a teenager's bedroom full (13) _____of_____ electronic devices and computer games. While computer games (14) _____are_____ considered to be mainly a teenage pastime, social media and browsing the internet are popular with both teenagers and adults. Another pastime which teenagers have (15) _____in_____ common with adults is watching television. Interestingly, none of these activities involve having a discussion about important issues – something which was popular in (16) _____the_____ past.

Part 3

For questions 17–24, read the text below. Use the word given in capitals at the end of some of the lines to form a word that fits in the gap in the same line. There is an example at the beginning (0).

Bringing families closer

A recent survey conducted by a leading scientific magazine has (0) _____surprisingly_____ revealed **SURPRISE**
that electronic devices do not weaken relationships within families. In fact, the opposite is true –
they actually bring children and parents together.

There has been a huge (17) _____growth_____ in the number of parents who have become **GROW**

involved in their children's (18) _____educational_____ activities online. This appears to **EDUCATE**

(19) _____strengthen_____ bonds between family members, as they work and play together on a **STRONG**
range of devices.

One further (20) _____conclusion_____ reached in a report based on the survey is that children's **CONCLUDE**

(21) _____competitive_____ needs are satisfied. This occurs because children consistently beat their **COMPETE**

parents at computer-based games. The survey must come as a great (22) _____relief_____ **RELIEVE**

to parents, many of whom were originally (23) _____doubtful_____ about the wisdom of **DOUBT**

having so many devices at home. After all, no parent wants their child to become anti-social and

uncommunicative, which used to be a common fear.

Parents no longer have any reason to be (24) _____suspicious_____ of these tools, which now **SUSPECT**

play an essential role in modern life.

Part 4

For questions 25–30, complete the second sentence so that it has a similar meaning to the first sentence, using the word given. Do not change the word given. You must use between two and five words, including the word given. Here is an example (0).

Example:

0 This is my first fishing trip.

NEVER

I _____ *have never been on* _____ a fishing trip before.

25 I first met Sarah twelve years ago, and I still know her now.

FOR

I _____ *'ve / have known Sarah for* _____ twelve years.

26 I don't remember Mary being such a difficult person in the past.

USE

Mary _____ *didn't / did not use to be* _____ such a difficult person.

27 How did you persuade Dad to lend you his car?

TALK

How did you _____ *talk Dad into lending* _____ you his car?

28 The growth of these plants was very slow in my back garden.

GROW

These plants _____ *didn't / did not grow (very) quickly / fast* _____ in my back garden.

29 I think what she said at the press conference was true.

TRUTH

I think _____ *she told the truth* _____ at the press conference.

30 She talks nonsense all the time and I can't stand it.

NERVES

It really _____ *gets on my nerves* _____ that she talks nonsense all the time.

B2 Practice: ECCE

Grammar

For questions 1–20, choose the word or phrase that best completes the sentence or conversation.

1 Simon isn't in. He has ___ to the theatre.
A been
B gone ⃝
C went
D done

2 My laptop ran out of power an hour ___ .
A ago ⃝
B since
C away
D lately

3 Did we ___ go to the same nursery school?
A would
B used to
C use to ⃝
D using to

4 Those jeans ___ too much money!
A are costing
B costs
C is costing
D cost ⃝

5 My cousin ___ in Australia at the moment.
A studies
B is studying ⃝
C study
D is study

6 ___ your ridiculous story.
A I don't believe ⃝
B I not believe
C I'm not believing
D I don't believing

7 Who's been ___ my cheese?
A ate
B eaten
C eating ⃝
D eat

8 We've ___ got past Level 2 of this game.
A ever
B no
C done
D never ⃝

9 I ___ having lunch when the phone rang.
A am
B was ⃝
C will
D did

10 I hope they ___ arguing again yesterday.
A wasn't
B aren't
C didn't
D weren't ⃝

11 I've been having a lot of bad dreams ___ .
A since
B recently ⃝
C ever
D always

12 I've ___ dinner so I'm not hungry.
A already eaten ⃝
B just ate
C still eaten
D never ate

13 They ___ living in the big city.
A would
B used to
C are getting used to ⃝
D are being used to

14 ___ you always brush your teeth at night?
A Are
B What
C Why
D Do ⃝

15 Where ___ your father work?
A is
B does ⃝
C are
D do

16 We saw some great shows ___ year.
A last ⃝
B ago
C next
D once

17 'Do you want to come out?'
'I haven't finished writing this essay ___ .'
A still
B ever
C yet ⃝
D just

18 'I'm exhausted.'
'___ you been working all afternoon?'
A Are
B Do
C Did
D Have ⃝

19 Steve ___ basketball for three years.
A play
B has played ⃝
C did play
D is playing

20 We ___ swimming for ages.
A didn't be
B weren't
C haven't
D haven't been ⃝

Vocabulary

For questions 21–40, choose the word or phrase that most appropriately completes the sentence.

21 I can't ___ eating when I'm this ill.
A face
B mouth
C head
D foot

22 I've got so much work to do! It's really getting me ___ .
A in
B on
C up
D down

23 The audience ___ into applause at the end.
A snapped
B banged
C burst
D popped

24 Calm down! There's no need to ___ out.
A run
B freak
C crash
D flash

25 Many music festivals are ___ in the UK every summer.
A had
B given
C played
D held

26 Why don't you come ___ with us to the park?
A under
B along
C for
D round

27 We don't have a plan, so let's just play it by ___ .
A heart
B ear
C nose
D neck

28 You must get into this university at all ___ .
A costs
B prices
C events
D possibilities

29 Did you fall ___ with your best friend again?
A over
B for
C out
D in

30 We were on the ___ of our seats all through the film.
A edge
B side
C corner
D top

31 In other ___ , I don't want to go out tonight.
A words
B verbs
C ways
D things

32 Don't ___ a fool of yourself!
A show
B do
C mark
D make

33 The celebration has its ___ in an ancient tradition.
A nerves
B skin
C roots
D terms

34 I know this poem by ___ .
A head
B mouth
C stomach
D heart

35 You shouldn't ___ up your feelings.
A box
B carton
C pack
D bottle

36 Emma and Anna are great friends. They hit it ___ the first time they met.
A off
B on
C out
D over

37 It took him years to get ___ the loss of his mother.
A out
B over
C off
D on

38 With ___ , we cannot come to your party.
A regret
B agony
C panic
D curiosity

39 I'm sorry, we had to ___ off the meeting.
A tell
B make
C call
D come

40 Despite the rain, the festival is expected to go ___ .
A along
B away
C around
D ahead

Unit 5

Awareness

1 Which of these sentences are correct (C) and incorrect (I)?

1 We had just arrived when the show began. _C_
2 The manager hadn't being informed. _I_
3 They had been played non-stop for hours. _I_
4 Had you been searching for a long time? _C_
5 The teacher had been waiting for everyone to calm down. _C_

6 She decided not to go because she hadn't been enjoying it last time. ___
7 We had wrote to them about this before. ___
8 The children had been swimming all morning. ___
9 I hadn't heard about the new head teacher. ___
10 He'd been working for age. ___

How many did you get right? ☐

Grammar

Past perfect simple

Affirmative	Negative	Questions
I / He / She / It / We / You / They **had ('d) watched.**	I / He / She / It / We / You / They **had not (hadn't) watched.**	**Had** I / he / she / it / we / you / they **watched?**
Short answers		
Yes, I / he / she / it / we / you / they had.	**No,** I / he / she / it / we / you / they hadn't.	

Spelling: walk → walk**ed**, love → lov**ed**, travel → trave**lled**, study → stu**died**, play → pl**ayed**

We use the past perfect simple for an action or situation that finished before another action, situation or time in the past.
*I **had watched** every one of her films before I interviewed her.*

> **Note**
> Some verbs are irregular and do not follow these spelling rules. See a list of irregular verbs on pages 172–173.

> **Note**
> Some common time expressions that are often used with the past perfect simple are: *before, after, when, already, for, for a long time, for ages, just, never, once, since 2019 / July, yet*, etc.
> *The footballer hadn't played **for a long time** because of his injury.*

Past perfect continuous

Affirmative	Negative	Questions
I / He / She / It / We / You / They **had ('d) been reading.**	I / He / She / It / We / You / They **had not (hadn't) been reading.**	**Had** I / he / she / it / we / you / they **been reading?**
Short answers		
Yes, I / he / she / it / we / you / they **had.**	**No,** I / he / she / it / we / you / they **hadn't.**	

Spelling: make → mak**ing**, run → ru**nning**, tidy → ti**dying**

We use the past perfect continuous:
- for actions that started in the past and were still in progress when something happened.
*The audience **had been waiting** half an hour before the band came on stage.*
- for actions that were in progress in the past and had an effect on a later action.
*Steve was exhausted because he **had been training** hard all day.*

> **Note**
> Some common time expressions that are often used with the past perfect continuous are: *all day / night / week, for years / a long time / ages, since*. We can use *How long ...?* with the past perfect continuous in questions.
> ***How long** had it been raining before they cancelled the tennis tournament?*

5

Grammar exercises

2 **Choose the correct option to complete the sentences.**

1 When her parents arrived, *she had done* / had been doing her homework for three hours.
2 As soon as she got home, she realised she had left / *had been leaving* her glasses at work.
3 My brother *had tried* / had been trying to repair the TV for two hours before I called him.
4 Lisa had never seen / *had never been seeing* such a beautiful painting.
5 Amanda *had worked* / had been working as a waitress for three years before she became a singer.
6 By the time the film ended, she had fallen / *had been falling* asleep on the sofa.
7 What had they seen / *had they been seeing* that made them so frightened?
8 *Had you lived* / Had you been living in the house for long before the fire destroyed it?

3 **Complete the sentences with the past perfect simple or past perfect continuous form of the verbs.**

1 Mary _____ *had been studying* _____ (study) for ten hours before she went to bed.
2 How long _____ *had you been cleaning* _____ (you / clean) your room for when your mother arrived yesterday?
3 I _____ *had been driving* _____ (drive) for three hours when the accident happened.
4 She told the doctor that she _____ *hadn't slept* _____ (not / sleep) for two nights.
5 Until I found this job, I _____ *had been searching* _____ (search) for almost ten months without success.
6 Until yesterday, he _____ *had never ridden* _____ (never / ride) a motorbike before.
7 By the time I got to the theatre, the play _____ *had started* _____ (start).
8 We still _____ *hadn't finished* _____ (not / finish) cooking by the time our guests arrived.

4 **Choose the correct time expression (a–c) to complete the sentences.**

1 She had been waiting for an opportunity like this ___ years.
   (a) for   **b** since   **c** already
2 What exactly had they been doing ___ ?
   a today   **(b)** all day   **c** next time
3 Mark had never been to a Formula 1 race ___ .
   a after   **b** just   **(c)** before
4 ___ I had spoken, I regretted it.
   (a) As soon as   **b** While   **c** Until
5 ___ had you been practising for?
   a What time   **(b)** How long   **c** When
6 We had ___ met two years before, and I had asked for his advice.
   a never   **b** always   **(c)** already

5 **Complete the sentences with one word in each gap.**

1 By the _____ *time* _____ I was 11, I'd learned to play five different musical instruments.
2 We hadn't been on holiday _____ *for* _____ a very long time.
3 Tina had _____ *been* _____ training all afternoon and now she felt tired.
4 _____ *Had* _____ you looked under the bed for your laptop before you asked to borrow Simon's?
5 It was a disappointing match. We had been looking forward to it _____ *all* _____ season.
6 She had done a lot of research _____ *before* _____ she interviewed the professor.
7 No, we had _____ *not* _____ heard of the actor – that's why we didn't know he was famous.
8 _____ *What* _____ had they done to win first prize in the competition?

6 **Write questions for the answers.**

1 **A:** *How long had you been trying to get in touch with her* ?
  B: I'd been trying to get in touch with her for three months.

2 **A:** *Had he been told about the new deadline* ?
  B: Yes, he had been told about the new deadline.

3 **A:** *How many pairs of shoes had she tried on (before she found a pair she liked)* ?
  B: She had tried on three pairs of shoes before she found a pair she liked.

4 **A:** *What had you been doing / Where had you been working* ?
  B: I had been working in the garden.

5 **A:** *Had he been crying* ?
  B: No, he hadn't been crying. He'd been sleeping.

6 **A:** *How many times had you met her before* ?
  B: I'd met her twice before.

7 **A:** *When had she spoken to him* ?
  B: She had spoken to him the day before yesterday.

8 **A:** *Where had they just been* ?
  B: They had just been to the circus.

7 **Correct the sentences where necessary. Tick those which do not need correcting.**

1 I hadn't sold any paintings since ages.
  I hadn't sold any paintings for ages.

2 Maria had been dancing with Paulo all night.
  ✓

3 Mum was upset because the twins had been fight again.
  Mum was upset because the twins had been fighting again.

4 How long had it been for you had checked your emails?
  How long had it been since you had checked your emails?

5 Had they been practise for the concert for a long time?
  Had they been practising for the concert for a long time?

6 We voted after everyone has had the chance to give their opinion.
  We voted after everyone had had the chance to give their opinion.

Vocabulary

Phrasal verbs

8 **Match the phrasal verbs (1–8) with their meanings (a–h).**

1	catch on	*b*	**a**	be as good as
2	catch up on	*h*	**b**	become popular
3	come in for	*f*	**c**	not be punished for doing something wrong
4	come up with	*g*	**d**	(of time) pass
5	get away with	*c*	**e**	circulate or spread
6	go around	*e*	**f**	receive (criticism or praise)
7	go by	*d*	**g**	suggest an idea or plan
8	live up to	*a*	**h**	find out what's been happening

9 Complete the sentences with the correct form of the phrasal verbs from Exercise 8.

1 There is a rumour _____*going around*_____ that a famous athlete is visiting our school.
2 Tom is reading the paper to _____*catch up on*_____ all the latest news.
3 The photographer _____*came in for*_____ a lot of criticism for his last exhibition.
4 Ella has _____*come up with*_____ a brilliant idea to help the local community.
5 Do you think that meeting a celebrity would _____*live up to*_____ your expectations?
6 The new style of trainers wasn't very comfortable, so it never really _____*caught on*_____ .
7 People who cheat in exams should never _____*get away with*_____ it.
8 I can't believe that two whole weeks have _____*gone by*_____ and there hasn't been any rain!

Prepositions

10 Choose the correct option to complete the sentences.

1 Have you ever made a fool of yourself at / (in) / by / behind public?
2 The audience seldom know what goes on at / in / by / (behind) the scenes of a theatre.
3 Success always comes (at) / in / by / behind a price – and that price is usually years of hard work.
4 She hopes to follow at / (in) / by / behind her aunt's footsteps and become an architect.
5 Can I talk to you at / (in) / by / behind private? I have something important to tell you.
6 At / In / (By) / Behind all accounts, this is the best film she has ever made.

Collocations and expressions

11 Complete the sentences with the correct form of these words.

draw   lead   lose   see   seize   set

1 I love science. I don't think I will ever _____*lose*_____ my passion for it.
2 Malala Yousafzai has _____*led*_____ the way in fighting for the rights of girls to education.
3 Famous sports people should _____*set*_____ a good example by playing fairly.
4 When Dan had a holiday job at the theatre, he _____*seized*_____ the chance to talk to the actors.
5 We played a joke on Dad, but he didn't _____*see*_____ the funny side of it!
6 Some celebrities don't like to _____*draw*_____ attention to themselves in public.

Words easily confused

12 Complete the sentences with the correct form of these words. Use each word at least once.

1 gap   interval   pause

a The dog must have escaped through a(n) _____*gap*_____ in the fence.
b The play was so bad that we left during the _____*interval*_____ .
c There are _____*pauses*_____ in the online lesson which give you time to practise.

2 borrow   hire   lend   rent

a Harold denied that I had _____*lent*_____ him the money.
b We've _____*rented*_____ a villa for the whole summer.
c If I were you, I wouldn't _____*borrow*_____ money from anyone.
d They _____*hired*_____ a children's entertainer for the party.

3 amount   extent   range

a You can choose from a wide _____*range*_____ of books at this shop.
b I agree with you to some _____*extent*_____ , but we differ on a few points.
c They received a large _____*amount*_____ of money to build a new concert hall.

4 | memorise   recognise   remember   remind |

a He'd changed so much that I didn't _recognise_ him.
b _Remember_ to switch off the lights when you leave.
c The actors spent a long time trying to _memorise_ their lines for the play.
d _Remind_ me to phone Grandad this evening.

Word formation   verb → noun

13 Use the word in capitals to form a word that fits in the gap.

1 It can take a long time and a lot of work to make your dreams a _reality_ . **REALISE**
2 I've never forgotten the _encouragement_ that my piano teacher gave me. **ENCOURAGE**
3 The painter took many _influences_ from other artists to create his style. **INFLUENCE**
4 The airline is one of the football team's biggest _sponsors_ . **SPONSOR**
5 Remember that _failure_ can be an important part of the learning process. **FAIL**
6 Very few writers achieve _success_ with their first book. **SUCCEED**
7 What was the _inspiration_ for the band's new album? **INSPIRE**
8 You need a lot of _determination_ to find your dream job. **DETERMINE**

Sentence transformation

14 Complete the second sentence so that it has a similar meaning to the first sentence, using the word given. Do not change the word given. You must use between two and five words.

1 Mary didn't start eating until all the family had sat down.
BEFORE
Mary waited until all the family _had sat down before_ she started eating.

2 When we got home, she was still painting the room.
FINISHED
She _hadn't / had not finished painting_ the room when we arrived.

3 Natalie graduated from university, then travelled around the world.
AFTER
Natalie travelled around the world _after graduating / after she had graduated_ from university.

4 Serena had some interesting ideas for our project.
UP
Serena _came up with_ some interesting ideas for our project.

5 Lots of people praised Mark's essay in the school magazine.
CAME
Mark's essay in the school magazine _came in for_ a lot of praise.

6 The presentation was interesting, so it felt like the time passed quickly.
BY
The time seemed to _go by_ quickly because the presentation was interesting.

7 Everybody says this is a terrible novel.
ACCOUNTS
By _all accounts_ , this is a terrible novel.

8 The musician wore dark glasses because he didn't want people to see him.
DRAW
The musician wore dark glasses because he didn't want to _draw attention to_ himself.

Unit 6

1 **Which of these sentences are correct (C) and incorrect (I)?**

1 Dan was in bed for an hour when we got home. _I_

2 We never found out what had happened. _C_

3 By the time he was 14 he had since become rich. _I_

4 Had the audience stopped clapping when you left the stage? _C_

5 They were starving because they hadn't had breakfast. _C_

6 Did you been waiting long? _I_

7 I was annoyed because I had worked hard on the project. _C_

8 Someone had drink all the milk. _I_

9 We hadn't been driving long when we got a puncture. _C_

10 They had woke in the night to find their tent had been stolen. _I_

How many did you get right? ☐

Grammar

Past simple, past perfect simple and past perfect continuous

When we want to show in which order actions happened in the past, we use the past perfect for the action that happened first in the past and we use the past simple for the actions that followed.

He **had been working** as a mechanic when a football agent **discovered** him and signed him to Manchester City. (First, he had been working as a mechanic and then a football agent discovered him.)

In time clauses with words like *after, as soon as, before, by the time, once, until* and *when*, you can use either the past simple or the past perfect to refer to an earlier event, with no important difference in meaning.

As soon as I (had) finished my homework, I went out.

I went out as soon as I (had) finished my homework.

Grammar exercises

2 **Choose the correct option to complete the sentences.**

1 When I ⟨saw⟩/ had seen Bill yesterday, he hadn't sold his car.

2 The plane *already took off /* ⟨had already taken off⟩ when we arrived at the airport.

3 As soon as she got home, she realised that somebody *broke /* ⟨had broken⟩ in and stolen all her medals.

4 When I ⟨arrived⟩/ had arrived at the cinema, my friend Alice had already bought the tickets.

5 After I *ran /* ⟨had been running⟩ for an hour, I stopped to have a drink.

6 By the time Zak ⟨phoned⟩/ had phoned Amelia, she had already arranged to go out.

7 That was the first time I *ever sang /* ⟨had ever sung⟩ on stage.

8 The moment the bus arrived, I realised that I *left /* ⟨had left⟩ my wallet at home.

3 **Complete the sentences with one word in each gap.**

1 We _____did_____ not feel like going out the other night.

2 By the time the photographer arrived, the guests _____had_____ left.

3 David and Megan had only _____been_____ playing in the band for a few weeks.

4 _____Did_____ Greta have enough time to practise before the competition?

5 Where _____had_____ they met before?

6 I didn't want to leave _____until_____ I had shown everyone my certificate.

7 She hadn't performed on stage _____since_____ her last year at school.

8 We had been _____having_____ a lovely time when we realised that we were at the wrong party.

4 Complete the sentences with the past simple, past perfect simple or past perfect continuous form of the verbs.

1 The teacher _____told_____ (tell) us that he _had been teaching_ (teach) for ten years.

2 She _____tried_____ (try) to explain how she _had come up with_ (come up with) her invention.

3 By the time I _____got_____ (get) to the concert hall, the choir _had been singing_ (sing) for over half an hour.

4 I _____didn't relax_____ (not / relax) until I _had finished_ (finish) my presentation.

5 We _had been looking_ (look) for a hotel room since we _____arrived_____ (arrive) in the city, and we were exhausted.

6 John _hadn't been riding_ (not / ride) very long when he _____realised_____ (realise) that he _____had forgotten_____ (forget) to bring his packed lunch.

7 How long _had you been walking_ (you / walk) in the mountains when it _____started_____ (start) to rain?

8 _____Did you see_____ (you / see) the children when they _____got_____ (get) home last night? They _____were_____ (be) very dirty and really tired! What _had they been doing_ (they / do)?

5 Complete the sentences with these time expressions.

| after | already | by the time | for | since | until |

1 I only started taking driving lessons _____after_____ I had bought a new car.

2 The train had already left _____by the time_____ we reached the station.

3 Susanna had been waiting for me _____since_____ four o'clock.

4 They had been trying to solve the problem _____for_____ three hours when they finally found the solution.

5 She had _____already_____ done her homework by the time her friend came to see her.

6 He didn't leave _____until_____ he had paid the bill.

6 Use the prompts to write sentences with the past simple and past perfect.

1 Sally / not / finish writing her essay / when / I call her
Sally hadn't finished writing her essay when I called her.

2 As soon as / I finish the race / I realise / I run my fastest time
As soon as I finished the race, I realised I had run my fastest time.

3 They / not / start the ceremony / until / all the guests arrive
They didn't start the ceremony until all the guests had arrived.

4 By the time / he be 25 / he / become a successful designer
By the time he was 25, he had become a successful designer.

5 After / the famous actor / win an Oscar / she retire
After the famous actor had won an Oscar, she retired.

6 We / not / serve the cake / until / everyone / finish the main course
We didn't serve the cake until everyone had finished the main course.

7 Natalie / not graduate from university / when / they offer her a job
Natalie hadn't graduated from university when they offered her a job.

8 I / finish / my homework / by the time / I go to bed
I had finished my homework by the time I went to bed.

7 **Write questions for the answers.** *Possible answers*

1 **A:** *W___n did you finish your homework* _____ ?

   B: I finished my homework an hour ago.

2 **A:** *H___ you been talking for a long time* _____ ?

   B: Yes, we'd been talking for quite a long time.

3 **A:** *W___re had they been travelling / What had they been doing* _____ ?

   B: They had been travelling around South America.

4 **A:** *H___ you heard the song before* _____ ?

   B: No, I hadn't heard the song before.

5 **A:** *D___ you think it was a good idea at the time* _____ ?

   B: Yes, I thought it was a good idea at the time.

6 **A:** *W___re had they been performing / What had they been doing* _____ ?

   B: They had been performing in small clubs and at parties.

7 **A:** *W___n did the journalist interview the writer / Who did the journalist interview last week* _____ ?

   B: The journalist interviewed the writer last week.

8 **A:** *W___ was she excited* _____ ?

   B: She was excited because she had just spoken to an astronaut.

Vocabulary

Phrasal verbs

8 **Match the phrasal verbs (1–8) with their meanings (a–h).**

1	live for	*g*	**a**	begin
2	live on	*d*	**b**	respect and admire
3	look down on	*e*	**c**	investigate or examine
4	look into	*c*	**d**	mainly eat a particular kind of food
5	look up to	*b*	**e**	think you are better than someone else
6	make up for	*h*	**f**	not have the opportunity to enjoy something
7	miss out on	*f*	**g**	have something or someone as the most important thing in your life
8	start out	*a*	**h**	when something good replaces something bad

9 **Complete the sentences with the correct form of the phrasal verbs from Exercise 8.**

1 The head teacher promised to _____*look into*_____ the accusations of cheating in his school.

2 She thinks she's so great. She _____*looks down on*_____ everyone!

3 No one should have to _____*miss out on*_____ an education.

4 I've always _____*looked up to*_____ my grandmother. She made an important discovery in chemistry.

5 Do you think that having money would _____*make up for*_____ losing your privacy?

6 My uncle is a famous journalist who _____*started out*_____ at a local newspaper.

7 I love Italian food. I could _____*live on*_____ pasta very happily!

8 Sara is very passionate about music. In fact, you could say she _____*lives for*_____ it.

Prepositions

10 Choose the correct option to complete the sentences.

1 I haven't been sleeping well because I've been *on / to /* under */ without* a lot of pressure.
2 He wasn't able to do PE that day on */ to / under / without* account of his bad leg.
3 Much *on /* to */ under / without* our astonishment, we won the match 6–1.
4 Don't worry, we have everything *on / to /* under */ without* control.
5 He couldn't make it to the ceremony, so his manager accepted the award on */ to / under / without* his behalf.
6 That was *on / to / under /* without a doubt the most terrifying rollercoaster ride I have ever been on.

Collocations and expressions

11 Complete the sentences with these words.

anywhere   doors   fame   name   nowhere   success

1 The band came out of _____nowhere_____ . A year ago, no one had heard of them.
2 If you don't practise the guitar regularly, you'll never get _____anywhere_____ with it.
3 Everyone knows the TV presenter now – she's a household _____name_____ .
4 He's talented, but knowing a film producer certainly opened _____doors_____ for him.
5 The secret of my _____success_____ is not being afraid to fail sometimes.
6 My sister's claim to _____fame_____ is that she won a national science competition when she was ten.

Words easily confused

12 Complete the sentences with the correct form of these words. Use each word at least once.

1 prescription   receipt   recipe   review

a You can't exchange goods without a _____receipt_____ .
b The play received excellent _____reviews_____ .
c I found the _____recipe_____ for this meal on an app.
d You need a _____prescription_____ to get this medicine.

2 charge   fee   payment   reward   tip

a I won't leave a _____tip_____ if I'm not satisfied with the service.
b A _____reward_____ has been offered for information leading to the return of the stolen medals.
c We deliver and install the system at no extra _____charge_____ .
d The _____fees_____ are so high that few parents can afford to send their children to that school.
e Unless we receive _____payment_____ within a week, your order will be cancelled.

3 company   factory   firm   industry

a She works for a law _____firm_____ in the capital.
b The inventor saw her idea being made into reality at the _____factory_____ .
c All the managers here have _____company_____ cars.
d This area depends heavily on the film _____industry_____ .

4 disgrace   gossip   rumour   scandal

a There's a _____rumour_____ going round that the singer is leaving the band.
b I'm not interested in celebrity _____gossip_____ , so I don't read that magazine.
c Many people have called for the players to resign after the cheating _____scandal_____ .
d The way the celebrity was treated by photographers was a _____disgrace_____ !

6

Word formation   noun → noun

13 Use the word in capitals to form a word that fits in the gap.

1 Sadly, our _____*friendship*_____ ended when the band split up.   **FRIEND**
2 The world's leading _____*scientists*_____ all agree that global warming is real.   **SCIENCE**
3 He left school at 16 and got a job in a _____*bakery*_____ .   **BAKER**
4 Some famous journalists started out as _____*bloggers*_____ on the internet.   **BLOG**
5 In the oral test, the _____*examiner*_____ will ask you questions about your life.   **EXAM**
6 Green eyes are a common _____*characteristic*_____ in our family.   **CHARACTER**
7 The time has come for _____*action*_____ , not words.   **ACT**
8 I have only one _____*criticism*_____ of the play – it was incredibly boring.   **CRITIC**
9 What _____*nationality*_____ are you?   **NATION**
10 The football team receives a large amount of _____*sponsorship*_____ from a mobile phone company.   **SPONSOR**

Sentence transformation

14 Complete the second sentence so that it has a similar meaning to the first sentence, using the word given. Do not change the word given. You must use between two and five words.

1 Dad didn't go to bed until my brother had come home.
   WAITED
   Dad _____*waited until my brother had*_____ come home before he went to bed.

2 It was the first time our teacher had shouted at us.
   NEVER
   Our teacher _____*had never shouted at us*_____ before.

3 Which famous people do you respect and admire?
   LOOK
   Which famous people do you _____*look up to*_____ ?

4 Truly great people don't think they're better than other people.
   DOWN
   Truly great people don't _____*look down on*_____ other people.

5 Football is the most important thing in Malcolm's life.
   FOR
   Malcolm _____*lives for*_____ football.

6 Because of her illness, Stella couldn't go to the award ceremony.
   ACCOUNT
   Stella couldn't go to the award ceremony _____*on account of*_____ her illness.

7 That was the best party this year, definitely.
   DOUBT
   That was _____*without doubt*_____ the best party this year.

8 The police are investigating the disappearance of the painting.
   INTO
   The police _____*are looking into*_____ the disappearance of the painting.

1 **Which of these sentences are correct (C) and incorrect (I)?**

1 I've decided I'm not going join the army. ⊥
2 Will you come this way, please? C
3 We'll had left this place by the weekend. ⊥
4 Shall we going to a restaurant this evening? ⊥
5 By the time you'll get home, you'll be exhausted. ⊥

6 I think I'll get a taxi home tonight. C
7 You'll have been working here since two years tomorrow. ⊥
8 Look out! That dog is going to bite you. C
9 After I'm going to have a bath, I'm going out. ⊥
10 He'll be doing his final exam this time next week. C

How many did you get right? ☐

Grammar

will

Affirmative	Negative	Questions
I / He / She / It / We / You / They **will** drive.	I / He / She / It / We / You / They **will not (won't)** drive.	**Will** I / he / she / it / we / you / they drive?
Short answers		
Yes, I / he / she / it / we / you / they **will**.	**No**, I / he / she / it / we / you / they **won't**.	

We use *will*:
- for decisions made at the time of speaking.
It's hot in here. I'll open the window.
- for predictions.
Buses won't have drivers in the future.
- for promises.
I'll book tickets tonight, I promise.
- for threats.
If you don't clear the table, I won't take you to the cinema.
- to talk about future facts.
The new game will be released in May.
- after verbs like *think, believe, be sure, expect*, etc. and before words like *probably, maybe*, etc.
I'm sure the new shopping centre will be popular.
- to offer to do something for someone.
I'll help you with that.
- to ask someone to do something.
Will you make me a sandwich, please?

We use *shall* with *I* and *we* in questions or when we want to make a suggestion or an offer.
Where shall we eat?
Shall we have lunch before the show?
Shall I park the car on the street?

We can use *should* instead of *will* to make a prediction when we're not 100% sure.
Our guests should be here soon, I expect.
Don't worry – it shouldn't be a problem to get a refund.

be going to

Affirmative	Negative	Questions
I am ('m) **going to** drive. He / She / It **is** ('s) **going to** drive. We / You / They **are** ('re) **going to** drive.	I am ('m) **not going to** drive. He / She / It **is not** (**isn't**) **going to** drive. We / You / They **are not** (**aren't**) **going to** drive.	**Am** I **going to** drive? **Is** he / she / it **going to** drive? **Are** we / you / they **going to** drive?
Short answers		
Yes, I **am**. **Yes**, he / she / it **is**. **Yes**, we / you / they **are**.	**No**, I'm **not**. **No**, he / she / it **isn't**. **No**, we / you / they **aren't**.	

We use *be going to* for:
- future plans.

*Jane **is going to buy** an electric car.*
- predictions for the near future based on present situations or evidence.

*Look at the queue! It**'s going to take** a long time to get a table.*

> **Note**
>
> Some common time expressions that are often used with *will* and *be going to* are: *this week / month / summer, tonight, this evening, tomorrow, tomorrow morning / afternoon / night, next week / month / year, at the weekend, in April, in a few minutes / hours / days, on Tuesday, on Saturday morning,* etc.
> *I**'ll tell** you all about the concert **tonight**.*

Future continuous

Affirmative	Negative	Questions
I / He / She / It / We / You / They **will be** work**ing**.	I / He / She / It / We / You / They **will not** (**won't**) **be** work**ing**.	**Will** I / he / she / it / we / you / they **be** work**ing**?
Short answers		
Yes, I / he / she / it / we / you / they **will**.	**No**, I / he / she / it / we / you / they **won't**.	

Spelling: dance → danc**ing**, travel → trave**lling**, ti**dy** → ti**dying**

We use the future continuous for:
- actions in progress at a specific time in the future.

*We**'ll be arriving** at the airport at this time next week.*
- plans and arrangements for the future.

*Parents **will be attending** a meeting about the new school.*

> **Note**
>
> Some common time expressions that are often used with the future continuous are: *this time next week / month / summer, this time tomorrow morning / afternoon / night,* etc.
> ***This time tomorrow**, he**'ll be working** in the new office.*

Future perfect simple and future perfect continuous

Affirmative	Negative	Questions
I / He / She / It / We / You / They **will have worked / been working**.	I / He / She / It / We / You / They **will not** (**won't**) **have worked / been working**.	**Will** I / he / she / it / we / you / they **have worked / been working**?
Short answers		
Yes, I / he / she / it / we / you / they **will**.	**No**, I / he / she / it / we / you / they **won't**.	

Spelling: walk → walk**ed**, dance → danc**ed**, travel → trave**lled**, ti**dy** → ti**died**, play → play**ed**

We use the future perfect simple to talk about:

- something that will be finished by or before a specific time in the future.

*The builders **will have finished** by the end of this week.*

- the length of time that an action will have lasted for at a point of time in the future.

*I**'ll have worked** here for three years next month.*

We use the future perfect continuous when we are looking back to the past from a point in the future. We can use it to talk about events or situations that will happen over a period of time and may have a result.

*By the end of tomorrow, I**'ll have been studying** all day, so I'll be tired.*

Time phrases

When we use time phrases such as *when, before, after, until, once, by the time,* etc. to talk about the future, we use them with a present or a present perfect tense. We do not use them with a future tense.

***After** I **have been** shopping, I'll meet a friend for lunch.*

***By the time** he **gets** to work, he'll be soaking wet.*

We use the present perfect simple to emphasise that the first action must be finished before the second starts.

***Once** you **have bought** the ticket, you can go anywhere in the park. (You need to buy the ticket and then you will be able to go anywhere in the park.)*

> **Note**
>
> Some verbs are irregular and do not follow these spelling rules. See a list of irregular verbs and their past participles on pages 172–173.

> **Note**
>
> Other tenses that describe the future are the present simple for timetabled events, and the present continuous for plans and arrangements.
> *The train to Manchester **leaves** at three o'clock.*
> *My sister **is moving in** to her new flat next week.*

> **Note**
>
> Some common time phrases that are often used with the future perfect simple and continuous are: *by the end of the week / month / year, by this time tomorrow, by tomorrow morning / ten o'clock / 2023,* etc.

Grammar exercises

2 **Choose the correct option to complete the sentences.**

1 I promise I'll never forget / I won't be forgetting your birthday again.
2 I'll work / I'll be working at 9 p.m. – I won't be home at that time.
3 Wait a minute. I'll call / I'll be calling a taxi now.
4 Sue will have been working / will work here for ten years by the end of the month.
5 Dan won't eat / won't have eaten so let's take him a sandwich.
6 Our friends will be finishing / will have finished eating by the time we arrive at the restaurant!
7 When I get home in the afternoon, my brother will be playing / will play basketball in the park.
8 Don't forget. The plane lands / will land at 7 p.m.

3 **Complete the sentences with *will* or the future continuous of the verbs.**

1 I _____'ll / will help_____ (help) you carry the sofa. Don't worry.
2 I think he _____'ll / will be_____ (be) here soon.
3 Don't call me at 6 p.m. – _____'ll / will be driving_____ (drive) home at that time.
4 This time tomorrow we _____'ll / will be having_____ (have) lunch in the new restaurant.
5 I really don't know where _____'ll / will be working_____ (work) this time next year.
6 It's an amazing building. I'm sure you _____'ll / will like_____ (like) it.

7

4 Complete the sentences with the *will* or *be going to* form of the verbs.

1 _____*Will you open*_____ (you / open) the door for me, please?
2 I've decided I _____*'m going to buy*_____ (buy) a flat.
3 Look at the red sky! It _____*'s going to be*_____ (be) a nice day tomorrow.
4 Is your bike not working? I _____*'ll / will have*_____ (have) a look at it for you.
5 I promise I _____*'ll / will be*_____ (be) on time for the cinema this evening.
6 We _____*'re going to play*_____ (play) tennis this evening. The court is booked for 6 p.m.

5 Complete the sentences with the future continuous, future perfect simple or future perfect continuous of the verbs.

1 By the end of next month, I _____*'ll have been singing*_____ (sing) in the choir for ten years.
2 If Martin is with them, they _____*'ll be talking*_____ (talk) about architecture.
3 I _____*'ll be working*_____ (work) late this evening, so don't wait up for me.
4 By the year 2030, we _____*'ll have built*_____ (build) 100,000 new homes.
5 We _____*'ll be staying*_____ (stay) with my aunt until we find another flat.
6 At the end of the year, Dr Green _____*will have been teaching*_____ (teach) at this university for thirty years.

6 Choose the correct option (a–b).

1 Can you come shopping with us tomorrow morning?
   a Sorry, but I'll see my dentist tomorrow morning.
   (b) Sorry, but I'm seeing my dentist tomorrow morning.

2 I'd really like to meet you on Saturday.
   (a) Great! I'm not doing anything then.
   b Great! I don't do anything then.

3 What are you thinking about?
   a This time tomorrow, I will fly to New York.
   (b) This time tomorrow, I'll be flying to New York.

4 This is the second time you've lied to me.
   (a) Sorry, Mum. I'll never lie to you again.
   b Sorry, Mum. I won't be lying to you again.

5 Can you give Tom this parcel for me, please?
   a Of course I can. I will have seen Tom today.
   (b) Of course I can. I am seeing Tom today.

6 Are you reading another book?
   a Yes, I will be finishing it by this evening.
   (b) Yes, I will have finished it by this evening.

7 Complete the sentences with one word in each gap.

1 I'm going ___*to*___ do my maths homework now.
2 By noon, I will ___*have*___ painted my room blue.
3 Will you ___*be*___ attending the seminar this afternoon?
4 He's not ___*going*___ to finish this by six o'clock.
5 ___*Is*___ Simon going to cycle this evening?
6 When ___*will*___ you have completed your design?
7 By the time the meal ___*is*___ ready, I'll be starving!
8 Sara will have ___*been*___ waiting for hours by now.

Vocabulary

Phrasal verbs

8 Match the phrasal verbs (1–8) with their meanings (a–h).

1	hang out	b	a	go on holiday or a break
2	hang up	d	b	spend time with somebody socially
3	hang on	g	c	change the subject you are talking about
4	move in	e	d	stop a telephone conversation
5	move out	h	e	start living in a place
6	move on	c	f	start feeling comfortable in a place
7	settle down	f	g	wait for a short while
8	get away	a	h	leave the place you live in

9 Complete the sentences with the correct form of the phrasal verbs from Exercise 8.

1 We _____*moved out*_____ of our flat when my little brother was born.

2 Please _____*hang on*_____ a minute. I'll see if I can find your order.

3 It took us a while to _____*settle down*_____ in our new house, but we really love it now.

4 The Ross family like to try to _____*get away*_____ to the countryside twice a year.

5 He's going to redecorate before he _____*moves in*_____ to his new place.

6 Terry is _____*hanging out*_____ with his friends at the shopping centre.

7 Let's _____*move on*_____ to another subject, shall we?

8 Samantha _____*hung up*_____ the phone before we had finished talking!

Prepositions

10 Choose the correct option to complete the sentences.

1 One of the advantages **of** / among / on living in the city is that everything you need is nearby.

2 We agreed to buy the house of / among / **on** condition that they lowered the price.

3 London is of / **among** / on the most expensive cities in the world to live in.

4 Sammy got the job as a result **of** / among / on his qualifications and experience.

5 We get our post delivered to us of / among / **on** a daily basis.

6 We didn't like the flat because, of / **among** / on other things, it didn't have any windows.

Collocations and expressions

11 Complete the sentences with the correct form of these words.

consideration	ghost	place	talk	town	world

1 These directions aren't very clear. They're all over the _____*place*_____ !

2 This town is becoming like a _____*ghost*_____ town. Bands don't play here anymore.

3 I've got the best of both _____*worlds*_____ – I live in the city, but near a huge park.

4 Tom and Kate really went to _____*town*_____ on their wedding. They spent a lot of money.

5 Her new exhibition is the _____*talk*_____ of the town.

6 The architect took the views of the local residents into _____*consideration*_____ .

7

Words easily confused

12 Complete the sentences with the correct form of these words. Use each word at least once.

1 annoy   disturb   matter   mind   object

  a It doesn't _____ *matter* _____ what you wear to the party.

  b What really _____ *annoys* _____ me is people walking slowly while they look at their phones.

  c I don't want to be _____ *disturbed* _____ . Please leave me alone.

  d Dan _____ *objects* _____ to anyone parking in front of his house.

  e Would you _____ *mind* _____ helping me with the luggage?

2 attendance   attention   care   notice

  a Jill attracted the waiter's _____ *attention* _____ by waving.

  b The students took no _____ *notice* _____ of the 'No swimming' signs and dived into the lake.

  c Please pay _____ *attention* _____ to what I'm saying.

  d These boxes must be handled with _____ *care* _____ .

  e Your _____ *attendance* _____ record in this class is very poor.

3 approval   attitude   opinion   view

  a From my point of _____ *view* _____ , it's a waste of time.

  b What provoked their hostile _____ *attitude* _____ towards you?

  c My boss showed her _____ *approval* _____ of the way I ran the office by giving me a pay rise.

  d What's your _____ *opinion* _____ of the new process?

4 alike   identical   same   similar

  a It doesn't matter which way you go – the distance is _____ *identical* _____ by either route.

  b The new shop sells the _____ *same* _____ types of clothes as the old shop.

  c They get on well together because they're so much _____ *alike* _____ .

  d Your house is _____ *similar* _____ to mine, but yours has a bigger garden.

Word formation   adjective → opposite adjective

13 Use the word in capitals to form a word that fits in the gap.

  1 We didn't tip the waiter because he was very _____ *impolite* _____ .   **POLITE**

  2 It is very _____ *unlikely* _____ that they'll move to the countryside – they love the city.   **LIKELY**

  3 You can wear what you like at our office – we are very _____ *informal* _____ .   **FORMAL**

  4 Don't drive past the red traffic light – that's _____ *illegal* _____ !   **LEGAL**

  5 He's so _____ *dishonest* _____ that I don't think he has ever told the truth in his life!   **HONEST**

  6 It was really _____ *irresponsible* _____ of you to let Dan borrow your car – he hasn't got a licence!   **RESPONSIBLE**

  7 I'm afraid my new hairstyle makes me look rather _____ *unattractive* _____ .   **ATTRACTIVE**

  8 Your office is very _____ *disorganised* _____ . I'm surprised you ever find anything!   **ORGANISED**

  9 What a(n) _____ *extraordinary* _____ film that was. Incredible!   **ORDINARY**

  10 The shop is open at such _____ *irregular* _____ times – we never know when we can go there.   **REGULAR**

Sentence transformation

14 **Complete the second sentence so that it has a similar meaning to the first sentence, using the word given. Do not change the word given. You must use between two and five words.**

1 Our party is on Saturday afternoon at our house.

HAVING

We _____ *'re / are having a party at* _____ our house on Saturday afternoon.

2 If you don't hurry, we'll arrive after the film starts.

STARTED

If you don't hurry, _____ *the film will have started* _____ by the time we arrive.

3 I started building the wall on Monday, and it's now Wednesday.

HAVE

By Thursday, I _____ *'ll / will have been building* _____ the wall for four days.

4 We never really began to feel comfortable in the village.

SETTLED

We never really _____ *settled down* _____ in the village.

5 They like to go on holiday every winter.

AWAY

They like to _____ *get / go away* _____ every winter.

6 Because of the roadworks, we had to go a different way.

ACCOUNT

We had to go a different way _____ *on account of* _____ the roadworks.

7 Who do you like to spend time with socially?

HANG

Who do you _____ *like to hang out* _____ with?

8 If you don't like your flatmates, you should leave the flat.

OUT

You should _____ *move out (of the / your flat)* _____ if you don't like your flatmates.

1 Which of these sentences are correct (C) and incorrect (I)?

1 Take the rubbishes outside, please. ⊥
2 There is some good news for you in this letter. C
3 Hurry up! We don't have many time. ⊥
4 The police were asking questions about Carol. C
5 We're still waiting for some new equipments. ⊥

6 He gave me a useful advice. ⊥
7 How much brothers do you have? ⊥
8 Few people go to the theatre these days. C
9 Can you give me an information, please? ⊥
10 He didn't invite many friends to the party. C

How many did you get right? ☐

Grammar

Countable nouns

Most nouns are countable and have singular and plural forms.

shop → shop**s**   lorry → lorr**ies**   boy → boy**s**   potato → potato**es**
beach → beach**es**   lea**f** → lea**ves**   wo**man** → wo**men**   **foo**t → **fee**t

We often use *a* or *an* with singular countable nouns.
a road   an avenue

We can use *some*, *any* or a number (for example, *three*) with plural countable nouns.
*There are **some** dogs in the park.*
*Are there **any** trees in your garden?*
*I haven't been to the cinema for **three** years.*

We can use singular or plural verb forms with countable nouns depending on whether we are talking about one item or more.
*A **bike** is useful when you live in a big city.*
***Lorries** are noisy and cause a lot of congestion.*

Some plural countable nouns don't end in *-s*. Remember to use a plural verb form with them.
*He ran for miles and now his **feet are** sore.*

Uncountable nouns

Some nouns are uncountable. They do not have plural forms.

advice	food	health	knowledge	music	time
biology	fruit	history	luggage	progress	traffic
chocolate	fun	homework	medicine	research	water
furniture	information	money	rubbish	weather	

We don't use *a* or *an* with uncountable nouns. We can use *some* and *any*.
*I'd like **some** food, please.*   *I haven't got **any** money with me.*

We always use singular verb forms with uncountable nouns.
***Is** this information correct?*   *The traffic **was** awful!*

Some uncountable nouns end in *-s*. Remember to use a singular verb form with them.
*The **news** this morning was shocking.*   ***Maths is** my favourite subject.*

Nouns that can be countable or uncountable

Many nouns can be either countable or uncountable. Sometimes there is only a small difference in meaning.
*Would you like **some** tea? (uncountable)*   *Would you like **a** tea? (countable, a cup of tea)*

Sometimes there is a very different meaning.

Countable	Uncountable
The new meeting **room** is very comfortable.	Is there any more **room** on the bus?
The car park was full. There were no **spaces**.	There isn't enough **space** in this office!

Nouns that are always plural

Some nouns are never used in the singular form (with a particular meaning) and always take a plural verb.
I didn't like the **clothes** in the shop window.
I can't read that sign. I think I might need **glasses**.
The **police** were talking to people in the street.

Quantifiers

We use *some* with both uncountable and plural countable nouns in affirmative sentences and in requests or offers.
I bought **some headphones** this weekend.
Could I have **some advice**, please?
Would you like **some help** to carry those?

We use *any* with both uncountable and plural countable nouns in negative sentences and in questions.
There isn't **any furniture** in the apartment.
Have you seen **any** good **films** lately?

We use *a lot of / lots of* with both uncountable and plural countable nouns.
Lots of people visited the exhibition.
There was **a lot of rubbish** in the park.

We use *(a) little* (or *a bit of*) with uncountable nouns and *(a) few* with plural countable nouns in affirmative sentences. We use *a little / a few* to emphasise that there is a positive amount (i.e. more than zero). We use *little / few* to emphasise a negative amount (i.e. not as much / many as expected).
We've done **a little** research already. (= more than none)
There is **little** research on the subject. (= not enough)
A few residents came to look at the plans. (= a reasonable number)
Few residents wanted a new motorway. (= hardly any)

We use *much* with uncountable nouns and *many* with plural countable nouns in negative sentences and in questions.
How **much** luggage are you taking?
There aren't **many** students in this part of the city.

We can use *as much / many as* to talk about a surprisingly large number.
As many as 80,000 people watched the match in the stadium.

all, whole, every and each

Every and *each* always take a singular noun. *Every* suggests a larger number, but both words are often possible.
Each / Every house in the street has its own garden.
When we use *all* with a singular countable noun, it means 'from beginning to end'.
I worked **all** day on Saturday. (= from morning to evening)
Whole has a similar meaning, but it's an adjective, not a quantifier, so it usually comes after *a / the*.
I worked **the whole** day.

Quantifiers with and without of

After some quantifiers, we add *of* before a noun.
a lot of commuters, **plenty of** light, **a bit of** space, etc.
After some quantifiers, we don't normally add *of* before a noun.
several people, **a little** time, **most** people, etc.
However, we need to add *of* before *the*, a possessive (e.g. *my*) or a pronoun (e.g. *us*).
several **of the** people, a little **of my** time, most **of them**
We can usually omit *of* after *all* and *both*, with no change of meaning.
all (of) the traffic, both (of) my shoes

8

Grammar exercises

2 **Complete the sentences with the plural form of the nouns.**

1 There were some intelligent _____ women _____ at the meeting. (woman)
2 The archeologists made some interesting _____ discoveries _____ . (discovery)
3 The shop had a display of _____ toys _____ in the window. (toy)
4 James couldn't reach the top three _____ shelves _____ of the bookcase. (shelf)
5 The rose _____ bushes _____ in her garden looked beautiful. (bush)
6 Could you go to the market and buy six _____ tomatoes _____ , please? (tomato)
7 The _____ photos _____ of the city from the air were amazing. (photo)
8 If your _____ teeth _____ are hurting, you should see a dentist. (tooth)

3 **Decide if these nouns countable or uncountable. Complete the table.**

| boy | city | citizen | countryside | damage | furniture | leaf | potato |
| progress | research | shelf | street | stress | traffic | tree | weather |

Countable	_boy_	_citizen_	_potato_	_street_
	city	_leaf_	_shelf_	_tree_
Uncountable	_countryside_	_furniture_	_research_	_traffic_
	damage	_progress_	_stress_	_weather_

4 **Complete the sentences with *a*, *an*, *some* or *any*.**

1 We would like ____ some ____ information about the rooms in your hotel.
2 Mum, I need ____ some ____ money to buy ____ a ____ new notebook.
3 I watched ____ an ____ unusual film at the cinema yesterday.
4 We haven't bought ____ any ____ new furniture for years!
5 I'll get you __ a / some __ coffee. Would you like milk and sugar with it?
6 No, thank you. We don't need ____ any ____ advertising at the moment.

5 **Complete the sentences with *few*, *a few*, *little*, *a little* or *a lot*.**

1 ____ Few ____ people applied for the job, so they put another advertisement on the website.
2 The village is in a beautiful area, with very ____ little ____ pollution.
3 Jack has ____ a lot ____ of friends in this town. It seems that everybody likes him.
4 I gave my teacher ____ a few ____ ideas for the class project. He liked them a lot.
5 In ____ a few ____ years, most people will be using electric cars.
6 I have ____ a little ____ free time today. How about going to the cinema?
7 'Mum, I need ____ a lot ____ of help to fix my bike,' said Lauren.
8 The cyclist had ____ little ____ patience with the driver who was rude to him.

6 **Write questions using *How much* or *How many*.**

1 **A:** _How many times have you been to France_ ? **B:** I've been to France twice.
2 **A:** _How much money do you have / have you got_ ? **B:** I have £16.
3 **A:** _How many days is it to your birthday_ ? **B:** It's three days to my birthday.
4 **A:** _How many people were (there) at your party_ ? **B:** There were 20 people at my party.
5 **A:** _How much time does it take to learn the piano_ ? **B:** It takes a lot of time to learn the piano.
6 **A:** _How much milk do we need_ ? **B:** We just need a little milk.

7 Choose the correct option to complete the sentences.

1 My friend and I go running for an hour *all* / every Saturday.
2 Each / *Whole* house in the street is painted a different colour.
3 The planners spent the whole / *all* afternoon in a meeting.
4 *All* / Each competitor has an individual number.
5 Sam has cycled to school every / *whole* day this week.
6 I waited *whole* / all day for the new furniture to arrive.
7 The journalist said that the council was spending as much / *many* as £5 million on the project.
8 The organisers say they expect as *much* / many as 20,000 people to attend the festival.

8 Complete the sentences with one word in each gap.

1 Can I have a few ____*of*____ your peanuts, please?
2 There are ____*some*____ fresh yoghurts in the fridge.
3 No, thank you. I don't want ____*any*____ money.
4 I'm afraid the news ____*is*____ not good.
5 There aren't ____*many*____ places to play in this town – just a park and the village hall.
6 ____*Lots*____ of students live in this part of the city.
7 The traffic ____*is / was*____ really bad this morning.
8 My feet ____*are*____ hurting quite badly at the moment.

Vocabulary

Phrasal verbs

9 Match the phrasal verbs (1–8) with their meanings (a–h).

1	get across	*e*	a	have a good relationship with
2	get at	*h*	b	stand up
3	get round to	*c*	c	finally do something which you meant to do
4	get in	*d*	d	be chosen or accepted into an institution
5	get on	*a*	e	succeed in making someone understand something
6	get out of	*g*	f	succeed in a competition or exam
7	get through	*f*	g	avoid doing something which you don't want to do
8	get up	*b*	h	be able to reach something

10 Complete the sentences with the correct form of the phrasal verbs from Exercise 9.

1 It is important to ____*get on*____ with your colleagues.
2 I've got lots of homework, and I must ____*get round to*____ doing it before the weekend.
3 Our team ____*got through*____ the second round of the competition, then we were beaten 4–0.
4 Everyone ____*got up*____ out of their seats and applauded when he walked onto the stage.
5 Put the biscuits on the top shelf, so that the dog can't ____*get at*____ them.
6 The message I am trying to ____*get across*____ is 'be safe'.
7 Sam was very happy when he ____*got in*____ to his first choice of university.
8 If I can ____*get out of*____ going into town, I will. I really don't feel like it.

8

Prepositions

11 **Choose the correct option to complete the sentences.**

1 You can do what you like this weekend (as) / for / in far as I'm concerned.
2 I'm just going to sit here and relax as / (for) / in the moment – then I'll start work.
3 It wasn't such a bad film – (as) / for / in a matter of fact, I really enjoyed it.
4 They used to meet as / for / (in) secret in the park after school.
5 Why don't we go somewhere else as / (for) / in a change?
6 You need to submit your application as / for / (in) writing.

Collocations and expressions

12 **Complete the sentences with these words.**

| fail | increase | jungle | lane | life | temptation |

1 I can never resist the _____*temptation*_____ to buy fresh bread from the bakery.
2 The city is sometimes referred to as an urban _____*jungle*_____ .
3 Do you like living life in the fast _____*lane*_____ ?
4 This train is never late. It arrives at 7.43 every day, without _____*fail*_____ .
5 My parents came from very different walks of _____*life*_____ .
6 The number of people cycling to work is on the _____*increase*_____ . It went up by 12% last year.

Words easily confused

13 **Complete the sentences with the correct form of these words. Use each word at least once.**

1 | lay | lie | scatter | spread |

   a The demonstrators _____*scattered*_____ when the riot police appeared.
   b On average, our hens _____*lay*_____ one egg a day.
   c The detectives _____*spread*_____ out and searched the field for clues.
   d Could you help me _____*lay*_____ the table, please?
   e _____*Lie*_____ down if you feel tired and need to rest.

2 | age | period | term | time |

   a In this day and _____*age*_____ , up-to-date information is vital.
   b We get our school reports at the end of _____*term*_____ .
   c Do you remember the _____*time*_____ when we got lost in Rome?
   d He spent a long _____*period*_____ of his life working in China.

3 | condition | position | situation | state |

   a We've bought a second-hand car in excellent _____*condition*_____ .
   b The _____*situation*_____ got worse and worse until war broke out a year later.
   c Finding herself in a _____*position*_____ of power has changed her completely.
   d Your children are in an excellent _____*state*_____ of health.

4 | damage | harm | injury | pain | wound |

   a He still bears the scars of a _____*wound*_____ on his right leg.
   b A serious back _____*injury*_____ forced him to miss most of last season.
   c Brenda was in quite a lot of _____*pain*_____ after the operation.
   d Fortunately, the storm did little _____*damage*_____ to our property.
   e A short walk round the park won't do you any _____*harm*_____ !

Word formation   adverbs

14 Use the word in capitals to form a word that fits in the gap.

1 When everyone is sitting _comfortably_ , I will begin.   **COMFORT**
2 If you are not aware of what you are doing, you are acting _unconsciously_ .   **CONSCIOUS**
3 People who speak _offensively_ are never very popular.   **OFFEND**
4 The economy is _steadily_ getting stronger every year.   **STEADY**
5 It was _extraordinarily_ kind of him to let you stay in his house.   **EXTRAORDINARY**
6 I don't _generally_ agree with what she says, but she is making sense today.   **GENERAL**
7 Peter drives so _dangerously_ that nobody will get in the car with him.   **DANGER**
8 The light comes on _automatically_ when someone enters the room.   **AUTOMATIC**
9 If you didn't work so _carelessly_ , you wouldn't make so many mistakes.   **CARE**
10 The director made the actors rehearse the scene _repeatedly_ until it was perfect.   **REPEAT**

Sentence transformation

15 Complete the second sentence so that it has a similar meaning to the first sentence, using the word given. Do not change the word given. You must use between two and five words.

1 Not many students went on the school trip last week.
FEW
There was a school trip last week, but _few (of the) students_ went.

2 We have very little money, so we must spend carefully.
MUCH
We _don't have / do not have / haven't got / have not got much_ money, so we must spend carefully.

3 Simon has very few friends in this school.
MANY
Simon _doesn't have / does not have / hasn't got / has not got many_ friends in this school.

4 I tried, but I couldn't make him understand my concerns.
ACROSS
I tried, but I couldn't _get my concerns across_ to him.

5 It is impossible to avoid the end-of-term exam.
GET
You can't _get out of (taking / sitting)_ the end-of-term exam.

6 My sister and I have a really good relationship.
WELL
My sister and I _get on well_ with each other.

7 I don't mind mind if they pay me at the end of the month.
CONCERNED
As _far as I'm / I am concerned_ , they can pay me at the end of the month.

8 He asked me to write it down.
PUT
He asked me _to put it in_ writing.

B2 Practice: First

Part 1

For questions 1–8, read the text below and decide which answer (A, B, C or D) best fits each gap. There is an example at the beginning (0).

Recycling in the office

One of the most exciting **(0)** ___ in the field of recycling is a machine that can clean used photocopier paper. The device, **(1)** ___ a decopier, uses a mixture of chemicals and a brush, and leaves the paper completely clean. **(2)** ___ to the manufacturers, the machine is **(3)** ___ of cleaning one sheet of paper at least five times. This is because the damage **(4)** ___ to the paper by the cleaning chemicals is compensated for by a special chemical which increases its strength.

It is predicted that the machine will **(5)** ___ on despite the high cost. The initial price of £30,000 will be too high for small companies, but they will be able to **(6)** ___ one for a reasonable monthly sum, or wait for a cheaper version to come out. Multinational companies will have a golden **(7)** ___ to help the environment and save money. What is more, the machine will, to a great **(8)** ___ , provide a way to improve security, as it offers an alternative to shredding confidential documents.

	A		B		C		D	
0	A	revelations	(B)	inventions	C	discoveries	D	concoctions
1	(A)	called	B	named	C	known	D	described
2	A	Listening	B	Speaking	C	Accounting	(D)	According
3	(A)	capable	B	able	C	possible	D	potential
4	A	made	B	exposed	C	inflicted	(D)	done
5	(A)	catch	B	get	C	carry	D	bring
6	A	take	B	lend	(C)	rent	D	borrow
7	A	chance	(B)	opportunity	C	occasion	D	possibility
8	A	length	(B)	extent	C	range	D	amount

Part 2

For questions 9–16, read the text below and think of the word which best fits each gap.
Use only one word in each gap. There is an example at the beginning (0).

A commute with a view

At 3,650 metres above sea level, La Paz, in Bolivia, is (0) _____the_____ highest capital city in the world. Spread (9) _____out_____ over the sides of a deep valley, it combines spacious residential areas, a modern commercial centre and overcrowded areas with people living on (10) _____top_____ of each other in narrow streets and traditional houses.

La Paz is also home to the world's largest (11) _____and_____ highest urban public transport system. However, this does not consist (12) _____of_____ buses or trains, as you might expect, but cable cars. Opened (13) _____in_____ 2014, the network links the commercial centre of La Paz with the neighbouring city of El Alto, (14) _____which_____ is one of Bolivia's most rapidly-growing cities as people migrate from rural areas in search of employment.

The cable car network, known (15) _____as_____ 'Mi Teleférico' ('my cable car') has changed the lives of the inhabitants of El Alto who work in La Paz, as many do. Daily commutes which (16) _____used_____ to take two or three hours each way can now take half as long, or even less. And the view is certainly better!

Part 3

For questions 17–24, read the text below. Use the word given in capitals at the end of some of the lines to form a word that fits in the gap in the same line. There is an example at the beginning (0).

A better place to live

An Italian animal charity recently carried out a very (0) _____successful_____ operation.   **SUCCESS**

They managed to transfer five unhappy tigers from an extremely small and (17) _____uncomfortable_____   **COMFORT**

cage in Italy to much more (18) _____luxurious_____ surroundings in England. This is just one of   **LUXURY**

several wonderful examples of (19) _____international_____ cooperation between animal welfare   **NATIONAL**

organisations. The tigers' arrival at their new home has brought hope to people whose lives are

dedicated to the prevention of (20) _____cruelty_____ to animals on a daily basis.   **CRUEL**

Of course, such happy endings are not always possible. (21) _____Unfortunately_____ , not all animals   **FORTUNATE**

can be liberated from the often desperately (22) _____unhealthy_____ conditions in which they are   **HEALTH**

discovered. There are many reasons for this, but the most common one is delays in legal

procedures within the animals' host country.

Added to this is the fact that many courts are (23) _____insensitive_____ to the needs of animals   **SENSE**

in captivity. Concern for animal welfare is not the same across different cultures. In order to end

this (24) _____unnecessary_____ suffering, a greater understanding of the problem must be promoted   **NECESSITY**

worldwide.

Part 4

For questions 25–30, complete the second sentence so that it has a similar meaning to the first sentence, using the word given. Do not change the word given. You must use between two and five words, including the word given. Here is an example (0).

Example:

0   She has always admired and respected her older sister.

LOOKED

She has always _____ *looked up to* _____ her older sister.

25   The rent was lower than I had expected.

AS

The rent _____ *wasn't / was not as high as* _____ I had expected.

26   This is her first chess tournament.

NEVER

She _____ *'s / has never competed in / been in / entered a* _____ chess tournament before.

27   I've never looked after a dog before.

USED

I _____ *'m / am not used to looking* _____ after a dog.

28   His answer to the first question was wrong.

MISTAKE

He _____ *made a mistake* _____ in the first question.

29   Karen will never let you pay her share of the bill.

INSISTS

Karen _____ *always insists on paying* _____ her share of the bill.

30   Tim has suggested a brilliant idea for a holiday!

COME

Tim has _____ *come up with* _____ a brilliant idea for a holiday!

B2 Practice: ECCE

Grammar

For questions 1–20, choose the word or phrase that best completes the sentence or conversation.

1 When we arrived, the band ___ home.
   A had already went
   B have already went
   C had already gone
   D have already gone

2 They had been waiting ___ five hours.
   A since
   B until
   C yet
   D for

3 She ___ my letter by now.
   A receives
   B will have received
   C will be receiving
   D will receive

4 We'd finished by the ___ they got here.
   A hour
   B minute
   C time
   D second

5 ___ you close the window for me, please?
   A Are
   B Do
   C Will
   D Shall

6 She had never tried octopus ___ that day.
   A before
   B for
   C at
   D when

7 It ___ the first time she had driven a fast car.
   A was
   B is
   C had been
   D did

8 Does the soup need ___ more salt?
   A a little
   B a few
   C many
   D a lot of

9 Shall we just try and calm down ___ a moment?
   A for
   B at
   C with
   D by

10 '___ we go out tonight?'
   'Yes, let's.'
   A Are
   B Shall
   C Have
   D Do

11 After I ___ lunch, I'm going to bed.
   A will have
   B am having
   C have
   D had

12 I'd like ___ cheese and biscuits, please.
   A any
   B few
   C some
   D much

13 ___ you been informed about the meeting before it happened?
   A Have
   B Did
   C Had
   D Will

14 What are you ___ to study at university?
   A want
   B will
   C having
   D going

15 I was late because someone had ___ my keys.
   A hid
   B hidden
   C hiding
   D hide

16 You ___ left by the time I arrive, won't you?
   A will
   B have
   C going to
   D will have

17 Mum ___ at Grandma's house yet.
   A don't arrive
   B won't arrive
   C won't have arrived
   D hadn't arrived

18 Not too ___ cake for me, thanks.
   A many
   B lots
   C much
   D few

19 What ___ to win first prize in the competition?
   A had they done
   B did they
   C will they have done
   D do they

20 Sorry, but I haven't got ___ cash.
   A no
   B none
   C some
   D any

REVIEW 2

Vocabulary

For questions 21–40, choose the word or phrase that most appropriately completes the sentence.

21 I'll ___ into the possibility of forming a coding club.
A see
B hide
C watch
D look *(circled)*

22 How can I ___ up for forgetting your birthday?
A live
B make *(circled)*
C give
D come

23 I still haven't got ___ to writing to my mother.
A over
B round *(circled)*
C up
D through

24 That was delicious! Can I have the ___ ?
A receipt
B review
C recipe *(circled)*
D prescription

25 It's a nice idea, but I don't think it will ___ on.
A take
B have
C catch *(circled)*
D bring

26 As a ___ of fact, I do care about you.
A thing
B matter *(circled)*
C figure
D concept

27 Please ___ on a minute – I need to finish this call.
A wait
B hang *(circled)*
C move
D stay

28 Why does he look ___ on people?
A up
B over
C down *(circled)*
D round

29 George has become a household ___ since he acted in a TV series.
A face
B name *(circled)*
C man
D title

30 Koala bears ___ on eucalyptus leaves.
A eat
B drink
C are
D live *(circled)*

31 His latest novel ___ in for a lot of harsh criticism.
A came *(circled)*
B went
C ran
D fell

32 I'm catching ___ with my cousin on Saturday.
A down
B up *(circled)*
C along
D on

33 As far as I'm ___ , he can do what he wants.
A cared
B concerned *(circled)*
C known
D bothered

34 Greg has been ___ a lot of pressure.
A on
B at
C under *(circled)*
D over

35 The meeting was held ___ private.
A to
B on
C under
D in *(circled)*

36 It's a great restaurant, by all ___ .
A stories
B sayings
C bills
D accounts *(circled)*

37 Let's ___ somewhere for the weekend.
A get away *(circled)*
B go along
C get around
D go over

38 Shall we cycle into town, ___ a change?
A from
B for *(circled)*
C by
D in

39 I didn't understand the point he was trying to get ___ to us.
A in
B on
C across *(circled)*
D at

40 They really went to ___ on the food for the party!
A town *(circled)*
B world
C place
D zone

1 Which of these sentences are correct (C) and incorrect (I)?

1 We must to finish this by the end of the day. ___I___

2 You don't have to bring your computer. ___C___

3 They shouldn't eating so much cake. ___I___

4 He might be right about that. ___C___

5 Tonya ought join an athletics club. ___I___

6 Could you be explain this problem to me? ___I___

7 She needn't type out the whole report. ___C___

8 May I borrow your laptop? ___C___

9 Would you talking more quietly, please? ___I___

10 You should try to get some sleep. ___C___

How many did you get right? ☐

Grammar

Modals of permission

We can use *can* or *may* to ask for and give permission. *May* is formal and a little old-fashioned.
***Can** I come to the technology fair with you?*
*You **can** work on the science project with us, if you like.*
***May** I leave the class?*
*You **may** come into the examination hall now.*

We can use *be allowed to* to talk about permission (given by other people).
*When I was younger, I **was allowed** to play computer games at weekends, but I **wasn't allowed to** play them on school days.*

Modals of obligation

We use *must / mustn't* to talk about rules.
*Lab coats **must** be worn when doing science experiments.*
*You **must not** play around in the laboratory.*

We use *have to*, *need to* and *not be allowed to* to talk about rules (made by other people).
*We **have to / need to** wear lab coats for science experiments.*
*They told us we **weren't allowed to** play around in the laboratory.*

We use *not have to*, *not need to* or *need not* to say there is no rule (i.e. you can choose what to do).
*You **don't have / need to** wear safety goggles, but it's a good idea if you do.*
*You **needn't** bring a helmet – we have lots that you can borrow.*

Note

The nine main modal auxiliary verbs in English are: *can, could, may, might, shall, should, will, would* and *must*. Unlike most other verbs:

• they have no 's' for the *he / she / it* form: *he can*, not *he ~~cans~~*.

• they have no *-ing* form and no past participle.

• they are followed by an infinitive (without *to*): *I should ~~to~~ go*.

• we make negatives by adding *not* or *n't*: *can't, shouldn't, mightn't, won't*. There is no contraction for *may not*.

• we make questions by moving the modal verb before the subject: ***Should** I go?*

Note

Need to is usually used like a normal verb, but it can also be used as a modal verb, without *to*, in questions and negatives, although it sounds slightly old-fashioned.

9

Requests, recommendations, etc.

We can use *can, could, will* and *would* to make requests. *Could* and *would* are more polite.
Can / Could / Will / Would *you charge my tablet, please?*

We use *must* to make strong recommendations and invitations.
*You **must** check out the latest photography app – it's brilliant!*
*You **must** come round for dinner with us soon.*

We use *should* to ask for and give advice and to state our expectations.
*You **should** get some rest – you look exhausted.* (= giving advice)
***Should** I get a newer phone?* (= asking for advice)
*I think you **should** ask before you use my tablet.* (= I expect you to do it)

We can use *ought to* instead of *should* to give advice, but it is not usually used in questions.
*You **ought to** revise before the test.*

We can use *be supposed to* to talk about other people's expectations.
*What **are we supposed to** do for homework?* (= What does our teacher expect us to do?)
*I **was supposed to** empty the dishwasher, but I forgot.*

We can use *could* to make weak suggestions.
*You **could** come along later, if you want.*

Modals of ability

We use *can / could / be able to* to talk about general ability in the present and past.
Be able to is a little more formal than *can* or *could*.
*Sally **can / is able to** count to ten in French and she's only five!*
*My sister **could / was able to** ride a bike when she was three.*

We can use *will be able to* to talk about future ability.
*I can't program a computer now, but hopefully I'**ll be able to** by the end of my course.*

To talk about ability or inability on a specific past occasion, we can use *couldn't* but not *could*.
Use *was able to* instead (or *managed to*).
*Unfortunately, I **couldn't / wasn't able to / didn't manage to** find my phone last night.*
*Luckily, I **was able to / managed to** find my phone last night.* (not: ~~I could find~~ …)

We can use *be capable of* to talk about the maximum limit of someone's / something's abilities.
*This drone **is capable of** flying for more than 30 minutes, apparently.*

Modals of logical deduction and probability

We use *must, may, might, could* and *can't* to make logical deductions about the present, i.e. to work something out based on evidence.

We use:
- *must* to say that we are sure that something is true.
*He **must be** happy, because he's studying his favourite subject.* (= I'm sure he is)
- *may, might* and *could* to say that we are not sure whether something is true or not.
*She **might** be the inventor – she looks familiar.* (= I'm not sure)
- *can't* to say that we are sure that something isn't true.
*He **can't** be a physicist; he doesn't like physics!* (= I'm sure he isn't)

We use *will / won't, should / shouldn't, may, might* and *could* to talk about the probability of future events.
The exam will / won't be very easy. (= I'm sure)
The exam should be very easy / shouldn't be too difficult. (= it's likely)
The exam may / might / could be easier than we think. (= it's possible)

Grammar exercises

2 **Choose the correct option to complete the sentences.**

1 Fortunately, *we can /* [were able to] reach the airport in time for our flight yesterday.

2 [Can I] */ Am I able to* use your phone charger, please?

3 Although I tried hard, I *could /* [couldn't] beat the club champion.

4 I'd like to *can /* [be able to] choose my own working hours.

5 *Can you /* [Could you] hear the teacher clearly this morning?

6 Both his sisters *can /* [were able to] play a reasonably good game of chess at the age of five.

7 We *can /* [could] see most of the city from our old house on the top of the hill.

8 Yes, you [can] */ could* borrow my games console at the weekend.

9 He *can't /* [wasn't able to] persuade his parents to let him go on holiday with his friends last summer.

10 Sally *couldn't /* [won't be able to] come to lunch tomorrow – she's working.

3 **Complete the sentences with *must / mustn't* or *don't / doesn't have to*.**

1 You _____*don't have to*_____ come with me if you don't want to.

2 Everyone _____*must*_____ obey the law.

3 She _____*doesn't have to*_____ rush. She's got plenty of time.

4 Pete has a good broadband connection at home, so he _____*doesn't have to*_____ go to the office every day.

5 Children _____*mustn't*_____ touch electrical wires.

6 You _____*must*_____ play your music quietly, or you will wake the baby.

7 I _____*don't have to*_____ go to bed early tonight – there's no school tomorrow!

8 Drivers _____*mustn't*_____ use their phones while driving.

4 **Write advice using *should / ought to* or *shouldn't*.** *Possible answers*

1 I always hurt myself when I jump down the stairs.
   You shouldn't jump down the stairs!

2 Stephan doesn't practise the piano very much.
   He should / ought to practise more.

3 My head hurts and I have got a fever.
   You should / ought to see a doctor.

4 I can't close this suitcase because there are too many clothes in it.
   You should / ought to take some clothes out.

5 Eating ice cream really hurts my teeth.
   You should / ought to see a dentist. / You shouldn't eat ice cream.

6 Pam really wants to buy a pet.
   She should / ought to buy a dog.

7 I get upset when I don't get 100% in a test.
   You shouldn't get upset.

8 I always write down my password so I don't forget it.
   You shouldn't write down your password.

5 Rewrite the sentences using *may* or *might (not)*.

1 It is possible that these are my headphones, but I am not sure.
These *may / might be my headphones* .

2 Perhaps this is the app Kate mentioned.
This *may / might be the app Kate mentioned* .

3 Perhaps she is browsing the internet.
She *may / might be browsing the internet* .

4 It is possible that he will not pass his exams.
He *may not / might not pass his exams* .

5 It is possible that Jack and Adam are flying the drone, but I am not sure.
Jack and Adam *may / might be flying the drone* .

6 Perhaps Jonathan is not at the meeting.
Jonathan *may not / might not be at the meeting* .

6 Rewrite the sentences using *can't* or *must*.

1 I am sure Susan isn't at work now. She left the office an hour ago.
Susan *can't be at work now* .

2 I am sure my brother is talking on the phone now. The line is busy.
My brother *must be talking on the phone now* .

3 I am sure that Ben isn't studying in his room. I saw him in the garden.
Ben *can't be studying in his room* .

4 I am sure she is at the office now. I just spoke to her on the phone.
She *must be at the office now* .

5 I am sure my father isn't cooking again. I saw him cooking two hours ago.
My father *can't be cooking again* .

6 I don't think my printer is broken. It was working ten minutes ago.
My printer *can't be broken* .

7 Complete the second sentence so that it has a similar meaning to the first sentence, using the word given. Do not change the word given. You must use between two and five words.

1 It isn't necessary for you to upgrade your phone.
You *don't / do not have to upgrade* your phone. **HAVE**

2 I am sure Oscar is at the dentist's.
Oscar *must be at* the dentist's. **BE**

3 I am sure this isn't the place we are looking for.
This *can't be the place* we are looking for. **BE**

4 It is possible that we will win the game.
We *might win* the game. **MIGHT**

5 I advise you to save your work regularly.
You *ought to save your work* regularly. **OUGHT**

6 Molly managed to finish her report in one day.
Molly *was able to finish* her report in one day. **WAS**

7 It isn't necessary for you to buy a present for me.
You don't *need to buy me* a present. **NEED**

Vocabulary

Phrasal verbs

8 Match the phrasal verbs (1–8) with their meanings (a–h).

1 back up — *b* — **a** turn on a computer, light, etc.
2 break down — *g* — **b** make a spare copy of something on a computer
3 come up — *e* — **c** illegally enter another computer system
4 hack into — *c* — **d** talk more loudly
5 plug in — *h* — **e** appear on a screen
6 shut down — *f* — **f** turn off a computer
7 speak up — *d* — **g** suddenly stop working
8 switch on — *a* — **h** connect a machine to an electricity supply

9 Complete the sentences with the correct form of the phrasal verbs from Exercise 8.

1 Martin was arrested for ___*hacking into*___ a company's computer system.
2 My laptop ___*broke down*___ last week and I can't afford to get it repaired.
3 It's too dark in here. Can you ___*switch on*___ the light, please?
4 How many results ___*came up*___ when you searched for information?
5 I felt silly when I realised that the computer wasn't broken – it was simply not ___*plugged in*___ .
6 You'll need to ___*speak up*___ because we can't hear you very well.
7 It was past midnight when I finally ___*shut down*___ my computer and went to bed.
8 Always ___*back up*___ your work, because you might lose it forever if you don't.

Prepositions

10 Complete the sentences with these words. Use each word at least once.

at   for   in   on

1 We've arranged ___*for*___ someone to fix your car on Tuesday morning.
2 You shouldn't stare ___*at*___ a screen for longer than 20 minutes.
3 Too much screen time can result ___*in*___ eye problems.
4 I spoke to her ___*on*___ the phone last night.
5 If you write down your password, it's ___*at*___ risk of being discovered.
6 Dropping your phone in water is very bad ___*for*___ it!

Collocations and expressions

11 Complete the sentences with these words.

answering   cash   sewing   time   vending   washing

1 I am wearing the same clothes again because our ___*washing*___ machine is broken.
2 If I had a ___*time*___ machine, I'd go back to the age of the dinosaurs.
3 Is there a ___*vending*___ machine near here? I need a drink.
4 Fewer people are using ___*cash*___ machines because they can pay with cards or phones.
5 Have you got a ___*sewing*___ machine? My jeans need to be repaired.
6 I hate talking to ___*answering*___ machines. I usually just hang up without saying anything.

9

Words easily confused

12 Complete the sentences with the correct form of these words. Use each word at least once.

1 | bring   carry   fetch   take |

a I think I'll ___take___ the children to the Science Museum tomorrow.

b We ordered tea and you've ___brought___ us coffee.

c Could someone help me ___carry___ this TV – it's really heavy!

d Please could you ___fetch___ that cable for me?

2 | avoid   ban   block   forbid   prevent |

a This device ___prevents___ the engine from overheating.

b How can I ___avoid___ speaking to her when we work in the same office?

c He was ___banned___ from the video call for shouting.

d Taking photographs in this area is strictly ___forbidden___ .

e I didn't trust the sender of the message, so I ___blocked___ the number.

3 | affect   cause   happen   lead |

a What ___happened___ to your car?

b Drones can ___cause___ accidents if they fly too close to planes.

c The floods ___affected___ several houses close to the river.

d Several different factors ___led___ to the development of the internet.

4 | expand   extend   increase   rise |

a Many technology companies have ___increased___ their profits.

b Silicon Valley ___extends___ along much of the Santa Clara Valley in California.

c They're thinking of ___expanding___ their business.

d If the temperature ___rises___ any higher, turn on the air conditioning.

e Gases ___expand___ when heated.

Word formation   mixed

13 Use the word in capitals to form a word that fits in the gap.

1 This motorbike has a very ___powerful___ engine. **POWER**

2 The boy who saved me won a medal for ___bravery___ . **BRAVE**

3 I use a ___wireless___ printer, so I don't need a cable to connect it to my laptop. **WIRE**

4 Were you able to open the ___attachment___ I sent you? **ATTACH**

5 The ___government___ is planning to increase taxes again. **GOVERN**

6 The two companies formed a ___partnership___ and became very successful. **PARTNER**

7 I'm so ___unlucky___ – I have never won anything in my life. **LUCK**

8 That was an ___amazing___ thing to do! **AMAZE**

Sentence transformation

14 Complete the second sentence so that it has a similar meaning to the first sentence, using the word given. Do not change the word given. You must use between two and five words.

1 I'm sure that Simon isn't 19 years old.

BE

Simon _____*can't / cannot be*_____ 19 years old.

2 I advise you to go and see this film.

OUGHT

You _____*ought to go*_____ and see this film.

3 It wasn't necessary for them to prepare a meal for us.

HAVE

They _____*didn't / did not have to*_____ prepare a meal for us.

4 You should turn off your computer, to save energy.

SHUT

You should _____*shut down*_____ your computer, to save energy.

5 I can go to work on my bike if my car stops working.

BREAKS

If my car _____*breaks down*_____ , I can go to work on my bike.

6 Always make a copy of your files.

BACK

Always _____*back up*_____ your files.

7 Heavy rain can sometimes cause floods in the streets near the river.

RESULT

Heavy rain can _____*sometimes result in*_____ floods in the streets near the river.

8 Someone is coming to replace my printer today. I've made a plan.

ARRANGED

I've _____*arranged for someone*_____ to come and replace my printer today.

Awareness

1 **Which of these sentences are correct (C) and incorrect (I)?**

1 Tom might taken your coat by mistake. ⊥
2 You should have been practised more. ⊥
3 I could have been a great footballer. C
4 He can't have driving home last night – he doesn't have a car. ⊥
5 That must have been a very exciting race. C

6 I would lent it to you if you had asked. ⊥
7 We needn't have hurried because the show started late. C
8 Sorry, should I asked permission first? ⊥
9 Would you have gone if you had been invited? C
10 He shouldn't have been said that to her. ⊥

How many did you get right? ☐

Grammar

Perfect modals

We can use a modal auxiliary verb + *have* + past participle to talk about the past.

- We can use *must have, may have, might have, could have* and *can't have* to make logical deductions about the past.

*Landing on the moon **must have been** very exciting.* (= I'm sure it was)
*Maria **may / might / could have picked up** your headphones, but I'm not sure.*
*They **can't have driven** here – they haven't got a car.* (= I'm sure they didn't)

- We can use *would have, could have, might have* and *should have* or *ought to have* to imagine the unreal past.
*I **would have lent** you my phone charger, but you didn't ask me.*
*Tom **could have been** an engineer, but he decided to become an artist instead.*
*You **should / ought to have taken** your laptop back to the shop.* (= Why didn't you?)

- We use *needn't have* to say someone did something although it wasn't necessary. This is slightly different from the meaning of *didn't need to*.
*I **needn't have printed** the document – they had extra copies.* (= I did it, but it wasn't necessary)
*I **didn't need to print** the document – they said they had copies for everyone.* (= it wasn't necessary)

Grammar exercises

2 Write the words in order.

1 might / arrived / She / not / yet / have
She might not have arrived yet.

2 out / gone / have / My parents / may
My parents may have gone out.

3 wanted / to come / Simon / not / have / might
Simon might not have wanted to come.

4 listening / might / been / have / I / to music
I might have been listening to music.

5 well / Daniel / last night / been / not / might / feeling / have
Daniel might not have been feeling well last night.

6 your / may / You / broken / finger / have
You may have broken your finger.

3 Complete the sentences with *can't have* or *must have* and the correct form of the verbs.

1 A: Did they go to the cinema yesterday?
B: They ___*must have gone*___ (go) because there was no one at home when I called.

2 Kate is exhausted. She ___*must have worked*___ (work) hard in the garden today.

3 Susan's telephone wasn't working yesterday. She ___*can't have phoned*___ (phone) you.

4 She hadn't seen him before, so she ___*can't have recognised*___ (recognise) him.

5 I called her twice, but she didn't answer the phone. She ___*must have been*___ (be) asleep.

6 A: John translated the email for me.
B: John doesn't speak French, so he ___*can't have translated*___ (translate) it.

7 Emma has been at home all day. You ___*can't have seen*___ (see) her at the restaurant.

8 She asked me for money again. She ___*must have spent*___ (spend) all the money I gave her.

4 Rewrite the sentences using *should have* / *shouldn't have*.

1 Tom was supposed to be sleeping.
Tom ___*should have been sleeping*___ .

2 Julia was supposed to bring all the documents.
Julia ___*should have brought all the documents*___ .

3 My brother tried to fix his phone, but he made it worse.
My brother ___*shouldn't have tried to fix his phone*___ .

4 She didn't arrive on time for the rehearsal.
She ___*should have arrived on time for the rehearsal*___ .

5 Ben lied to his parents.
Ben ___*shouldn't have lied to his parents*___ .

6 My sister didn't mention the accident.
My sister ___*should have mentioned the accident*___ .

5 Rewrite the sentences using *needn't have* or *didn't need to.*

1 It was unnecessary for you to bring all this food. You're very kind.
You _____ *needn't have brought all this food* _____ .

2 It wasn't necessary for me to get up early this morning; that's why I slept until late.
I _____ *didn't need to get up early this morning* _____ .

3 I didn't go shopping today. I went yesterday.
I _____ *didn't need to go shopping today* _____ .

4 She watered the flowers this morning, but it rained later.
She _____ *needn't have watered the flowers* _____ .

5 We didn't cook today. We had booked a restaurant.
We _____ *didn't need to cook today* _____ .

6 I studied for the test, but it was incredibly easy.
I _____ *needn't have studied for the test* _____ .

6 Complete the second sentence so that it has a similar meaning to the first sentence, using the word given. Do not change the word given. You must use between two and five words.

1 Perhaps your son took your car.
Your son _____ *may / might / could have taken* _____ your car.   **HAVE**

2 I'm sure that you didn't see Mark in the city centre.
You _____ *can't have seen* _____ Mark in the city centre.   **CAN'T**

3 I am sure someone has fixed this computer. It's much faster now.
Someone _____ *must have fixed* _____ this computer.   **MUST**

4 Thank you very much for the present. It wasn't necessary.
You _____ *needn't have brought* _____ a present.   **BROUGHT**

5 You didn't ask your parents first.
You _____ *should have asked your parents* _____ first.   **ASKED**

6 It was too big, so I didn't buy it.
I _____ *would have bought it* _____ if it had been smaller.   **BOUGHT**

Vocabulary

Phrasal verbs

7 Match the phrasal verbs (1–8) with their meanings (a–h).

1	be taken in	*e*	**a**	find	
2	get hold of	*a*	**b**	pay close attention to something to avoid anything bad happening	
3	key in	*g*	**c**	join a computer network	
4	log in	*c*	**d**	make the volume or heat lower	
5	log out	*h*	**e**	be fooled or cheated by someone	
6	turn down	*d*	**f**	make the volume or heat higher	
7	turn up	*f*	**g**	type information into a computer or other machine	
8	watch out for	*b*	**h**	disconnect from a computer network	

8 Complete the sentences with the correct form of the phrasal verbs from Exercise 7.

1 I can't _log in_ to this account without a password.
2 Do you know where I can _get hold of_ some good speakers?
3 Can you _turn down_ your music, please? I'm trying to work.
4 What problems should I _watch out for_ when I'm setting up a video call?
5 Don't _be taken in_ by emails asking for your bank details.
6 _Turn up_ the heating. It's freezing in here!
7 Always remember to _log out_ from your email account when you are using a public computer.
8 Could you _key in_ this data for me, please?

Prepositions

9 Complete the sentences with these words. Use each word at least once.

1 We've been experimenting *with* / *within* / *without* different designs for the app.
2 Our service engineer will call you *with* / *within* / *without* the next few days.
3 Please respond to this message *with* / *within* / *without* delay.
4 We managed to keep our spending on the project *with* / *within* / *without* budget.
5 The classrooms are equipped *with* / *within* / *without* tablets and a high-speed broadband connection.
6 How long do you think you could do *with* / *within* / *without* your phone?

Collocations and expressions

10 Complete the sentences with these words.

attention   business   consideration   control   convenience   difference

1 When you mark my exam, please take into _consideration_ the fact that I was ill.
2 I have left my essay on your desk for you to read at your _convenience_ .
3 It makes no _difference_ what I do – the screen is blank.
4 I'm sorry, but what happens from now on is beyond my _control_ .
5 It's none of your _business_ how much money I earn!
6 Try to catch the waiter's _attention_ – I want to ask for the bill.

Words easily confused

11 Complete the sentences with the correct form of these words. Use each word at least once.

1 arrive   get   reach

a After an hour's walk, we _got_ to the Science Museum.
b She _arrived_ at the technology fair in an electric car.
c The plane is due to _reach_ the airport in 20 minutes.

2 angle   corner   edge   margin

a Leave the bag in the _corner_ , next to the desk.
b Let's look at the problem from a different _angle_ .
c Don't write in the _margin_ because that's where the teacher makes her comments.
d They stood at the water's _edge_ and gazed at the sunset.

3 certainly   likely   probably

a Don't worry. There's _probably_ a simple reason why they're late.
b It's _likely_ that Smith will win the race. She's the current champion.
c I'm _certainly_ not going to lend him my headset again! He broke it.

10

Word formation   mixed

12 Use the word in capitals to form a word that fits in the gap.

1 All of the _____performers_____ in the computer game were professional actors.   **PERFORM**

2 That's the _____tiniest_____ camera I have ever seen.   **TINY**

3 We see our cousins _____virtually_____ every week on a video call.   **VIRTUAL**

4 I _____accidentally_____ spilled coffee all over my keyboard.   **ACCIDENT**

5 I _____truly_____ believe that the wheel is the greatest invention.   **TRUE**

6 Virtual _____reality_____ is used in education, medicine and sport, as well as gaming.   **REAL**

7 Thank you. Your _____kindness_____ is really appreciated.   **KIND**

8 He was lucky to be _____alive_____ after an accident like that!   **LIVE**

Sentence transformation

13 Complete the second sentence so that it has a similar meaning to the first sentence, using the word given. Do not change the word given. You must use between two and five words.

1 It was a bad idea to spend so long browsing the internet.
SPENT
You _____shouldn't / should not have spent_____ so long browsing the internet.

2 I didn't know about the exhibition, so I didn't go.
WOULD
I _____would have gone to_____ the exhibition if I had known about it.

3 I am certain she was sleeping when I phoned her.
BEEN
She _____must have been sleeping_____ when I phoned her.

4 Many people were fooled by a text which asked for their bank details.
TAKEN
Many people were _____taken in by_____ a text which asked for their bank details.

5 You should install anti-virus software as soon as possible.
WITHOUT
Install anti-virus software _____without delay_____ .

6 You won't get those emails back, no matter what you do.
DIFFERENCE
It _____makes no difference_____ what you do, you won't get those emails back.

7 I was trying to make her notice me, so that I could ask her for help.
CATCH
I was trying _____to catch her attention_____ , so that I could ask her for help.

8 You have no right to know my password, so don't ask me for it.
NONE
My password _____is none of your business_____ , so don't ask me for it.

1 **Which of these sentences are correct (C) and incorrect (I)?**

1 Have you finished tidy your room? ___I___
2 Your bungalow will be cleaned daily. ___C___
3 I'm pleased to hear that you have recovered. ___C___
4 She persuaded him going on the rollercoaster. ___I___
5 It's not worth to worry about it. ___I___

6 We weren't allowed to use mobile phones. ___C___
7 The teacher made me write the essay again. ___C___
8 I wasn't expecting meet anyone I knew. ___I___
9 Steve had difficulty understanding the instructions. ___C___
10 Do you remember visiting this place before? ___C___

How many did you get right? ☐

Grammar

-*ing* form

We can use the -*ing* form:

- as the subject of a sentence or clause.

Running *is my favourite type of exercise.*
*Are you sure that **swimming** straight after lunch is a good idea?*

- after prepositions.

*I'm so excited about **coming** to visit you.*

- after the verb *go* when we talk about activities.

*Emma goes **skiing** every winter.*

We also use the -*ing* form after certain verbs and phrases:
admit, avoid, be used to, can't help, can't stand, deny, dislike,
(don't) mind, enjoy, fancy, (don't) feel like, finish, forgive, hate,
have difficulty, imagine, involve, it's no good, it's no use, it's (not) worth, keep, like, love, miss, practise, prefer,
prevent, regret, risk, spend time.
*I **don't feel like cooking** tonight.*
*It's **worth paying** a little bit more for a better bike.*

to + infinitive

We use *to* + infinitive:

- to explain purpose.

*We went into town **to buy** tickets for the concert.*

- after adjectives such as *easy, difficult, afraid, scared, happy, glad, pleased, sad,* etc.

*I find it **difficult to do** exercise first thing in the morning.*

- after *too* + adjective or adjective + *enough*.

*It was **too wet to play** tennis outside.*
*It wasn't **cold enough to snow**.*

We also use *to* + infinitive after certain verbs and phrases:
afford, agree, appear, arrange, begin, choose, decide, expect, fail, forget, hope, learn, manage, mean, need,
offer, plan, prepare, pretend, promise, refuse, seem, start, want, would like.
*Anna and I **agreed to run** the race together.*
***Would you like to come** to the cinema with us?*

Infinitive (without to)

We use the infinitive (without to) after:
- modal verbs.

They **could win** the tournament.
- had better to give advice.

We **had better run** or we'll miss the train.
- would rather to talk about preference. We often use the word than.

I **would rather play** basketball **than** volleyball.

> **Note**
>
> We use let + object + infinitive when we want to say that we give permission for someone to do something, and it is only used in the active voice. In the passive we can use the verb be allowed to.
> Her parents **let her stay out** later at weekends.
> She **is allowed to stay out** later at weekends.

> **Note**
>
> We use make + object + infinitive when we want to say that we force a person to do something in the active voice. However, in the passive make is followed by to + infinitive.
> The coach **made us practise** hitting the ball at the net.
> We **were made to practise** hitting the ball at the net (by the coach).

> **Note**
>
> After the verb help, we can use either to + infinitive or the infinitive (without to). Both forms mean exactly the same.
> Can you **help me (to) learn** to juggle?

-ing form or to + infinitive?

Some verbs can be followed by an -ing form or to + infinitive with no change in meaning. Some common ones are begin, bother, continue, hate, like, love and start.
They've **started doing / to do** yoga on Tuesday evenings.
Sam has **continued playing / to play** hockey after leaving school.
I **hated doing / to do** jigsaw puzzles when I was a child.

There are other verbs that can be followed by an -ing form or to + infinitive, but the meaning changes. Some common ones are forget, go on, mean, regret, remember, stop and try.
I'll never **forget scoring** the winning goal in the final. (I'll always remember that it happened.)
I **forgot to bring** my trainers. (I didn't remember to bring my trainers, so I don't have them with me.)

We **went on running** through the rain. (We continued to run.)
She **went on to run** her fastest time ever. (She had been running, then after the point the speaker is referring to, she ran her fastest time ever.)

Being in the swimming team **means training** before school. (That's what it involves.)
I **meant to bring** my goggles, but I forgot. (I planned / intended to bring them.)

I **regret not going** to the trials for the basketball team. (I didn't go to the trials, but now I wish I had.)
We **regret to inform** you that the match has been cancelled. (We're sorry that we have to tell you this.)

My dad **remembers seeing** Usain Bolt in the Olympics. (He saw Usain Bolt and remembers seeing him.)
I **remembered to take** my helmet when I cycled to school. (I remembered first and then I took my helmet.)

We **stopped playing** because we were thirsty. (We didn't continue playing.)
We **stopped to have** a drink. (We stopped doing something so we could have a drink.)

Try calling the box office about the tickets. (See if you can call the box office about the tickets.)
I'll **try to book** tickets this afternoon. (I'll make an effort to book tickets this afternoon.)

Grammar exercises

2 Choose the correct option to complete the sentences.

1 It's no use *talking* / *to talk* to Adam – he won't listen to you.

2 You were so *lucky get* / *to have got* tickets for the cup final.

3 It was so kind of you *to take* / *taking* me to the theatre.

4 We should *learn* / *to learn* some Spanish before our trip.

5 My sister denied *taking* / *to take* my headphones without asking.

6 Sam couldn't afford *going* / *to go* on holiday this year.

7 We had better *to hurry* / *hurry*, or else we will miss the train.

8 Cara avoided *driving* / *to drive* in the rush hour when she lived in Paris.

9 My parents don't let me *staying up* / *stay up* late during the week.

10 Liam reminded me *entering* / *to enter* the race.

3 Complete the sentences with the *-ing* or infinitive form (with or without *to*) of the verbs.

1 Do you feel like ___*going*___ (go) out or would you rather ___*stay*___ (stay) in tonight?

2 Did they manage ___*to carry*___ (carry) the new canoe to the river?

3 I always enjoy ___*eating*___ (eat) out with friends.

4 I'd like ___*to eat*___ (eat) in a Chinese restaurant this weekend.

5 Oh no. I forgot ___*to lock*___ (lock) the door! I'd better ___*go*___ (go) back and ___*do*___ (do) it now.

6 After ___*spending*___ (spend) two weeks away, she looked forward to ___*seeing*___ (see) us all.

7 He pretended ___*to be*___ (be) sick in order to avoid ___*going*___ (go) to the circus.

8 I love amusement parks, but I'm scared of ___*riding*___ (ride) on rollercoasters.

4 Use the prompts to write sentences with the *-ing* or infinitive form (with or without *to*).

1 I / not remember / get / a letter from you
   I don't remember getting a letter from you.

2 it / be / very kind / you / send / me / flowers / yesterday
   It was very kind of you to send me flowers yesterday.

3 they / try / prevent / the spectators / from / run onto the pitch / last night
   They tried to prevent the spectators from running onto the pitch last night.

4 they / accuse him of / sell fake tickets / last month / and finally / he admit / do it
   They accused him of selling fake tickets last month and finally he admitted doing it.

5 it / take / her / ages / get over / her illness / last year
   It took her ages to get over her illness last year.

6 there / be / no point in / complain about / spend / so much money on the car
   There's no point in complaining about spending so much money on the car.

7 he / be / the only student / pass / the exam
   He was the only student to pass the exam.

8 my brother / spend / most of his free time / listen to music and / play computer games
   My brother spends most of his free time listening to music and playing computer games.

9 it / be / important / for me / relax / outdoors / and / be / close to nature
   It's important for me to relax outdoors and (to) be close to nature.

10 it / be / impossible / for me / meet / you right now
   It's impossible for me to meet you right now.

5 Rewrite the sentences using these verbs.

| accuse | admit | agree | apologise | deny | promise | refuse | suggest |

1 My sister said, 'No, I didn't take your sunglasses.'

My sister _____*denied taking*_____ my sunglasses.

2 Oscar said to me, 'No, I won't give you any money.'

Oscar _____*refused to give*_____ me any money.

3 Dan said to Beth, 'I am so sorry I spoiled our holiday.'

Dan _____*apologised for spoiling*_____ their holiday.

4 Martha said, 'Let's go sailing this weekend.'

Martha _____*suggested going*_____ sailing that weekend.

5 Anna said to me, 'Yes, I'll help you with your homework.'

Anna _____*agreed to help*_____ me with my homework.

6 My brother said to me, 'You took my racket.'

My brother _____*accused me of taking*_____ his racket.

7 I said, 'Yes, I borrowed your ball without asking .'

I _____*admitted borrowing*_____ my sister's ball without asking.

8 'Don't worry, Freddie. I'll take you to the park tomorrow,' said his father.

Freddie's father _____*promised to take*_____ him to the park the next day.

6 Correct the sentences where necessary. Tick those which do not need correcting.

1 She couldn't cope with worked for so many hours a day.

She couldn't cope with working for so many hours a day.

2 Pam would rather to drink coffee than tea.

Pam would rather drink coffee than tea.

3 She admitted to steal the money from the safe.

She admitted stealing the money from the safe.

4 Mr Anderson can't stand to be in the office all day.

Mr Anderson can't stand being in the office all day.

5 They postponed going to see their grandparents.

✓

6 I don't remember arranging a meeting for today.

✓

7 Mike advised me working overtime to earn money for my holiday.

Mike advised me to work overtime to earn money for my holiday.

8 I don't enjoy to be in crowded places.

I don't enjoy being in crowded places.

7 Complete the sentences about you. *Students' own answers*

1 I really can't afford _____ .

2 I spend my spare time _____ .

3 My parents don't let me _____ .

4 I am old enough _____ .

5 I really can't stand _____ .

6 I avoid _____ .

Vocabulary

Phrasal verbs

8 Match the phrasal verbs (1–8) with their meanings (a–h).

1	feel up to	*g*	**a**	meet with socially
2	get together	*a*	**b**	stop doing or trying to do something
3	give up	*b*	**c**	try to impress other people
4	knock over	*h*	**d**	show someone a place
5	run into	*e*	**e**	meet someone by chance
6	show around	*d*	**f**	arrive somewhere, usually unexpectedly
7	show off	*c*	**g**	be well or confident enough to do something
8	show up	*f*	**h**	hit someone / something and make them / it fall to the ground (including with a vehicle)

9 Complete the sentences with the correct form of the phrasal verbs from Exercise 8.

1 Let's stay at home tonight. I still don't _____*feel up to*_____ going out.
2 Every year the old school friends _____*get / got together*_____ for a meal.
3 The guide who _____*showed*_____ us _____*around*_____ the museum was really friendly.
4 Ben is _____*showing off*_____ because he wants to impress his teacher.
5 Zoe did gymnastics for six years, but she _____*gave up*_____ last year.
6 Our cat has been _____*knocked over*_____ by a car twice, but he's still OK!
7 I _____*ran into*_____ my old tennis coach at the supermarket yesterday.
8 We waited for half an hour for Simon to _____*show up*_____ , but he never did.

Prepositions

10 Choose the correct option to complete the sentences.

1 *On* / *In* / *At* second thoughts, I'd rather go to the tennis match tomorrow.
2 I'm *to* / *in* / *at* two minds about whether or not to go rock climbing this weekend.
3 If you're *on* / *in* / *at* a loose end, why not come round to my house and play computer games?
4 Athletics appeals *to* / *in* / *at* people in many different countries.
5 Shall we move *on* / *in* / *at* to the next point you wanted to discuss?
6 Has James told you his great idea? I think he's really *onto* / *into* / *out of* something.

Collocations and expressions

11 Complete the sentences with the correct form of *play*, *go* or *do*.

1 How often do you _____*go*_____ climbing?
2 My aunt _____*does*_____ yoga three times a week.
3 The only sport I enjoy _____*playing*_____ is volleyball.
4 Gary has been _____*doing*_____ karate for five years, and now he has a black belt.
5 Do you want to _____*go*_____ bungee jumping with me next week?
6 I've _____*played / been playing*_____ chess since I was eight years old, but I'm still not good at it.

11

Words easily confused

12 Complete the sentences with the correct form of these words. Use each word at least once.

1 **lead   medal   trophy   victory**

   a The captain of the winning team held up the winners' _____trophy_____ .
   b With 400 metres of the race left, Jo was in the _____lead_____ by a few metres.
   c Three great goals gave the team a memorable _____victory_____ .
   d Very few gymnasts have won five Olympic gold _____medals_____ .

2 **logical   reasonable   sensible   sensitive**

   a She wears sunglasses because her eyes are _____sensitive_____ to light.
   b He's so _____sensitive_____ that he gets upset when you criticise him.
   c Julia was _____sensible_____ enough to stop driving when she got too tired.
   d I tried to be _____reasonable_____ , but they refused to cooperate.
   e There's no _____logical_____ explanation for what happened.

3 **abandon   desert   disappear   mislay**

   a The weather was so bad that they had to _____abandon_____ the search for the missing sailors.
   b Everyone _____deserted_____ the beach when it started to rain.
   c As the fog came down, the mountains slowly _____disappeared_____ from view.
   d I seem to have _____mislaid_____ my goggles. Have you seen them?

4 **accurate   exact   precise**

   a My watch always tells the right time. It's very _____accurate_____ .
   b The winners received a(n) _____exact_____ copy of the original trophy.
   c You said the film starts around eight o'clock. Can you be more _____precise_____ , please?

Word formation   mixed

13 Use the word in capitals to form a word that fits in the gap.

   1 The team should be congratulated on such a _____memorable_____ performance.   **MEMORY**
   2 Before you go to university, you need to decide what subject you want to _____specialise_____ in.   **SPECIAL**
   3 There is a _____suspicious_____ looking man hanging around outside the stadium.   **SUSPECT**
   4 Tim decided not to play in the match because of the _____weakness_____ in his shoulder.   **WEAK**
   5 The crowd watched in _____amazement_____ as the stunt rider performed his tricks.   **AMAZE**
   6 This club has a large _____membership_____ , consisting of people of all ages.   **MEMBER**
   7 Lucy is really _____competitive_____ . She loves racing against other people.   **COMPETE**
   8 I don't just _____dislike_____ boxing, I hate it.   **LIKE**

Sentence transformation

14 **Complete the second sentence so that it has a similar meaning to the first sentence, using the word given. Do not change the word given. You must use between two and five words.**

1 'Let's go ice skating at the weekend,' said Julia.
   SUGGESTED
   Julia ___*suggested going ice skating*___ at the weekend.

2 Driving without a licence is illegal.
   TO
   It's ___*illegal to drive without*___ a licence.

3 I'd buy these skis, but I don't have enough money.
   AFFORD
   I ___*can't / cannot afford to buy*___ these skis.

4 Jenny's mother thinks Jenny should join the basketball team.
   WANTS
   Jenny's mother ___*wants her to join*___ the basketball team.

5 The referee made the goalkeeper take the kick again.
   WAS
   The goalkeeper ___*was made to take*___ the kick again.

6 I can't decide whether or not to go surfing tomorrow.
   MINDS
   I'm ___*in two minds about*___ whether or not to go surfing tomorrow.

7 I'm too tired to go for a run tonight.
   UP
   I don't ___*feel up to going*___ for a run tonight. I'm really tired.

8 I unexpectedly met Ian while I was watching the football match.
   RAN
   While I was watching the football match, ___*I ran into*___ Ian.

1 Which of these sentences are correct (C) and incorrect (I)?

1 I'd like to know when are you arriving. ⊥
2 You aren't very helpful, aren't you? ⊥
3 Wasn't that a great match? C
4 Why you didn't tell me about this? ⊥
5 Could you to give me directions to the bank? ⊥

6 Let's go to the beach, shall we? C
7 Don't talk so quickly, do you? ⊥
8 Doesn't she look lovely in that dress? C
9 I'm very late, aren't I? C
10 Do you know if Isabel is coming today? C

How many did you get right? ☐

Grammar

Question tags

Question tags are short questions at the end of a sentence. They are formed with a modal or an auxiliary verb + a subject pronoun (*I, you, he, she, it, we* or *they*) or *there*.
We usually use an affirmative question tag after a negative sentence, and a negative question tag after an affirmative sentence.
She has played all over the world, **hasn't she?**
You can't solve this puzzle, **can you?**
There were a lot of goals, **weren't there?**

When a sentence contains a verb in the present simple or the past simple (and doesn't use the verb *be*), *we use do / does, don't / doesn't* and *did / didn't* in the question tag.
Ben loves windsurfing, **doesn't he?**
They played really well, **didn't they?**

We use question tags when we want:
• someone to agree with what we are saying.
That was a delicious meal, **wasn't it?**
• to make sure that what we are saying is right.
We go to the same gym, **don't we?**

Some question tags are irregular. Notice the way these tags are formed.
I am in the team, **aren't I?**
Everyone is happy, **aren't they?**
Let's go to the beach, **shall we?**
Don't drive so fast, **will you?**
Wear a helmet, **won't you?**

Indirect questions

Indirect questions are used when we want to sound more formal, polite or distant. For indirect questions, we use the word order of a normal statement. We don't always need to use a full stop at the end.
I'd like to know when *the tickets go on sale.*
I wonder where *the football ground is.*

Questions for which the answer is *yes* or *no* use the word *if* or *whether*.
Do you know **if** *Marco is coming to the training session today?*
Could you tell me **whether** *I need to bring my own racket?*

Negative questions

Negative questions can be used:

- to show that we are surprised or doubtful.

Haven't you seen that film yet?

Why didn't you want to play yesterday?

- when we expect someone to agree with us.

Wow! Wasn't that an amazing race?

Don't the new team tracksuits look great?

Grammar exercises

2 Choose the correct option to complete the sentences.

1 I'd *wonder / like* to know where you bought those trainers.

2 *Would / Could* you mind telling me where the exit is?

3 I don't *mind / suppose* you know how to get to the station from here.

4 Do you know *what / if* the other team has arrived yet?

5 I *suppose / wonder* if she would like to come to the art gallery.

6 *Do / Could* you tell me whether it's going to rain today?

7 I *could / would* like to ask you why the tickets are so expensive.

3 Complete the indirect questions.

1 Where is the changing room?

Could you tell me *where the changing room is* ?

2 How much does this cost?

I wonder if you know *how much this costs* .

3 When do the tickets go on sale?

I'm not sure if you know *when the tickets go on sale* .

4 Is that Wembley Stadium over there?

Do you know *if that is Wembley Stadium over there* ?

5 Did the children enjoy the show?

I'd like to ask you *if / whether the children enjoyed the show* .

6 What's the time?

Would you mind *telling me the time / what the time is* ?

4 Match the sentences (1–8) with the question tags (a–h).

1 You went to the practice on Monday,   [e]   **a** won't they?

2 There aren't any goggles by the pool,   [g]   **b** does it?

3 Let's turn off the television,   [f]   **c** aren't I?

4 They never win away from home,   [h]   **d** has she?

5 They'll be here soon,   [a]   **e** didn't you?

6 She's never beaten you at tennis,   [d]   **f** shall we?

7 It doesn't hurt,   [b]   **g** are there?

8 I am right,   [c]   **h** do they?

5 Complete the questions with question tags.

1 I'd better leave now, _____*hadn't I*_____ ?

2 Patrick can't drive, _____*can he*_____ ?

3 He broke the world record last year, _____*didn't he*_____ ?

4 Help me with this assignment, _____*will / won't you*_____ ?

5 Let's go swimming, _____*shall we*_____ ?

6 Those are your boots, _____*aren't they*_____ ?

6 Complete the negative questions.

1 _____*Hasn't*_____ the weather been terrible recently?

2 Why _____*wasn't*_____ Martha home until after midnight?

3 _____*Wouldn't*_____ it be great if Mum and Dad bought an electric car?

4 _____*Haven't*_____ you heard the news about the Olympics?

5 _____*Weren't*_____ they happy to have Sports Day at school yesterday?

6 _____*Isn't / Wasn't*_____ it a lovely day?

7 Complete the sentences with one word in each gap.

1 Do you know _____*if / whether*_____ Simon is at home?

2 They don't enjoy losing, _____*do*_____ they?

3 _____*Why*_____ didn't they phone a taxi?

4 I'd _____*like*_____ to know where you got those tickets.

5 Let's go to the park, _____*shall*_____ we?

6 Everyone loves chocolate, don't _____*they*_____ ?

Vocabulary

Phrasal verbs

8 Match the phrasal verbs (1–8) with their meanings (a–h).

1 believe in	*g*	**a** get out of bed later than usual
2 burst out	*e*	**b** move at the same speed as someone / something
3 cut down on	*h*	**c** become successful or popular very quickly
4 keep up with	*b*	**d** reject an invitation
5 sleep in	*a*	**e** begin doing something suddenly
6 stand back	*f*	**f** move a short distance from something
7 take off	*c*	**g** be sure that something is right
8 turn down	*d*	**h** reduce the number or amount of something

9 Complete the sentences with the correct form of the phrasal verbs from Exercise 8.

1 The doctor advised my uncle to _____*cut down on*_____ the amount of sugar he eats.

2 Finn _____*turned down*_____ his place at a university in London because he wanted to live near the sea.

3 I used to go running with Sarah, but she was so fast that I couldn't _____*keep up with*_____ her.

4 Sorry I'm late. I _____*slept in*_____ this morning because my alarm didn't go off!

5 When Ellen saw the funny photo of herself, she _____*burst out*_____ laughing.

6 When did your tennis career really start to _____*take off*_____ ?

7 Steve _____*believes in*_____ always being honest with people, even if they might be offended.

8 You should _____*stand back*_____ from the edge of the cycle track or you might get hit.

Prepositions

10 Choose the correct option to complete the sentences.

1 Why don't you want to come to the beach? What's wrong *for* / *of* / (*with*) you?

2 We can't afford another car, so this one will just have to do (*for*) / *of* / *with* the moment.

3 Is this just a rehearsal or is it (*for*) / *of* / *with* real?

4 Gymnastics requires a combination *for* / (*of*) / *with* strength and flexibility.

5 I am writing *for* / *of* / (*with*) reference to our recent stay at your hotel in Monaco.

6 Tom's new bike is just (*for*) / *of* / *with* mountain biking – not cycling to work.

Collocations and expressions

11 Complete the sentences with these words.

| come | hold | know | make | put | take |

1 I'm afraid I don't ___*know*___ the first thing about rugby.

2 It's fun playing tennis with my friends because we don't ___*take*___ ourselves too seriously.

3 Don't ___*put*___ your life at risk when you're climbing. Wear a helmet.

4 They are getting better, but they've never ___*come*___ close to winning a tournament.

5 Practising for a few minutes every day will really ___*make*___ a difference.

6 The club he played for as a boy will always ___*hold*___ an important place in his heart.

Words easily confused

12 Complete the sentences with the correct form of these words. Use each word at least once.

1 | notice | observe | see | watch |

  a The zoologist spent days ___*observing*___ the behaviour of the lions.

  b Can you ___*see*___ the top of the mountain?

  c It's such a small stain that no one will ___*notice*___ it.

  d Would you rather ___*watch*___ television or go out?

2 | coast | port | resort | seaside | shore |

  a A day at the ___*seaside*___ would be good fun.

  b Cannes is a popular tourist ___*resort*___ .

  c We had a wonderful holiday sailing on the west ___*coast*___ of Ireland.

  d Our boat sank, but we were able to swim to the ___*shore*___ .

  e Large cruise ships are too big for this small ___*port*___ .

3 | commentator | correspondent | editor | reporter |

  a A(n) ___*editor*___ decides which articles are included in a newspaper.

  b He's worked as an arts ___*correspondent*___ for the last ten years.

  c At the start of the football match, the ___*commentator*___ predicted a win for Brazil.

  d The ___*reporter*___ asked the manager some tricky questions at the press conference.

4 | qualification | skill | talent |

  a She has all the necessary ___*skills*___ for the job.

  b On paper, the candidate had plenty of ___*qualifications*___ , but very little experience.

  c Nowadays, ___*talent*___ scouts try to sign children at a very young age.

12

Word formation   mixed

13 Use the word in capitals to form a word that fits in the gap.

1 My father is a professional _____economist_____ who works for the government.   **ECONOMY**
2 Tanya stared at the chess board _____thoughtfully_____ and considered her next move.   **THOUGHT**
3 If you get a reputation for _____dishonesty_____ , nobody will want you on their team.   **HONEST**
4 The competitors weren't distracted by the _____presence_____ of so many spectators.   **PRESENT**
5 My _____preference_____ for a holiday destination is probably different from yours.   **PREFER**
6 We haven't got an _____endless_____ supply of money, you know.   **END**
7 You shouldn't argue with the referee, even if you _____disagree_____ with her decision.   **AGREE**
8 I can't do this puzzle – it's _____impossible_____ !   **POSSIBLE**

Sentence transformation

14 Complete the second sentence so that it has a similar meaning to the first sentence, using the word given. Do not change the word given. You must use between two and five words.

1 Are there any tickets left?
   WHETHER
   Could you _____tell me whether there are_____ any tickets left?

2 When does the train arrive in Coventry?
   WHEN
   I'd like to know _____when the train arrives_____ in Coventry.

3 I'm sure you'll agree that the concert was fantastic.
   WASN'T
   The concert _____was fantastic, wasn't it_____ ?

4 Step away from the doors, or you might fall out.
   STAND
   You might fall out if you _____don't / do not stand back_____ from the doors.

5 She was invited to the party, but she decided not to go.
   DOWN
   She _____turned down_____ the invitation to the party.

6 You should reduce the amount of chocolate you eat.
   CUT
   You _____should cut down_____ the amount of chocolate you eat.

7 Let's sit down and rest here for now.
   MOMENT
   For _____the moment_____ , let's sit down and rest here.

8 I'm writing about your job advert.
   REFERENCE
   I'm writing _____with reference to_____ your job advert.

Part 1

For questions 1–8, read the text below and decide which answer (A, B, C or D) best fits each gap. There is an example at the beginning (0).

A new breed of superstar

Nowadays, many people become household names through professions that were once **(0)** ___ of as simply respectable, rather than glamorous. Take lawyers, for example. Getting a job with a top law firm may not only ensure financial security due to the astronomical **(1)** ___ lawyers can command, but it may also bring the same superstar **(2)** ___ as that of a Hollywood actor – or lead to a career in politics. There are few people who do not **(3)** ___ the names of Bill and Hillary Clinton or Barak Obama.

But a person must be cut out to be a lawyer in order to be successful. Firstly, a persuasive character is essential. Secondly, the **(4)** ___ to judge character is vital, since a witness's **(5)** ___ to a question may be more significant than the answer given. **(6)** ___ , leadership qualities are fundamental. Top lawyers do not have the time to **(7)** ___ all the research necessary in a case by themselves. As a **(8)** ___ , they have to set an example for those under their command, so that they can count on the team to work conscientiously.

0	A looked	B regarded	C considered	**(D)** thought
1	A tips	B fares	C rewards	**(D)** fees
2	A level	B fame	**(C)** status	D stance
3	**(A)** recognise	B remind	C memorise	D retain
4	A certainty	B capability	C will	**(D)** ability
5	A look	**(B)** reaction	C action	D response
6	A Eventually	**(B)** Finally	C Ultimately	D Conclusively
7	**(A)** do	B take	C make	D carry
8	A end	B score	**(C)** result	D sum

Part 2

For questions 9–16, read the text below and think of the word which best fits each gap. Use only one word in each gap. There is an example at the beginning (0).

Robert Burns

Robert Burns, Scotland's greatest poet, (0) ___was___ born in 1759. From an early age he had to help his father on his farm, as (9) ___well___ as attend school lessons. When he was 22, he moved to Irvine, where he began to learn about making cloth. Shortly after (10) ___his___ arrival, the factory in which he was training was destroyed by fire, so he started a farm with his younger brother Gilbert.

While he was living on the farm, Robert concentrated (11) ___on___ writing poems. He fell for a local girl, Jean Armour, and wanted to marry her, but her father (12) _would / did_ not allow him to do so. This took Robert (13) ___by___ surprise, and since he could not (14) ___get___ used to the idea of being unable to marry her, he decided to leave the country. Just as he was about to leave, he was advised to publish some of the poems he (15) ___had___ written. He received a large sum of money for the poetry and was then (16) ___able___ to get married to Jean.

Part 3

For questions 17–24, read the text below. Use the word given in capitals at the end of some of the lines to form a word that fits in the gap in the same line. There is an example at the beginning (0).

Extreme sports

In the past few years, extreme sports have (0) ___greatly___ increased in popularity, **GREAT**

particularly among young, well-paid professionals. But why do people take up such apparently

(17) ___dangerous___ activities? What is the attraction of doing things like bungee jumping, **DANGER**

hang-gliding, or jumping off a cliff with a parachute? Extreme sports lovers say they get no **SATISFY**

(18) ___satisfaction___ from traditional sports or even (19) ___athletics___ . They **ATHLETE**

claim that their boring daily routine does not (20) ___enable___ them to live life to the **ABLE**

full. Only when putting their lives at risk do they feel truly alive.

Nowadays, there are extreme sports competitions in which those people courageous enough to

face the challenge of these (21) ___revolutionary___ new activities can win large cash prizes. **REVOLUTION**

This, in turn, has increased their popularity, and has resulted in the (22) ___creation___ of **CREATE**

a whole new industry which specialises in making (23) ___equipment___ and clothing for **EQUIP**

extreme games. It has become a multi-million dollar business. Often the (24) ___discovery___ **DISCOVER**

that certain games have become commercial causes other people to come up with even more

extreme sports and the cycle is repeated.

Part 4

For questions 25–30, complete the second sentence so that it has a similar meaning to the first sentence, using the word given. Do not change the word given. You must use between two and five words, including the word given. Here is an example (0).

Example:

0 Jake couldn't fix the computer himself.

MANAGE

Jake _____ *didn't manage to* _____ fix the computer himself.

25 The house was completely empty.

FURNITURE

There _____ *was no / wasn't any / was not any furniture in* _____ the house.

26 I'm sure they were asleep during the film.

MUST

They _____ *must have been asleep* _____ during the film.

27 My dentist's advice was to reduce the amount of sugar I ate.

ADVISED

My _____ *dentist advised me to cut* _____ down on sugar.

28 When we got to Dover, the ferry wasn't there.

ALREADY

The ferry _____ *had already left / gone / departed / sailed by* _____ the time we got to Dover.

29 Ingrid and Astrid have had many arguments in the past.

FALLEN

It's not the first time Ingrid _____ *has fallen out with* _____ Astrid.

30 You need to be determined as well as skilful in order to be a professional athlete.

CALLS

Being a professional athlete _____ *calls for skill(s)* _____ and determination.

B2 Practice: ECCE

Grammar

For questions 1–20, choose the word or phrase that best completes the sentence.

1 We might have been ___ about the start time.
   A mistook
   (B) mistaken
   C mistake
   D mistaking

2 Alex should never ___ bought that cheap car.
   (A) have
   B had
   C been
   D of

3 I'd like to ___ who stole my laptop.
   A tell
   (B) know
   C believe
   D suppose

4 Those ships are all from the same country, ___ ?
   (A) aren't they
   B aren't those
   C they are
   D those aren't

5 Why are you pretending ___ a bad leg?
   A having
   (B) to have
   C have
   D to having

6 ___ you ever tasted spinach?
   A Didn't
   B Aren't
   (C) Haven't
   D Weren't

7 Can you imagine ___ an Olympic medal?
   (A) winning
   B to win
   C win
   D to winning

8 Our car broke ___ on the way to the opera.
   A up
   B out
   C in
   (D) down

9 My dad made me ___ his car this morning.
   A cleaning
   B to clean
   (C) clean
   D to cleaning

10 It was very kind of you to help. You didn't ___ .
   A should
   B might
   (C) have to
   D may

11 Luckily, we ___ finish the match before it rained.
   (A) were able to
   B weren't able to
   C had to
   D wouldn't

12 They ___ have missed the train – I left them at the station with plenty of time to spare!
   A must
   B mustn't
   (C) can't
   D could

13 Let's have a game of tennis, ___ ?
   A have we
   B let we
   C will we
   (D) shall we

14 He ___ be a grandfather. He looks so young!
   A mustn't
   B needn't
   C couldn't
   (D) can't

15 When we were young, we ___ climb trees.
   A used
   (B) would
   C may
   D should

16 I prefer watching football ___ it.
   A playing
   B to play
   C play
   (D) to playing

17 You ___ have asked. You knew he would say 'no'.
   A couldn't
   B should
   (C) needn't
   D didn't

18 You really ___ to practise a bit more.
   A should
   (B) ought
   C must
   D could

19 Toby's a careless rider, ___ ?
   A is he
   B does he
   (C) isn't he
   D hasn't he

20 I think she'd rather ___ out than stay home.
   A to go
   (B) go
   C going
   D went

Vocabulary

For questions 21–40, choose the word or phrase that most appropriately completes the sentence.

21 I'm afraid what happens next is beyond my ___ .
A aim
B influence
(C) control
D ability

22 If you're at a loose ___ , we could go to the park.
A ending
B final
C finish
(D) end

23 Jo doesn't ___ up to going back to school yet.
(A) feel
B make
C look
D live

24 Simon has given ___ football to play more hockey.
A out
B on
(C) up
D over

25 When are you next ___ hiking in the mountains?
A coming
(B) going
C doing
D playing

26 It doesn't ___ any difference how much you offer to pay him.
A do
(B) make
C have
D hold

27 Can you ___ in to your Facebook account?
(A) log
B go
C key
D turn

28 There's a ___ machine selling snacks.
A cash
B washing
(C) vending
D sewing

29 Too much exercise can be bad ___ you.
(A) for
B of
C from
D at

30 Are we playing for ___ now?
A true
B honest
(C) real
D fact

31 On second ___ , let's just stay in and watch TV.
A beliefs
(B) thoughts
C thinks
D ideas

32 Why did he turn ___ the job?
A up
B off
(C) down
D around

33 What's wrong ___ the tablet? It isn't working.
A within
(B) with
C from
D for

34 We missed the flight because we slept ___ .
(A) in
B on
C under
D over

35 Don't forget to ___ some food with you.
A fetch
B carry
C hold
(D) bring

36 We're experimenting ___ a new IT system.
(A) with
B for
C from
D in

37 Let's all get ___ for a coffee and a chat.
A in
B around
C about
(D) together

38 Somebody has hacked ___ my computer and stolen my passwords.
A over
B on
(C) into
D off

39 Turn the music ___ . I can't hear it.
A down
B off
C out
(D) up

40 I'll give you a call ___ the next hour or so.
(A) within
B without
C among
D along

Awareness

1 **Which of these sentences are correct (C) and incorrect (I)?**

1 Our car was stole last week. _I_
2 I'm being attacked by a gang of youths. _C_
3 The suspect is been taken to the police station. _I_
4 You'll be being given a new identity badge. _I_
5 What will be done about the problems? _C_

6 This project must be finished by next week. _C_
7 He is believed that crime is falling. _I_
8 This street hasn't been cleaned for weeks. _C_
9 This area is being said to be the safest in the city. _I_
10 You won't be told about our decision until later. _C_

How many did you get right? ☐

Grammar

The passive

We use the passive when:
- the action is more important than who or what is responsible for it (the agent).

*The burglar **was arrested** yesterday evening.*
- we don't know the agent, or it is not important.

*Surveys **are used** to investigate people's preferences.*
- we want to draw particular attention to the agent by moving it to the end.

*The vandals **were caught** by a dog walker.*

> **Note**
>
> When it is important to mention the agent in a passive sentence, we use the word *by*. When we want to mention a tool or material, we use *with*.
> *The stolen goods **were found by** some children.*
> *The window **was broken with** a large rock.*
> *The house **is equipped with** a burglar alarm.*

The passive is formed with the verb **be** and a past participle. Notice how active verb forms change to passive forms. There is no passive form for the future continuous, present perfect continuous or past perfect continuous.

Tense	Active	Passive
present simple	take / takes	am / are / is taken
present continuous	am / are / is taking	am / are / is being taken
past simple	took	was / were taken
past continuous	was / were taking	was / were being taken
present perfect simple	have / has taken	have / has been taken
past perfect simple	had taken	had been taken
will	will take	will be taken

The object of the verb in the active sentence becomes the subject of the verb in the passive sentence. The verb *be* is used in the same tense of the main verb in the active sentence, together with the past participle of the main verb in the active sentence.
*They **were chasing** him. He **was being chased**.*
In this example we do not know who was chasing him and it is not very important, so we do not include this information in the passive sentence.

It's often possible to change a prepositional object in an active sentence into the subject of a passive sentence. The preposition remains in its original position after the verb, without an object.
*They didn't pay **for the magazines**.*
*The magazines weren't paid **for**.*

> **Note**
>
> After some verbs there are two objects, for example, *give*, *lend*, *send* and *show*. When we want to change an active sentence with two objects into the passive voice, one becomes the subject of the passive sentence and the other one remains an object. Which object we choose depends on what we want to emphasise. The structure is:
> subject [indirect object] + passive verb + direct object (+ *by* + agent).
> ***She** was given **the documents** (by her boss).*
> OR subject [direct object] + passive verb + indirect object (+ *by* + agent). When a direct object is followed by an indirect object, we have to use a preposition (*to*, *for*, etc.) in front of the indirect object.
> ***The documents** were given **to her** (by her boss).*

The passive: -ing form, infinitives and modal verbs

Tense	Active	Passive
-ing form	taking	being taken
Infinitive	take	be taken
to + infinitive	to take	to be taken
Modal	can take	can be taken

The criminals tried to avoid **being seen**.
This report had better **be completed** by the end of today.
She agreed **to be transferred** to another police station.
Any unusual activity **must be reported** as soon as possible.

We form the impersonal passive structure with: *it* + passive verb + *that* + clause.
Many people believe that poverty increases crime.
It is believed that poverty increases crime.

We form the personal structure with noun + passive verb + *to* + infinitive.
People say that alarms deter burglars.
Alarms are said to deter burglars.

Note

We often use verbs like *believe, consider, know, expect, say, suppose* and *think* in the passive. They can be used in an impersonal or a personal passive structure.

Grammar exercises

2 **Choose the correct option to complete the sentences.**

1   Fingerprints are *been* / being taken at the moment.
2   Two young men were *hurting* / hurt yesterday in an accident.
3   The detective is going to be promoted / *promote* next week.
4   He has never *be* / been suspected of theft before.
5   The jury will *be sat* / have been sitting for three weeks by the end of tomorrow.
6   Two football fans were arrested / *arresting* yesterday.
7   A window was *broke* / broken at school yesterday and I was *accusing* / accused of doing it.
8   The crime figures for the city are *publishing* / published every month.
9   Phones *don't* / aren't allowed in the courtroom.
10 A statement was *took* / taken immediately after the incident.

3 **Write sentences in the passive.**

1   They report the crime. The crime _____ *is reported* _____ .
2   They are reporting the crime. The crime _____ *is being reported* _____ .
3   They reported the crime. The crime _____ *was reported* _____ .
4   They were reporting the crime. The crime _____ *was being reported* _____ .
5   They have reported the crime. The crime _____ *has been reported* _____ .
6   They had reported the crime. The crime _____ *had been reported* _____ .
7   They will report the crime. The crime _____ *will be reported* _____ .
8   They are going to report the crime. The crime _____ *is going to be reported* _____ .
9   They will have reported the crime. The crime _____ *will have been reported* _____ .

13

4 Complete the sentences with the active or passive form of the verbs.

1 A message _____was sent_____ (send) to me yesterday.
2 Sam _____didn't invite_____ (not / invite) me to his party last Saturday.
3 The package _____was delivered_____ (deliver) to him by post.
4 He _____'s writing_____ (write) a report at the moment. He can't speak to you.
5 Your phone can't _____be repaired_____ (repair). You should _____get_____ (get) a new one.
6 Your letter _____hasn't been posted_____ (not / post) yet.

5 Write sentences in the passive.

1 You mustn't share your passwords with anyone.
   Passwords _mustn't be shared with anyone_ .
2 He must deliver this parcel right away.
   This _parcel must be delivered right away_ .
3 He can't have broken the vase.
   The _vase can't have been broken_ .
4 We must bring identification to the interview.
   Identification _must be brought to the interview_ .
5 She has to make all the preparations for the trial.
   All the preparations _for the trial have to be made / have to be made for the trial_ .
6 We don't have to clean the room now.
   The room _doesn't have to be cleaned now_ .
7 We should take the child to his parents' house.
   The child _should be taken to his parents' house_ .
8 He might have taken the book by mistake.
   The book _might have been taken by mistake_ .

6 Rewrite the sentences.

1 They believe that the suspect lives in the area.
   a It _is believed that the suspect lives in the area_ .
   b The suspect _is believed to live in the area_ .
2 They say that violent crime rates increase in hot weather.
   a It _is said that violent crime rates increase in hot weather_ .
   b Violent crime rates _are said to increase in hot weather_ .
3 They expect that he will get a fine for speeding.
   a It _is expected that he will get a fine for speeding_ .
   b He _is expected to get a fine for speeding_ .
4 People know that the inspector works very hard.
   a It _is known that the inspector works very hard_ .
   b The inspector _is known to work very hard_ .
5 People understand that politicians sometimes lie.
   a It _is understood that politicians sometimes lie_ .
   b Politicians _are understood to lie sometimes_ .
6 They think that the burglars came in through the bathroom window.
   a It _is thought that the burglars came in through the bathroom window_ .
   b The burglars _are thought to have come in through the bathroom window_ .

7 Complete the second sentence so that it has a similar meaning to the first sentence, using the word given. Do not change the word given. You must use between two and five words.

1 They told you to be here at ten.
You _____ *were told to be here* _____ at ten. **BE**

2 They are investigating the case at the moment.
The case _____ *is being investigated* _____ at the moment. **IS**

3 They have just fitted new locks.
New locks _____ *have just been* _____ fitted. **BEEN**

4 They might vandalise that old cinema.
That old cinema _____ *might be vandalised* _____ . **VANDALISED**

5 Someone gave me some helpful advice.
I _____ *was given* _____ some helpful advice. **WAS**

6 You had better pay that parking fine within 14 days.
That parking fine _____ *had better be paid* _____ within 14 days. **PAID**

7 We sell crime novels on the second floor.
Crime novels _____ *are sold* _____ on the second floor. **SOLD**

8 I hate it when my brother tricks me.
I can't _____ *stand being tricked* _____ by my brother. **STAND**

Vocabulary

Phrasal verbs

8 Match the phrasal verbs (1–8) with their meanings (a–h).

1 burn down — *f* — a not be punished for doing something wrong
2 do away with — *b* — b kill or get rid of
3 do up — *e* — c surrender to the police
4 get away with — *a* — d rob
5 give yourself up — *c* — e fix or decorate something, so that it looks good
6 give away — *h* — f destroy something (usually a building) with fire
7 hold up — *d* — g die
8 pass away — *g* — h give something to someone for free

9 Complete the sentences with the correct form of the phrasal verbs from Exercise 8.

1 The criminals _____ *got away with* _____ the crime because the police never found them.
2 They are _____ *giving away* _____ free bottles of water in the park today.
3 Three men _____ *held up* _____ the bank in the high street this afternoon, but they were soon arrested.
4 After they started the fire, the whole building _____ *burned / burnt down* _____ within minutes.
5 The kidnappers finally _____ *gave themselves up* _____ , and are now in jail.
6 My grandfather _____ *passed away* _____ peacefully in his sleep at the age of 85.
7 Have you heard that they are _____ *doing up* _____ the old clubhouse, to make it look nice again?
8 The pupils at our school hope to _____ *do away with* _____ school uniform soon, because it is very unpopular.

13

Prepositions

10 **Choose the correct option to complete the sentences.**

1 You can't do that – it's **against** / *under* / *to* the law.
2 Barry is *against* / **under** / *of* suspicion of having taken part in a robbery.
3 Eventually, she confessed *against* / *under* / **to** stealing the phone.
4 Come with us, sir. You are *against* / **under** / *of* arrest.
5 The murderer was sentenced *against* / *under* / **to** a lifetime in prison.
6 After a long trial, the suspect was found guilty *against* / *under* / **of** the crime.

Collocations and expressions

11 **Complete the sentences with the correct form of these words.**

| break | care | give | have | make | take |

1 You have to ___take___ responsibility for your actions – you can't blame anyone else.
2 My friend recommended the new crime drama, so I'm going to ___give___ it a go.
3 I don't want to ___make___ a fool of myself by forgetting what to say.
4 I couldn't ___care___ less about losing the money, but the wallet was a gift from my aunt.
5 I don't want to get a new phone, but I ___have___ no choice.
6 He is one of the few people I know who didn't have to ___break___ the law to get rich!

Words easily confused

12 **Complete the sentences with the correct form of these words. Use each word at least once.**

1 | accuse | commit | confess | suspect |

a Many people ___suspected___ Harry of stealing the phone, but they couldn't be sure.
b After checking the speed camera, the police ___accused___ Sue of dangerous driving.
c Do you think it's ever OK to ___commit___ a crime?
d After several hours of questioning, she finally ___confessed___ to the crime.

2 | glance | sight | view | vision |

a Just one ___glance___ at the man was enough to prompt the doctor to call an ambulance.
b The ___view___ from the helicopter was amazing.
c Stay out of ___sight___ until they've gone.
d These glasses will improve your ___vision___ .
e The police waited quietly, hoping to catch ___sight___ of the criminals.

3 | inhabitant | neighbour | resident | tenant |

a They don't own the flat. They're ___tenants___ .
b You can't park here. I'm afraid parking is only for ___residents___ .
c Our next-door ___neighbours___ were burgled yesterday.
d The ___inhabitants___ of this island have some very interesting customs.

4 | court | jury | sentence | trial |

a During the ___trial___ , several witnesses made false statements.
b The ___jury___ consisted of seven men and five women.
c If we can't agree on a solution, the matter will have to be settled in ___court___ .
d The blackmailer received a three-year prison ___sentence___ .

Word formation mixed

13 Use the word in capitals to form a word that fits in the gap.

1 Have you heard about the _____*robbery*_____ at the local shop today? **ROB**
2 I have always suspected that Mark was a _____*criminal*_____ . **CRIME**
3 The neighbours were worried after the second _____*burglary*_____ in two weeks. **BURGLAR**
4 _____*Terrorism*_____ is a problem for governments and citizens the world over. **TERROR**
5 Passengers were told to leave the airport after staff discovered a _____*suspicious*_____ package. **SUSPECT**
6 Offering money to a police officer is a serious _____*offence*_____ . **OFFEND**
7 You can't drive at that speed on this road – it's _____*illegal*_____ . **LEGAL**
8 Do you think _____*punishment*_____ is effective in preventing crime? **PUNISH**

Sentence transformation

14 Complete the second sentence so that it has a similar meaning to the first sentence, using the word given. Do not change the word given. You must use between two and five words.

1 They believe the event will be a huge success.
BELIEVED
It _____*'s / is believed the event*_____ will be a huge success.

2 Your dog can't have eaten your homework!
BEEN
Your homework _____*can't / cannot have been eaten*_____ by your dog!

3 They say that area is dangerous after dark.
SAID
That area _____*is said to be*_____ dangerous after dark.

4 She hates it when people lie to her.
STAND
She _____*can't / cannot stand being lied*_____ to.

5 You don't have to pay the bill straight away.
PAID
The bill doesn't _____*have to be paid*_____ straight away.

6 It is time to get rid of this ridiculous law.
AWAY
It is time _____*to do away with*_____ this ridiculous law.

7 People suspect she's a hacker.
SUSPICION
She's _____*under suspicion of being*_____ a hacker.

8 The shoplifters eventually admitted their crime and went with the police.
GAVE
The shoplifters eventually _____*gave themselves up*_____ to the police.

Awareness

1 **Which of these sentences are correct (C) and incorrect (I)?**

1 We have had smoke alarms installed in every room. _C_

2 I'm used to have my nails done every month. _I_

3 He got his wallet stolen on holiday. _I_

4 We'll have our car serviced soon. _C_

5 Did you get your photo taken by the police? _C_

6 Have you have had your hair trimmed? _I_

7 They were getting their bikes repaired when I saw them. _C_

8 What time are you to having your hair cut? _I_

9 She lost her passport, but got it replaced. _C_

10 Did you use to get your mum to clean your shoes? _C_

How many did you get right? ☐

Grammar

Causatives

We use the causative passive:

* to say that someone has arranged for someone else to do something for them.

*Many people **have locks fitted** to their garage doors.*

* to say that something unpleasant happened to someone.

*We **had our flat broken into** while we were on holiday.*

We form the causative with *have* + object + past participle. It can be used in a variety of tenses. When we want to mention the agent, we use the word *by*.

*My grandmother **has had** an alarm **fitted**.*

*We **used to have** our car **serviced** every year.*

*You **will have** your passport **checked** (**by** passport control).*

We use the causative active to say that someone asks or tells someone else to do something for them, when we want to emphasise the agent. We form the causative active with *get* + object + *to* + infinitive or *have* + object + infinitive (without *to*). It can be used in a variety of tenses. The version with *have* is much less common. We can only use it if the subject has the authority to tell other people to do things (e.g. he / she is the boss).

*Can you **get someone to fix** this?* (Can you ask / tell him / her to do it?)

*I'll **have an officer take** your fingerprints.* (I'll instruct him / her to do it.)

> **Note**
>
> For something that someone has arranged to have done, we can also use *get* + object + past participle. This structure is less formal. We don't usually use this to talk about unpleasant events.
>
> *I **got** my glasses **repaired** at the optician's.*

Grammar exercises

2 **Choose the correct option to complete the sentences.**

1 Dad (had) / has got his car washed yesterday.

2 It's going to be a hot summer. We must (get) / to have air conditioning put in.

3 It's three years since we last had the bedroom walls *paint* / (painted).

4 *I get* / (I'm getting) my computer fixed at the moment.

5 Terry is going to (have) / get her dad check her work before she hands it in.

6 The inspector is (having) / to get the whole house checked for fingerprints.

7 Sally (had) / got her arm broken in a climbing accident.

8 I'll *have* / (get) a plumber to have a look at our bathroom taps.

3 Complete the sentences with the causative form of the verbs.

1 We ____*had our roof repaired*____ last week. (our roof / repair)

2 She ____*hasn't had her passport photo taken*____ yet. (not / her passport photo / take)

3 He ____*'s having his ears checked*____ at the moment. (his ears / check)

4 They *were having the alarm replaced* when I called in this morning. (the alarm / replace)

5 Paul ____*has his carpets cleaned*____ once a year. (his carpets / clean)

6 We __*have had the flat redecorated*__ once since we moved in. (the flat / redecorate)

7 I *had already had my eyes tested* by nine o'clock yesterday. (already / my eyes / test)

8 I have called a plumber. I ____*'ll have the tap fixed*____ before you arrive. (the tap / fix)

4 Rewrite the sentences using the causative.

1 Someone stole my camera.
I *had my camera stolen* .

2 They are servicing my car.
I *'m having my car serviced* .

3 Someone broke into my aunt's house.
My aunt *had her house broken into* .

4 The hairdresser is going to cut my hair tomorrow.
I am *going to have my hair cut / going to have a hairdresser cut my hair tomorrow* .

5 An electrician fixed the TV for Mary.
Mary *had her TV fixed / had an electrician fix her TV* .

6 The dentist is filling one of my teeth.
I am *having one of my teeth filled / having the dentist fill one of my teeth* .

5 Write questions for the answers in bold. Use the causative.

1 *Who do you have your hair cut by* ?
I have my hair cut by **my brother**.

2 *Who are you going to get to service your car* ?
I'm going to get **Mr Walker** to service my car.

3 *When did you have your room painted* ?
I had my room painted **last month**.

4 *What do you need to get fixed* ?
I need to get **my watch fixed**.

5 *What do you get your little sister to clean* ?
I get my little sister to clean **my room**.

6 *How often do you have your teeth checked* ?
I have my teeth checked **every six months**.

7 *Why have you had your computer upgraded* ?
I've had my computer upgraded **because it was so slow**.

8 *Where will you be having your dress made* ?
I'll be having my dress made **at Divine Designs**.

6 Complete the second sentence so that it has a similar meaning to the first sentence, using the word given. Do not change the word given. You must use between two and five words.

1 They have already published three books of mine.
I've _____*already had*_____ three books published by them. **HAD**

2 We had our boiler fixed by a plumber.
We _____*got a plumber to fix*_____ our boiler. **GOT**

3 Our floor needs polishing before the party.
We must _____*get / have our floor polished*_____ before the party. **POLISHED**

4 Joe's mother washes his clothes.
Joe _____*gets his clothes washed by*_____ his mother. **GETS**

5 Is someone going to fix your teeth for you?
Are you _____*going to have your teeth*_____ fixed? **HAVE**

6 They will deliver Carol's new fridge tomorrow.
Carol will _____*have / get her new fridge delivered*_____ tomorrow. **DELIVERED**

Vocabulary

Phrasal verbs

7 Match the phrasal verbs (1–8) with their meanings (a–h).

1	go off	*g*	**a**	put someone in prison
2	own up	*d*	**b**	realise someone is trying to trick you
3	put away	*a*	**c**	leave or escape suddenly
4	put down	*e*	**d**	admit to doing something wrong
5	put off	*f*	**e**	write someone's name on a document
6	run away	*c*	**f**	make someone dislike something
7	see through	*b*	**g**	make a sudden loud noise
8	see to	*h*	**h**	deal with something that needs attention

8 Complete the sentences with the correct form of the phrasal verbs from Exercise 7.

1 He tried to trick me, but I _____*saw through*_____ his plan.
2 The cat looked terrified when the alarm _____*went off*_____ .
3 I think Eva broke your computer, but she'll never _____*own up*_____ to it.
4 They caught the criminal and _____*put*_____ him _____*away*_____ for 25 years.
5 Shall I _____*put down*_____ your name for the neighbourhood watch scheme?
6 Don't worry about the broken window – I'll _____*see to*_____ it when I get home.
7 The vandals _____*ran away*_____ when they heard the police sirens.
8 We were going to go to the park, but were _____*put off*_____ by the graffiti and vandalism.

Prepositions

9 **Choose the correct option to complete the sentences.**

1 Nobody likes being accused *of*/ *from* / *in* a crime they didn't commit.
2 Police arrested the teenagers *of* / *for*/ *in* vandalising the playground.
3 He picked up the jewellery and hid it *of* / *from*/ *in* sight in his jacket.
4 I don't think she'll go to prison – I'm sure she is innocent *of*/ *for* / *in* the crime.
5 After he was caught speeding through town, the man was banned *of* / *from*/ *in* driving for six months.
6 The police were watching her, as they suspected her *of*/ *for* / *in* committing several crimes.

Collocations and expressions

10 **Complete the sentences with these words.**

eye   justice   sentence   service   track   ways

1 Steve had to do community ___*service*___ when he got caught painting graffiti on the park walls.
2 If they ever catch the killer, he'll be given a life ___*sentence*___ .
3 The detective was so focused on the investigation that she lost ___*track*___ of time.
4 Sometimes, criminals can change their ___*ways*___ and stop committing crimes.
5 Keep a(n) ___*eye*___ on your bag – there are pickpockets in this part of town.
6 When the robbers were sent to prison, I felt that ___*justice*___ had been done.

Words easily confused

11 **Complete the sentences with the correct form of these words. Use each word at least once.**

1 **contain   form   hold   include   involve**

a My job ___*involves*___ travelling abroad quite frequently.
b The price ___*includes*___ airport taxes and transfers.
c Wood ___*forms*___ only a small part of the structure of these houses.
d Nobody knew exactly what the box ___*contained*___ .
e We need a suitcase that can ___*hold*___ at least 15 kg.

2 **inland   inner   interior   internal**

a We'd better get an ___*interior*___ decorator to do the work.
b His injuries are superficial and there's no ___*internal*___ bleeding.
c The village is about ten miles ___*inland*___ , not on the coast.
d There is a great deal of poverty in some ___*inner*___ city areas.

3 **carry out   celebrate   hold   perform**

a The next meeting will be ___*held*___ on 2nd March.
b They're ___*celebrating*___ their 25th wedding anniversary.
c A soldier must ___*carry out*___ orders without question.
d He enjoys ___*performing*___ magic tricks at children's birthday parties.

4 **bargain   discount   offer   sale**

a There's a(n) ___*discount*___ of 20% on all cameras this week.
b It was on special ___*offer*___ – that's why I only paid £10 for it.
c Wait until the ___*sales*___ start before you go shopping for clothes.
d I got a real ___*bargain*___ – these shoes were half price!

14

Word formation   verb → noun

12 Use the word in capitals to form a word that fits in the gap.

1 The police had to let him go because they had no _____*proof*_____ that he had committed a crime.   **PROVE**

2 Have you come to any _____*conclusion*_____ about the court case yet?   **CONCLUDE**

3 Being a police officer can be quite a dangerous _____*occupation*_____ .   **OCCUPY**

4 When Philip graduated, he became a professional _____*photographer*_____ .   **PHOTOGRAPH**

5 She had to have an _____*operation*_____ on her broken ankle.   **OPERATE**

6 We didn't realise the _____*significance*_____ of the news at the time.   **SIGNIFY**

7 The judge gave her a short sentence because she was a first-time _____*offender*_____ .   **OFFEND**

8 The high crime rate in the area influenced our _____*decision*_____ to move to the country.   **DECIDE**

Sentence transformation

13 Complete the second sentence so that it has a similar meaning to the first sentence, using the word given. Do not change the word given. You must use between two and five words.

1 She always has her hair cut by her aunt.
   GETS
   She always _____*gets her aunt to cut*_____ her hair.

2 Our grass needs cutting this weekend.
   CUT
   We should _____*have / get our grass cut*_____ this weekend.

3 Somebody will remove your plaster tomorrow.
   REMOVED
   You _____*will have / get your plaster removed*_____ tomorrow.

4 I saw Lucas vandalise a bus shelter and now I don't like him anymore.
   PUT
   Seeing Lucas vandalise a bus shelter _____*put me off*_____ him.

5 You'll get put in prison for a long time.
   AWAY
   They'll _____*put you away*_____ for a long time.

6 The jury decided that the suspect did not commit the crime.
   INNOCENT
   The jury decided that the suspect _____*was innocent of*_____ the crime.

7 After a few months in prison, he started behaving completely differently.
   WAYS
   After a few months in prison, he _____*changed his ways*_____ completely.

8 Someone will deal with this problem tomorrow.
   SEEN
   I'll get this problem _____*seen to*_____ tomorrow.

1 Which of these sentences are correct (C) and incorrect (I)?

1 If you'll fall off your bike, you'll hurt yourself. _I_

2 If you climb to the top, you'll be able to see the sea. _C_

3 I won't put her in the team unless she'll train harder. _I_

4 I'd buy the coat if I thought it suited me. _C_

5 She wouldn't shout so much if she would behave herself. _I_

6 If he hadn't missed his flight, he wouldn't have had to buy another ticket. _C_

7 If you would have had a map, you wouldn't have got lost. _I_

8 If I was you, I'd apologise immediately. _I_

9 If you boil water, it would turn into steam. _I_

10 Don't tell Wendy about the party if she phones. _C_

How many did you get right? ☐

Grammar

Zero conditional

If clause	Main clause
present simple	present simple

We use the zero conditional to talk about an action that always / usually happens or a situation that is always true. We can use *when* instead of *if*.
*If you **burn** fossil fuels, you **pollute** the atmosphere.*
***When** you **burn** fossil fuels, you **pollute** the atmosphere.*

First conditional

If clause	Main clause
present simple / continuous	*will* + infinitive

We use the first conditional to talk about the results of an action or situation that will probably happen now or in the future.
*If the volcano **erupts**, the village **will be destroyed**.*
*If the climate **gets** warmer, the sea level **will rise**.*

We can use *can, could, may* or *might* in the main clause instead of *will*. We can also use an imperative.
*If you **want** to be more environmentally friendly, you **could** install solar panels.*
*If you **don't want** to buy a drink, **bring** your own.*

Second conditional

If clause	Main clause
past simple / continuous	*would* + infinitive

We use the second conditional to talk about an action or a situation:
- that isn't true now.
*If **I had** the time, **I would write** a book.*
- that is unlikely in the future.
*If everyone **stopped** using plastic, fewer sea animals **would die**.*

We can also use the second conditional to give advice.
*If I **were** you, **I'd buy** an electric car.*

> ### Note
> We usually use *were* for all persons in second conditional sentences.
> *If Dan **were** here, he'd **choose** the vegetarian option.*

We can use *could* or *might* in the main clause instead of *would*.
You **could** stay in an eco-lodge if you **went** to Costa Rica.
I **might be able to** afford it if I **worked** through the summer.

Third conditional

If clause	Main clause
past perfect simple / continuous	*would* + *have* + past participle

We use the third conditional to imagine past events or situations that didn't actually happen. These are always hypothetical things because we cannot change the past.
If my dad **had gone** to university, he **would have been** a geologist. (He didn't go to university, so he isn't a geologist.)

We can use *could* or *might* in the main clause instead of *would*.
We **could have helped** you if we **hadn't been** on holiday.
If the meeting **had been** earlier, I **might have been** there.

Grammar exercises

2 **Choose the correct option to complete the sentences.**

1   If you are caught speeding, you *would get* / *get* a fine.
2   She *would* / *will* pass the exam if she studies hard.
3   Simon *didn't damage* / *wouldn't have damaged* the car if he had been more careful.
4   Unless we *put* / *don't put* the recycling in the right bin, they won't collect it.
5   If we *took* / *are taking* the bus instead of driving, it would help the environment.
6   If the baby *is* / *were* a girl, I'll call her Emily.
7   Sally *would be* / *is* very happy if she were offered the job.
8   She could have played football professionally if she *moved* / *had moved* to the USA.

3 **Complete the sentences with the first conditional.**

1   If I _____*find*_____ (find) your notebook, I _____*'ll give*_____ (give) it to you.
2   If you _____*don't know*_____ (not / know) the meaning, you _____*could / should look*_____ (look) in a dictionary.
3   We _____*'ll go*_____ (go) for a picnic if the weather _____*is*_____ (be) nice tomorrow.
4   They _____*won't believe*_____ (not / believe) you even if you _____*tell*_____ (tell) them the truth.
5   I _____*'ll wash*_____ (wash) the dishes if you _____*'re*_____ (be) tired.
6   We _____*won't get*_____ (not / get) any festival tickets unless we _____*go*_____ (go) earlier.
7   If the dog _____*doesn't stop*_____ (not / stop) barking, they _____*'ll call*_____ (call) the police.
8   She _____*won't come*_____ (not / come) to the party if you _____*don't invite*_____ (not / invite) her.

4 **Complete the sentences with the second conditional.**

1 She would like to buy a new hybrid car, but she doesn't have enough money.
   If she _____had_____ enough money, she _____would buy_____ a new hybrid car.

2 He eats a lot of red meat; that's why he's so unhealthy.
   If he _____didn't eat_____ a lot of red meat, he _____wouldn't be_____ so unhealthy.

3 She doesn't own a bike; that's why she can't cycle to work.
   She _____would be able to cycle_____ to work if she _____owned_____ a bike.

4 I get up late every morning, so I am always late for school.
   I _wouldn't always be_ late for school if I _____didn't get up_____ late every morning.

5 He doesn't have much free time, so he doesn't see his friends very often.
   If he _____had_____ more free time, he _____would see_____ his friends more often.

6 They play loud music every night; that's why we can't sleep.
   If they _____didn't play_____ loud music every night, we _____would be able to sleep_____ .

5 **Complete the sentences with the third conditional.**

1 If they _____had planted_____ (plant) more trees, the area _____wouldn't have flooded_____ (not / flood) so easily.

2 If I _____had known_____ (know) that there was a recycling bank here, I _would have brought_ (bring) my old clothes.

3 If I _____had seen_____ (see) you at the bus stop, I _would have offered_ (offer) you a lift.

4 I _would have called_ (call) you if I _____hadn't lost_____ (not / lose) your telephone number.

5 We _wouldn't have taken_ (not / take) a taxi if the buses _____hadn't been_____ (not / be) on strike.

6 They _would have gone_ (go) to the beach if it _____hadn't rained_____ (not / rain).

6 **Complete the second sentence so that it has a similar meaning to the first.**

1 Don't drive so much and you will help the environment.
   If you _don't drive so much, you'll help the environment_ .

2 Can I borrow your bike? I can give it back to you this afternoon.
   If you _lend me your bike, I'll given it back to you this afternoon_ .

3 Julia can't drink coffee because she gets a headache.
   When _Julia drinks coffee, she gets a headache_ .

4 Why don't you talk to her about your problem?
   If I were you, _I would talk to her about your problem_ .

5 Dan was thirsty because he left his water bottle in the park.
   If Dan _hadn't left his water bottle in the park, he wouldn't have been thirsty_ .

6 I was listening to music, so I didn't hear my phone ring.
   If I _hadn't been listening to music, I would have heard my phone ring_ .

7 **Complete the sentences with one word in each gap.**

1 I wouldn't be so confident if I _____were_____ him.

2 She would _____have_____ been happier if she had moved out of the city.

3 Martin doesn't travel by plane because it _____is_____ bad for the environment.

4 _____If_____ I had your email address, I'd send you the photo.

5 If I have enough time, I _____might / may_____ come and visit you – but I can't be sure.

6 When you put salt on ice, _____it_____ melts.

7 I won't call him if he _____is_____ still working.

8 If more people use solar energy, it _____will_____ become cheaper.

15

Vocabulary

Phrasal verbs

8 Match the phrasal verbs (1–8) with their meanings (a–h).

1	add to	d	**a**	make something fall by using a sharp tool at its base
2	block out	b	**b**	stop light or noise passing through
3	blow over	h	**c**	persuade someone to do something
4	blow up	e	**d**	increase the size, number or amount of something
5	cut down	a	**e**	destroy with an explosion
6	slow down	f	**f**	go or make something go less quickly
7	talk into	c	**g**	take all of something so there is nothing left
8	use up	g	**h**	(of a storm or argument) end without causing harm

9 Complete the sentences with the correct form of the phrasal verbs from Exercise 8.

1 We were lucky that the storm _____ blew over _____ quickly.

2 It wasn't easy, but I finally _____ talked _____ my parents _____ into _____ buying me an electric scooter.

3 Burning fossil fuels _____ adds to _____ the problem of climate change.

4 If we eat less meat, we will _____ use up _____ less land for farming.

5 I need some thick curtains to _____ block out _____ the sunshine in the morning.

6 They _____ blew up _____ the tower block to destroy it, because it was unsafe.

7 Using energy from the sun or wind will help _____ slow down _____ the rate of climate change.

8 If we _____ cut down _____ our rainforests, many species of plants and animals will disappear.

Prepositions

10 Choose the correct option to complete the sentences.

1 Unfortunately, this tiny umbrella doesn't offer much protection *from* / *with* / *of* the rain.

2 It's very difficult to live with the threat *from* / *with* / *of* poverty every day.

3 I'm not sure that I can cope *from* / *with* / *of* not eating meat.

4 Is the customer satisfied *from* / *with* / *of* her new electric car?

5 The group is trying to make more people aware *from* / *with* / *of* climate change.

6 Don't let Simon discourage you *from* / *with* / *of* joining the club.

Collocations and expressions

11 Choose the correct option to complete the sentences.

1 We all need to *do* / *play* our bit to avoid single-use plastics.

2 Do you think having fines for *putting* / *dropping* litter would stop people doing it?

3 We need to *take* / *do* action to protect some natural habitats.

4 I hope that, one day, we can *put* / *make* an end to global poverty.

5 How do you think we can *drop* / *tackle* the problem of increasing carbon emissions?

6 Everyone can *make* / *play* a part in slowing down climate change.

Words easily confused

12 **Complete the sentences with the correct form of these words. Use each word at least once.**

1 `course   dessert   meal   starter`

  a Breakfast is the most important _____ *meal* _____ of the day.
  b Apple pie and ice cream is my favourite _____ *dessert* _____ .
  c For the main _____ *course* _____ , I would like the vegan option, please.
  d I'll have soup for a _____ *starter* _____ , please.

2 `aisle   corridor   line   now`

  a Why are you in the _____ *corridor* _____ when you should be in your classroom?
  b They live in a street with two neat _____ *rows* _____ of identical bungalows.
  c I prefer a window seat to a(n) _____ *aisle* _____ seat when I'm flying.
  d Don't walk on the railway _____ *line* _____ .
  e The bride looked nervous as she walked down the _____ *aisle* _____ .

3 `consider   guess   reckon   wonder`

  a I _____ *wonder* _____ if Dad has already taken out the recycling.
  b Would you _____ *consider* _____ switching to a renewable energy provider?
  c Can you _____ *guess* _____ how many people there are in the world?
  d He _____ *reckons* _____ he lives a greener lifestyle than me.

4 `demonstration   display   exhibition   show`

  a Jim Jones has won first prize in the village flower _____ *show* _____ yet again.
  b It was the best firework _____ *display* _____ I have ever seen.
  c Can you give us a(n) _____ *demonstration* _____ of how the machine works?
  d All the major manufacturers were represented at the technology _____ *exhibition* _____ .

Word formation   verb or noun → adjective

13 **Use the word in capitals to form a word that fits in the gap.**

  1 This phone is completely _____ *useless* _____ without a battery.   **USE**
  2 We watched a very _____ *educational* _____ documentary about whales last night.   **EDUCATE**
  3 There has been a _____ *dramatic* _____ increase in the amount of land used for agriculture.   **DRAMA**
  4 Some species of dolphin are _____ *endangered* _____ – there aren't many of them left.   **DANGER**
  5 The pollution from the factory is totally _____ *unacceptable* _____ – we need to campaign   **ACCEPT**
     against it.
  6 Many sea birds died as a result of the oil spill. It was an _____ *ecological* _____ disaster.   **ECOLOGY**
  7 Energy from the sun or the wind is known as _____ *renewable* _____ energy.   **RENEW**
  8 The technology works, but it's too expensive to use on a _____ *massive* _____ scale   **MASS**
     at the moment.

Sentence transformation

14 Complete the second sentence so that it has a similar meaning to the first sentence, using the word given. Do not change the word given. You must use between two and five words.

1 The wall fell down because you didn't build it properly.
   HAD
   If _____ *you'd / you had built the wall* _____ properly, it wouldn't have fallen down.

2 We won't finish this job without Rob's help.
   US
   If _____ *Rob doesn't / does not help us* _____ , we won't finish this job.

3 It only works if you turn it on.
   UNLESS
   It _____ *doesn't / does not work unless* _____ you turn it on.

4 My advice to you is to forget about it.
   WERE
   If _____ *I were you, I'd / I would* _____ forget about it.

5 Molly was finally persuaded to come with us.
   TALKED
   We finally _____ *talked Molly into coming* _____ with us.

6 I'm going to let the boss know about this.
   AWARE
   I'm going to _____ *make the boss aware* _____ of this.

7 They want large organisations to stop using energy from fossil fuels.
   PUT
   They want to _____ *put an end to* _____ large organisations using energy from fossil fuels.

8 We'll solve the problem more effectively if we all help.
   BIT
   We'll solve the problem more effectively if we all _____ *do our bit* _____ .

Unit 16

Awareness

1 Which of these sentences are correct (C) and incorrect (I)?

1 Provided everyone agrees, we'll leave early. _C_
2 If you hadn't told me, I still don't know. _I_
3 She won't be able to help you otherwise she's busy. _I_
4 As long it doesn't cost too much, I'll buy it. _I_
5 Supposing we have some spare time, where shall we go? _C_

6 If he hadn't taken the wrong road, he'd be here by now. _C_
7 You are earning more money today if you had gone to university. _I_
8 He'll do the work on condition that you pay him in advance. _C_
9 I'm happy to come with you, provided my parents would give me permission. _I_
10 Be quiet, otherwise you won't know what to do. _C_

How many did you get right? ☐

Grammar

Mixed conditionals

If clause	Main clause
past perfect simple / continuous	*would* + infinitive
or	
past simple / continuous	*would* + *have* + past participle

A mixed conditional is where the two clauses in a conditional sentence refer to different times. They contain one clause from a second conditional and one from a third conditional.
*If our car **hadn't been stolen** (a few hours ago), **we'd be** home in bed (now).*
*If they **cared** about the environment (now, in general), they **wouldn't have flown** to Edinburgh (last week).*

Conditionals without *if*

We can use *provided / providing that, on condition that* and *as long as* to replace *if* in first conditional sentences. These phrases mean *if* and *only if*.
***Provided that I have** the time, **I'll come** and visit you this evening.*
***We'll go** to the beach tomorrow **on condition that** you **promise** to behave.*
***As long as** public transport is cheap, people **will use** it.*

We can use *unless* in first and second conditional sentences. It means the same as *if not*.
*She won't get to the meeting on time **if she doesn't get** a taxi.*
*She won't get to the meeting on time **unless she gets** a taxi.*

We can use *otherwise* to replace an *if* clause. It means *if not*.
***If you don't** drive more carefully, I'm not getting in the car with you.*
*Drive more carefully. **Otherwise**, I'm not getting in the car with you.*

We can use *suppose* or *supposing* in all conditional sentences, usually to ask questions. It means *imagine* or *what if*.
***Suppose / Supposing** you could live anywhere in the world, where would you choose?*
***Suppose / Supposing** we had run out of money, what would we have done?*

16

Grammar exercises

2 **Complete the sentences with a mixed conditional.**

1 If we ___hadn't missed___ (not / miss) our flight, we would be lying in the sunshine right now.
2 You ___wouldn't be___ (not / be) so tired now if you had gone to bed earlier.
3 If I didn't like chicken so much, I would ___would have become___ (become) a vegetarian years ago.
4 This town would still be beautiful if it ___hadn't been___ (not / be) polluted so badly.
5 If he didn't care about the environment, he ___wouldn't have installed___ (not / install) solar panels.
6 If I ___had___ (have) a refillable water bottle, I would have brought it with me now.

3 **Choose the correct option to complete the sentences.**

1 *Provided* / *Unless* / *Otherwise* we have enough money, we'll buy an electric car.
2 Some species will become extinct *on condition that* / *unless* / *otherwise* we protect their habitats.
3 We'd better hurry up, *provided* / *unless* / *otherwise* we'll be late.
4 *As long as* / *Unless* / *Supposing* it rains tomorrow, the whole family is going on a picnic.
5 Steven agreed to wash my bicycle, *on condition that* / *unless* / *otherwise* I helped him with his maths.
6 *Provided* / *Unless* / *Supposing* you lost your job tomorrow, what would you do?
7 Carbon emissions will decrease *as long as* / *supposing* / *otherwise* we stop burning fossil fuels.
8 Let's not stay too long, *on condition that* / *otherwise* / *unless* we won't get home before dark.

4 **Complete the second sentence so that it has a similar meaning to the first.**

1 Some animals will lose their habitats if we don't eat less meat.
   Unless *we eat less meat, some animals will lose their habitats* .
2 Don't call me if there isn't a problem.
   Unless *there's a problem, don't call me* .
3 We won't be able to sit together if we don't get on the boat now.
   Unless *we get on the boat now, we won't be able to sit together* .
4 We won't go swimming if it isn't hot.
   Unless *it's hot, we won't go swimming* .
5 If you don't ask him, he won't help you.
   Unless *you ask him, he won't help you* .
6 This species will become extinct if we don't take action soon.
   Unless *we take action soon, this species will become extinct* .

5 **Complete the sentences with the correct form of the verbs.**

1 Supposing you ___saw___ (see) someone dropping litter, what would you do?
2 Supposing they hadn't wanted to fly, ___would___ they ___have considered___ (consider) the train?
3 Supposing there aren't any vegetarian options, what ___will___ you ___eat___ (eat)?
4 Supposing she only ___travels___ (travel) by public transport, how long will the journey take?
5 Supposing he hadn't got the job, what ___would___ he ___have done___ (do) instead?
6 Supposing there ___had been___ (be) a storm, where would they have found shelter?

6 Complete the sentences with one word in each gap.

1 Don't say anything to Sam about this ____*unless / if*____ he asks you.
2 Yes, you can borrow my bike _____*as*_____ long as you look after it.
3 _*Providing / Provided*_ we use renewable energy, our carbon emissions will decrease.
4 He agreed to take the job on ____*condition*____ that he could work at home twice a week.
5 They'd be safely home by now if they ____*had*____ got on that last bus.
6 Supposing I gave you the money – what ____*would*____ you spend it on?
7 You'd better not be late, ____*otherwise / or*____ Jane will be furious.

Vocabulary

Phrasal verbs

7 Match the phrasal verbs (1–8) with their meanings (a–h).

1 freeze over — *b* — **a** tolerate
2 put up with — *a* — **b** (a surface of water) turn to ice
3 run out — *e* — **c** cause something to become extinct
4 soak up — *d* — **d** take in and hold water
5 take over — *f* — **e** use up or finish a supply of something
6 wear away — *h* — **f** take control
7 wear out — *g* — **g** make somebody feel very tired
8 wipe out — *c* — **h** make smaller or smoother over time

8 Complete the sentences with the correct form of the phrasal verbs from Exercise 7.

1 When our biology teacher was ill, the chemistry teacher ____*took over*____ the class for a few days.
2 Forests are important in fighting climate change because they ____*soak up*____ carbon dioxide.
3 Because people used to take a shortcut over the field, they had ____*worn away*____ a path in the grass.
4 Many people are worried that tigers will be completely ____*wiped out*____ by poachers.
5 We went skating on the lake, which had ____*frozen over*____ during the night.
6 Unlike fossil fuels, wind and solar power won't ____*run out*____ .
7 Tim moved to the countryside because he couldn't ____*put up with*____ the pollution in the city.
8 Elena was ____*worn out*____ because she had been working hard all day.

Prepositions

9 Choose the correct option to complete the sentences.

1 There has been a steep rise (in)/ *on* / *to* the number of bicycle thefts in the area.
2 James is a very honest man – you can rely *in* /(on)/ *to* him to tell you the truth.
3 It is important not to allow children to be exposed *in* / *on* /(to)too much violence in the cinema.
4 Does anyone object *in* / *on* /(to)the heating being turned down a bit?
5 Simone is really keen *in* /(on)/ *to* saving the environment.
6 The decision to put more bins in the playground resulted(in)/ *on* / *to* a reduction in the amount of litter.

16

Collocations and expressions

10 Complete the sentences with these words.

bee   cat   crocodile   fish   wolf   worm

1 When you manage to get someone to tell you something against their will, you ___worm___ the information out of them.

2 When someone is pretending to be sad, we say that they are crying ___crocodile___ tears.

3 A dangerous person who is pretending to be harmless is a ___wolf___ in sheep's clothing.

4 When you are trying to encourage people to say something nice about you, you ___fish___ for compliments.

5 Someone who is working very hard is as busy as a ___bee___ .

6 To let the ___cat___ out of the bag means to accidentally reveal a big secret.

Words easily confused

11 Complete the sentences with the correct form of these words. Use each word at least once.

1   bar   lump   piece   sheet   slice

   a That's an interesting ___piece___ of information.

   b Use a fresh ___sheet___ of paper for each question.

   c I'd like two ___slices___ of ham in my sandwich.

   d How much sugar do you take, one ___lump___ or two?

   e I've bought a ___bar___ of chocolate for you.

2   income   interest   investment   salary

   a The bank pays ___interest___ on my account twice a year.

   b As the managing director of a large company, she gets a large ___salary___ .

   c His ___income___ consists largely of rent he receives from property he owns.

   d Buying shares in renewable energy wasn't considered a wise ___investment___ at that time.

3   branch   compartment   department   ward

   a During my stay in hospital I shared a ___ward___ with nine other patients.

   b The train was nearly empty, with only a few passengers in each ___compartment___ .

   c The local ___branch___ of my bank has closed because more people are using internet banking.

   d He works for a government ___department___ , but I don't know which one.

4   earth   ground   land   soil

   a Sandy ___soil___ is no good for growing these flowers.

   b I found the bracelet lying on the ___ground___ outside.

   c Her family owns quite a lot of ___land___ .

   d What on ___earth___ are you doing?

Word formation   adverbs

12 Use the word in capitals to form a word that fits in the gap.

1 We had a _____*memorably*_____ awful holiday in Wales last winter.   **MEMORY**

2 The head teacher reacted _____*furiously*_____ when he heard what Sam had done.   **FURY**

3 It's a pity they decorated the town centre so _____*unattractively*_____ – more people   **ATTRACTIVE**
   would visit if it looked nicer.

4 The dog quickly ate the food on the plate, and then looked _____*guiltily*_____ at   **GUILT**
   its owner.

5 The match ended _____*controversially*_____ , with the losing team claiming that they   **CONTROVERSY**
   had been unfairly denied a penalty.

6 Stop behaving so _____*foolishly*_____ !   **FOOL**

7 The bus driver _____*skilfully*_____ steered the vehicle around the parked cars.   **SKILL**

8 The small boy _____*irritatingly*_____ repeated the same question again and again,   **IRRITATE**
   until his mother finally told him to be quiet.

Sentence transformation

13 Complete the second sentence so that it has a similar meaning to the first sentence, using the word
given. Do not change the word given. You must use between two and five words.

1 If you don't finish your dinner, you aren't allowed to watch TV.
   UNLESS
   You aren't allowed to watch TV _____*unless you finish*_____ your dinner.

2 Supposing I hadn't been here to help you – what would you have done?
   IF
   What _____*would you have done if*_____ I hadn't been here to help you?

3 If you promise to be home before midnight, you can go to the party.
   LONG
   You can go to the party _____*as long as you promise*_____ to be home before midnight.

4 Provided I can return it if I don't like it, I'll buy your computer.
   CONDITION
   I'll buy your computer _____*on condition that*_____ I can return it if I don't like it.

5 I'm not going to tolerate that loud music any longer.
   PUT
   I'm not going to _____*put up with*_____ that loud music any longer.

6 I'll drive if you are feeling too tired to continue.
   OVER
   I'll _____*take over*_____ the driving if you are feeling too tired to continue.

7 I can't believe he revealed the secret on live TV!
   CAT
   I can't believe he _____*let the cat out*_____ of the bag on live TV!

8 He's been looking after the children all day and now he's exhausted.
   WORN
   He _____*'s / is worn out*_____ after looking after the children all day.

Part 1

For questions 1–8, read the text below and decide which answer (A, B, C or D) best fits each gap. There is an example at the beginning (0).

Take care, it's a jungle out there

The (0) __ of young children playing happily in the garden is a joy to behold, especially when parents believe that they can come to no (1) __ there. Parents will admit that children could be stung by a bee or scratch themselves on the rose bushes, but these are not (2) __ occurrences. In most people's (3) __ , being at home means staying safe.

Unfortunately, however, about four thousand British toddlers are poisoned by plants each year. Some of them have to (4) __ time in hospital because their condition is considered serious. Most parents are not (5) __ of which plants are poisonous. Often the flowers that are the most attractive are the most deadly, but it's no use trying to get this (6) __ to a small child!

Safety in the garden depends on parents paying close (7) __ to what their children are doing. When they are quiet, it often means they are (8) __ up to something. Leaving children unattended in the garden can be a risk.

0	(A) sight	B scenery	C view	D vision
1	A injury	(B) harm	C damage	D hurt
2	(A) common	B many	C often	D usual
3	A idea	B attitude	(C) opinion	D thought
4	(A) spend	B earn	C pay	D win
5	(A) aware	B knowing	C conscious	D learned
6	A back	B around	C into	(D) across
7	A notice	(B) attention	C attendance	D care
8	A breaking	B going	(C) getting	D staying

Part 2

For questions 9–16, read the text below and think of the word which best fits each gap. Use only one word in each gap. There is an example at the beginning (0).

A man with a vision

Stamford Raffles was born aboard a ship off the coast of Jamaica **(0)** __in__ 1781. Instead of attending university, he worked for the East India Company **(9)** __as__ a clerk and studied hard in his spare **(10)** __time__ . At the age of 30, he became governor of Java, where he employed zoologists and botanists **(11)** __to__ discover all they could about the animals and plants on the islands. Raffles himself acquired a large collection of animals, including a Malayan sun bear that was brought up with his children. The bear often joined Raffles for dinner, eating fruit **(12)** __and__ drinking champagne.

On a trip to Europe in 1817, Raffles had the idea for the forming of a collection of living animals. After founding the colony of Singapore in 1819, Raffles **(13)** __got__ together with several influential scientists and aristocrats, **(14)** __who__ listened carefully to his ideas. He convinced them, and he was voted president of **(15)** __the__ Zoological Society of London. Raffles died suddenly in 1826. Sadly, the man whose idea it was to start London Zoo did not see its opening two years **(16)** __later__ , in 1828.

Part 3

For questions 17–24, read the text below. Use the word given in capitals at the end of some of the lines to form a word that fits in the gap in the same line. There is an example at the beginning (0).

A holiday in Mauritius

With holiday resorts the world over getting more **(0)** __crowded__ , any place offering **CROWD**

the opportunity of spending a holiday in a **(17)** __beautiful__ natural environment next **BEAUTY**

to endless sandy beaches is guaranteed to be a major **(18)** __attraction__ . But where **ATTRACT**

is one to find such a paradise in this day and age? Mauritius, an almost perfectly circular island

about 600 miles from the East African coast, can provide a wonderful, unspoiled location for just

such a holiday. The island has very little **(19)** __tourism__ at this point in its history. **TOUR**

This means that **(20)** __visitors__ today can enjoy its unspoiled scenery in relative calm, **VISIT**

undisturbed by fellow holidaymakers. It is true that there are not many sights on the island, but

(21) __boredom__ is never a problem since local organisations offer exciting fishing and **BORE**

sailing trips to **(22)** __hidden__ areas where you can see some of the most breathtaking **HIDE**

natural **(23)** __scenery__ in the world. Mauritius is guaranteed to leave the holidaymaker **SCENE**

(24) __completely__ relaxed. **COMPLETE**

Part 4

For questions 25–30, complete the second sentence so that it has a similar meaning to the first sentence, using the word given. Do not change the word given. You must use between two and five words, including the word given. Here is an example (0).

Example:

0   You mustn't use a calculator in the test.

ALLOWED

You are _____ *not allowed to use* _____ a calculator in the test.

25   She is still making her decision.

DECIDED

She _____ *hasn't / has not decided what* _____ to do yet.

26   I've only got a little luggage, so I don't need a trolley.

MUCH

I _____ *haven't got / have not got / don't have / do not have much* _____ luggage, so I don't need a trolley.

27   I am sure he has told her my secret.

MUST

He _____ *must have told her* _____ my secret.

28   Some of the paintings are still for sale.

BEEN

Some of the paintings _____ *haven't / have not been sold* _____ yet.

29   They gave me a computer because I wanted to work at home.

SO

They gave me a computer _____ *so (that) I could* _____ work at home.

30   The goods cannot leave the factory unless there is a signature on these papers.

SIGNED

These papers _____ *must be / have to be signed before* _____ the goods can leave the factory.

B2 Practice: ECCE

Grammar

For questions 1–20, choose the word or phrase that best completes the sentence.

1 If I ___ you, I wouldn't eat that much.
   A were
   B am
   C be
   D was

2 You will ___ shown to your room by this man.
   A be
   B being
   C have
   D having

3 We ___ new doors put in our house.
   A have had
   B have get
   C having
   D getting

4 If this car breaks down, we ___ be stuck here!
   A had
   B would have
   C will
   D can

5 ___ it rains tomorrow, what shall we do?
   A Providing
   B Supposing
   C Thinking
   D Imagining

6 You can wash the dishes, if you ___ to help.
   A are wanting
   B want
   C had wanted
   D would want

7 As ___ as you are happy, I am happy, too.
   A far
   B tall
   C long
   D wide

8 The bad news ___ given to my aunt yesterday.
   A is
   B was
   C were
   D are

9 He avoided ___ accused of fraud.
   A be
   B being
   C have
   D having

10 We hope ___ our new TV delivered today.
   A have
   B having
   C to have
   D had

11 He might be ___ to give you a lift.
   A can
   B able
   C how
   D want

12 You can't get in ___ you have a ticket.
   A unless
   B without
   C otherwise
   D would

13 We could ___ been the winners if we'd worked as a team.
   A of
   B had
   C would
   D have

14 We have to leave now, ___ we'll miss the bus.
   A unless
   B provided
   C otherwise
   D if

15 The boxer had his nose ___ in the fight.
   A broke
   B breaking
   C break
   D broken

16 I got my sister ___ my homework for me.
   A doing
   B to do
   C do
   D did

17 If you hadn't been sent off, we'd ___ holding that trophy now!
   A have
   B being
   C having
   D be

18 She'll do it, on ___ that you pay her.
   A situation
   B condition
   C provided
   D promise

19 They ___ all asked to participate.
   A be
   B were
   C have been
   D was

20 Look! I ___ my teeth whitened.
   A have
   B am having
   C have had
   D will get

Vocabulary

For questions 21–40, choose the word or phrase that most appropriately completes the sentence.

21 It's ___ the law to break the speed limit.
- (A) against
- B counter
- C versus
- D beside

22 I was in a deep sleep when my alarm went ___ .
- A in
- B out
- (C) off
- D on

23 She can see ___ your tricky scheme!
- A over
- B about
- (C) through
- D up

24 You can always rely ___ me to get the job finished.
- A of
- (B) on
- C for
- D to

25 The man turned out to be a wolf in ___ clothing.
- A dog's
- B cow's
- C goat's
- (D) sheep's

26 Are you ___ any suspicion for this crime?
- A with
- (B) under
- C over
- D beside

27 You should ___ yourself up to the police.
- A hold
- B put
- (C) give
- D take

28 I think it's time you ___ up to your crimes.
- (A) owned
- B showed
- C gave
- D turned

29 Mark will ___ over this project from now on, because I am giving up.
- A have
- (B) take
- C give
- D hold

30 The criminal was given a life ___ for murder.
- A jury
- B justice
- C service
- (D) sentence

31 Stop accusing me ___ cheating.
- A with
- (B) of
- C at
- D by

32 You can't do that – you're ___ the law!
- (A) breaking
- B making
- C taking
- D having

33 They had an argument, but it had ___ over by the evening.
- (A) blown
- B burst
- C gone
- D flown

34 We all play a(n) ___ in keeping our house tidy.
- A bit
- (B) part
- C end
- D action

35 That smell is really ___ me off my food.
- A getting
- B throwing
- C moving
- (D) putting

36 Two robbers ___ up a jewellery store in town.
- A took
- (B) held
- C brought
- D went

37 Let's go skating if the pond is frozen ___ .
- A out
- B hard
- (C) over
- D up

38 The woolly mammoth was ___ out during the Ice Age.
- A swept
- B brushed
- C cleaned
- (D) wiped

39 She won't be able to cope ___ such long hours!
- A on
- B after
- (C) with
- D at

40 I was talked ___ volunteering by my friends.
- A on
- B over
- C inside
- (D) into

Awareness

1 Which of these sentences are correct (C) and incorrect (I)?

1 She married a man her parents didn't approve of him. _⊥_

2 I really like the car I bought last year. _C_

3 Mr Fowler, that you met yesterday, is a famous author. _⊥_

4 The singer you like is only 16 years old. _C_

5 The printer that you bought it is faulty. _⊥_

6 The story that I told you is untrue. _C_

7 That's the place when I grew up. _⊥_

8 Do you remember the time where we first met? _⊥_

9 Eva, who was my babysitter years ago, has just got married. _C_

10 Nobody knows the reason why it happened. _C_

How many did you get right? ☐

Grammar

Relative clauses

Relative clauses give more information about a person, thing, place, etc. in a sentence. They are introduced by the following words:

- *who* for people
- *which* for things
- *whose* to show possession
- *when* for time
- *where* for places
- *why* for reason

Defining relative clauses

This type of relative clause gives us information that we need in order to understand who or what the speaker is talking about. We do not use commas to separate it from the rest of the sentence. We can use *that* instead of *who* and *which* in defining relative clauses.
*That's the café **where** I worked in the holidays.*
*We met some people **who / that** were very friendly.*

We often omit the relative pronoun from defining relative clauses, especially in informal English. But we can't omit it when it's the subject of the relative clause, and we never omit *whose*.
*The only exam (**which / that**) he didn't pass was French.* (subject = he)
*She's the other candidate (**who**) they interviewed for the job.* (subject = they)
*The person **who** answered the phone was very helpful.* (subject = the person)

Non-defining relative clauses

This type of relative clause gives us extra information which isn't necessary to understand the meaning of the main clause. We use commas to separate it from the rest of the sentence. We can't use *that* as the relative pronoun, and we can't omit the relative pronoun.
*My manager, **who wanted to start his own business**, left last week.*
*Her CV, **which we received yesterday**, is very impressive.*

Relative clauses with prepositions

When the relative pronoun is the object of a preposition, the preposition can come before *whom* (for people) or *which* (for things), but this is rather formal.
*This is the job advert **to which** I was referring.*
*The people **at whom** the course was aimed were mainly new managers.*

In everyday English, it's much more common to leave a short preposition in its original position, in which case the relative pronoun is often omitted from a defining relative clause.
*This is the job advert (**which / that**) I was referring **to**.*
*The people (**who / that**) the course was aimed **at** were mainly new managers.*

17

Grammar exercises

2 **Choose the correct option to complete the sentences.**

1 My mother was born at a time *when* / *which* her parents were working abroad.
2 Mrs Jenkins, *who* / *that* is sitting at the back of the hall, is the head teacher.
3 That's the man *which* / *that* I spoke to yesterday.
4 Mrs Black, *which* / *whose* husband also works here, is in charge of the company.
5 He didn't tell us the reason *why* / *which* he left his job.
6 The restaurant *which* / *where* we usually eat is the best in town.

3 **Complete the sentences with a relative pronoun.**

1 What is the name of the person _____*who / that*_____ manages the volunteers?
2 The watch _____*which / that*_____ I bought from your shop is not working anymore.
3 Does anyone know the reason _____*why / that*_____ Liam didn't turn up for training today?
4 Is that the place _____*where*_____ they are going to build the new office block?
5 That's the friend _____*whose*_____ mother is an electrician.
6 I'll never forget that summer _____*when*_____ we all worked together.

4 **Tick the sentences where the relative pronoun can be omitted.**

1 Tim, whose sister won the tennis championship, is very happy. ___
2 The gift that my friend gave me for my birthday was really great. ✓
3 I met a man whose mother is a famous musician. ___
4 Please return the book which I lent you. ✓
5 This is the factory that they are going to knock down. ✓
6 The supermarket where we usually shop is not too expensive. ___
7 The reason why I can't come to work is because I am unwell. ✓
8 Anna, who travels a lot on business, has visited many countries. ___

5 **Write sentences with a relative pronoun. Use commas where necessary.**

1 Jenny is a successful lawyer. Her husband is unemployed.

   Jenny, whose husband is unemployed, is a successful lawyer.

2 Sam has passed his driving test. He doesn't like taking the bus.

   Sam, who doesn't like taking the bus, has passed his driving test.

3 Many people earn a lot of money. They work overtime.

   Many people who work overtime earn a lot of money.

4 Mark runs a marketing company. He needs to find more clients.

   Mark, who runs a marketing company, needs to find more clients.

5 The Four Seasons Hotel is closing down. I stayed there for a week.

   The Four Seasons Hotel, where I stayed for a week, is closing down.

6 The book is on the table. I have been looking for it.

   The book (which / that) I've been looking for is on the table.

7 Last winter was a wonderful time for me. I worked in a ski resort.

   Last winter, when I worked in a ski resort, was a wonderful time for me.

8 She wasn't honest in her CV. I really don't know the reason.

   I really don't know (the reason) why she wasn't honest in her CV.

6 Match the beginnings of the sentences (1–6) with their endings (a–f). Complete the sentences with a relative pronoun.

1 An employee is a person _____*who / that*_____ [d]
2 A library is a building _____*where*_____ [a]
3 J.K. Rowling is an author _____*whose*_____ [e]
4 A microscope is an instrument _____*which / that*_____ [b]
5 1971 was the year _____*when*_____ [c]
6 A pilot is a person _____*who*_____ [f]

a books are stored.
b makes tiny things look bigger.
c the first email was sent.
d is paid to work for a company.
e books have sold millions of copies.
f flies a plane.

7 Complete the second sentence so that it has a similar meaning to the first sentence, using the word given. Do not change the word given. You must use between two and five words.

1 I met my wife in this place.
This _____*is (the place) where*_____ I met my wife. **WHERE**

2 That girl's mother is our doctor.
That's _____*the girl whose mother*_____ is our doctor. **WHOSE**

3 We ate a delicious meal last night.
The meal _____*that we ate last night*_____ was delicious. **THAT**

4 I got a new laptop for my last birthday.
My last birthday _____*was (the time) when*_____ I got a new laptop. **WHEN**

5 He didn't get the job because he didn't prepare for the interview.
Not preparing for the interview _____*was (the reason) why*_____ he didn't get the job. **WHY**

6 She volunteered there last year, and they offered her a job yesterday.
Yesterday they offered a job to the girl _____*who volunteered there*_____ last year. **WHO**

Vocabulary

Phrasal verbs

8 Match the phrasal verbs (1–8) with their meanings (a–h).

1 act as [h]
2 cut down on [c]
3 fill in [f]
4 get down to [d]
5 hold down [b]
6 keep to [g]
7 keep up [e]
8 work on [a]

a develop and improve
b keep a job
c reduce the number or amount of something
d start doing something properly
e continue
f complete a form
g stick with a plan
h do a job for a short time

9 Complete the sentences with the correct form of the phrasal verbs from Exercise 8.

1 Tim was never able to _____*hold down*_____ a job for long because he was always late!
2 Please _____*fill in*_____ this form and return it to the office as soon as possible.
3 Andrew is going to _____*act as*_____ office manager while Emma is away on holiday.
4 I need to _____*work on*_____ my time management skills before I ask for a promotion.
5 I'm trying to _____*keep to*_____ our original plan, but some things have to be changed.
6 You're doing a great job – _____*keep up*_____ the good work!
7 I think it's time we really _____*got down to*_____ work on this project.
8 We're _____*cutting down on*_____ the number of documents we print at work.

17

Prepositions

10 **Choose the correct option to complete the sentences.**

1 The city had been *over / through /* under attack for three days.
2 Ella's workspace isn't very tidy. There are papers all over */ through / under* her desk.
3 I often go for a run *over /* through */ under* the forest before work in the morning.
4 What time do you plan to pop over */ through / under* to my house this evening?
5 Don't worry. I have the situation *over / through /* under control.
6 Let me *over /* through */ under*! I'm a doctor.

Collocations and expressions

11 **Complete the sentences with the correct form of these verbs.**

get   give   go   make   miss   take

1 If his behaviour doesn't improve, he'll be _____ *given* _____ the sack.
2 She finally decided to _____ *take* _____ the initiative and phone her boss.
3 The workers decided to _____ *go* _____ on strike because they wanted more money.
4 Sarah worked until very late last night because she didn't want to _____ *miss* _____ the deadline for her work.
5 Five people had to be _____ *made* _____ redundant because the company had lost money.
6 You're never going to _____ *get* _____ a promotion if you keep being late for work!

Words easily confused

12 **Complete the sentences with the correct form of these words. Use each word at least once.**

1   discover   find out   invent   set up

  a It was Marie Curie who _____ *discovered* _____ the chemical element radium.
  b Two brothers _____ *set up* _____ the company 60 years ago.
  c One type of telescope was _____ *invented* _____ by Sir William Herschel.
  d Can you _____ *find out* _____ when the bus leaves, please?

2   allowance   pass   permission   permit

  a You need a(n) _____ *permit* _____ to fish in this part of the river.
  b My parents give me a weekly _____ *allowance* _____ , which I use to buy food and clothes.
  c Our manager gave us _____ *permission* _____ to come in later after we worked late the night before.
  d Please wear your _____ *pass* _____ so that security can see it easily.

3   earlier   former   past   previous

  a As a(n) _____ *former* _____ prime minister, she has many important contacts.
  b We should have caught a(n) _____ *earlier* _____ flight.
  c How much _____ *previous* _____ experience have you had?
  d She's not been well for the _____ *past* _____ few days.

4   fit   go with   match   suit

  a Red _____ *goes with* _____ both black and white.
  b If the jacket doesn't _____ *fit* _____ , you can exchange it for a larger size.
  c Jeans don't really _____ *suit* _____ him – he looks much better in smart trousers.
  d After buying a necklace, she searched for a pair of earrings to _____ *match* _____ .

Word formation prefixes

13 Use the word in capitals to form a word that fits in the gap.

1 There must be some kind of __*misunderstanding*__ – we didn't order any food.   **UNDERSTAND**

2 Where did you __*disappear*__ to earlier? You missed the meeting.   **APPEAR**

3 Try not to be so __*impatient*__ – some people work more slowly than others.   **PATIENT**

4 That was the most __*incredible*__ magic trick I have ever seen.   **CREDIBLE**

5 It took decades to __*rebuild*__ the city after the earthquake.   **BUILD**

6 Simon has been __*unemployed*__ ever since losing his job at the factory five years ago.   **EMPLOY**

7 I have arranged to __*repay*__ the loan, starting with £100 per month.   **PAY**

8 In spite of his mother's __*disapproval*__ , Mario decided to apply for a job as a stunt pilot.   **APPROVE**

Sentence transformation

14 Complete the second sentence so that it has a similar meaning to the first sentence, using the word given. Do not change the word given. You must use between two and five words.

1 She played her first professional football match in this stadium.
   WHERE
   This is __*the stadium where she played*__ her first professional football match.

2 She had an interview for a job in a summer camp yesterday.
   WAS
   The interview __*(that / which) she had yesterday was*__ for a job in a summer camp.

3 You didn't get the job because you dressed too informally.
   REASON
   The __*reason (why) you didn't / did not*__ get the job was because you dressed too informally.

4 That dog's owner is a police officer.
   WHOSE
   That's __*the dog whose owner*__ is a police officer.

5 We're trying to reduce the amount of electricity we use in the office.
   DOWN
   We're trying to __*cut down (on)*__ the amount of electricity we use in the office.

6 I'm going to start work on my novel properly this summer.
   GET
   This summer, I'm __*going to get (down) to*__ work on my novel.

7 They dismissed him from his last job.
   SACK
   He __*got / was given the sack*__ from his last job.

8 The factory workers have decided to stop working in protest against their working conditions.
   GO
   The factory workers have decided __*to go on strike*__ in protest against their working conditions.

1 Which of these sentences are correct (C) and incorrect (I)?

1 I found the boy hiding behind the sofa.   _C_

2 The girl was awarded first prize cried.   _I_

3 Having saw the film before, I didn't go with my friends to the cinema.   _I_

4 Walking home last night, my phone's battery went dead.   _I_

5 Not knowing what to do, I emailed you.   _C_

6 Seen from a distance, the insect looked green.   _C_

7 Looked through the window, I saw something move.   _I_

8 The man speaks at the moment is my uncle.   _I_

9 Having had a long holiday, my desk was full.   _I_

10 Having chosen the colours for her room, she went out to buy the paint.   _C_

How many did you get right? ☐

Grammar

Reduced relative clauses

When the relative pronoun is the subject of the relative clause, we can often reduce the relative clause (i.e. make it shorter) by using a present participle (verb + -ing) or past participle (verb + -ed or irregular form). The present participle has an active meaning; the past participle has a passive meaning. We can reduce both defining and non-defining relative clauses in the same way.

*Everyone **who works** in the building must carry their security pass.*
*Everyone **working** in the building must carry their security pass.*
*I work in a building **which is known** as 'The Gherkin'.*
*I work in a building **known** as 'The Gherkin'.*

The advantage of reduced relative clauses is that you can express your meaning in fewer words. The disadvantage is that the reader or listener has to work harder to work out the missing information, so you should only use them when the meaning is clear.

Participle clauses

Participle clauses are very similar to reduced relative clauses, but we use them for different purposes. They can start with a present participle (verb + -ing) or a past participle (verb + -ed or irregular form). We can use participle clauses to make sentences shorter. They can replace the subject and the verb in a sentence if the subject of both clauses is the same. We use a present participle if the verb is active and a past participle if the verb is passive. Participle clauses can replace full clauses with a range of conjunctions, including *because, after, when* and *if*.

***Wanting** his CV to stand out, Zak printed it on yellow paper. (= Because he wanted …)*
***Asked** what she thought, Kate said they should take on an assistant. (= After / When she was asked …)*
***Given** the chance, I'd travel and work abroad for a year. (= If I were given …)*

Because the reader or listener has to work harder to understand the missing information, you should only use participle clauses when the meaning is clear. We can make a participle clause negative by adding *not*.
***Not understanding** the question, I asked the interviewer to repeat it.*

Perfect participle clauses

We can use a perfect participle (*having* + past participle) to combine clauses that have the same subject:
• when one action is completed before another action.
***He had arrived** early, so he had a coffee.*
***Having arrived** early, he had a coffee.*

• when one action has been going on for a period of time before another action starts.
***She had been acting** as office manager for three months, so she asked for a promotion.*
***Having acted** as office manager for three months, she asked for a promotion.*

The perfect participle can be used for active and passive sentences.
• active: *having* + past participle ***Having sent** the email, she waited for a reply.*
• passive: *having been* + past participle ***Having been made redundant**, he was looking for a job.*
We can make a perfect participle clause negative by adding *not* or *never* at the beginning.
***Not / Never having created** a CV before, he asked for advice.*

Grammar exercises

2 **Choose the correct option to complete the sentences.**

1 *Checking* / *Check* the website that morning, Ben saw an interesting job advert.
2 *Having spoken* / *After spoken* to her manager, she applied for the position.
3 Students *wishing* / *wished* to take part in the careers fair must put their names down by the end of the week.
4 I'm interested in buying the car *advertising* / *advertised* on your website.
5 *Not being* / *Not been* able to speak German, I asked Rudi to translate for me.
6 The woman *interviewing* / *who interviewing* you was my aunt!

3 **Complete the sentences with the correct form of these verbs.**

call	live	offer	send	steal	study

1 A lot of the artwork _____ *sent* _____ in to our studio last week was excellent.
2 She was delighted when she received a letter _____ *offering* _____ her the job.
3 Police are looking for a car _____ *stolen* _____ from the car park last night.
4 A flood warning has been sent out to people _____ *living* _____ near the river.
5 Someone _____ *called* _____ Jacob left a message for you.
6 Every pupil _____ *studying* _____ languages in this school has the opportunity to spend a month abroad.

4 **Rewrite the sentences using a present participle clause.**

1 Because I knew the traffic would be bad, I went by train.
  Knowing the traffic would be bad, I went by train.

2 I'm not afraid of heights, so I don't mind climbing mountains.
  Not being afraid of heights, I don't mind climbing mountains.

3 While Christine was walking through the park, she thought about life in France.
  Walking through the park, Christine thought about life in France.

4 Because we didn't want to disturb the meeting, we waited outside.
  Not wanting to disturb the meeting, we waited outside.

5 I thought the dog might be hungry, so I gave it one of my sandwiches.
  Thinking the dog might be hungry, I gave it one of my sandwiches.

6 She didn't know David's phone number, so she couldn't contact him.
  Not knowing David's phone number, she couldn't contact him.

5 **Rewrite the sentences using a past participle clause.**

1 This song, which was written in the 1960s, remains one of the band's most popular.
  This song, written in the 1960s, remains one of the band's most popular.

2 The politician didn't know what to say when he was asked about the economy.
  Asked about the economy, the politician didn't know what to say.

3 I would have been able to finish the exam if I had been given more time.
  Given more time, I would have been able to finish the exam.

4 The man who was wanted by the police got on a plane to Brazil.
  The man wanted by police got on a plane to Brazil.

5 People all over the world admired Justin, but he didn't really like being famous.
  Admired by people all over the world, Justin didn't really like being famous.

6 The cat felt safe and happy because it was hidden under a pile of cushions.
  Hidden under a pile of cushions, the cat felt safe and happy.

6 Rewrite the sentences using a perfect participle clause.

1 As he had had a long holiday, Martin felt quite refreshed.

Having had a long holiday, Martin felt quite refreshed.

2 After we had made the arrangements for the conference, we had lunch.

Having made the arrangements for the conference, we had lunch.

3 Since I hadn't seen the presentation, I couldn't comment on it.

Not having seen the presentation, I couldn't comment on it.

4 After she had decided when she wanted to go, she bought her tickets.

Having decided when she wanted to go, she bought her tickets.

5 Because he hadn't had a bath for a couple of days, he felt dirty.

Not having had a bath for a couple of days, he felt dirty.

6 As we had heard the news already, we weren't taken by surprise.

Having heard the news already, we weren't taken by surprise.

Vocabulary

Phrasal verbs

7 Match the phrasal verbs (1–8) with their meanings (a–h).

1	move on	c	a	employ	
2	pick up	b	b	learn	
3	stand out	e	c	start something new	
4	take off	f	d	remove money from your bank account	
5	take on	a	e	be easy to see or notice	
6	take out	d	f	have a short holiday	
7	take round	h	g	fill an amount of time or space	
8	take up	g	h	walk around a place with somebody to show it to them	

8 Complete the sentences with the correct form of the phrasal verbs from Exercise 7.

1 Redecorating the office _____ _took up_ _____ the whole weekend.

2 She's been working here for too long, and now thinks it's time to _____ _move on_ _____ .

3 I'd like to _____ _take_ _____ Monday _____ _off_ _____ because I'll be studying all weekend.

4 The beach café is _____ _taking on_ _____ extra staff during the summer.

5 Max, will you _____ _take_ _____ Eva _____ _round_ _____ the office, please?

6 How much money did you _____ _take out_ _____ this morning?

7 What can I do to make my CV _____ _stand out_ _____ from everyone else's?

8 I didn't study Spanish – I _____ _picked_ _____ it _____ _up_ _____ when I worked in Spain.

Prepositions

9 Choose the correct option to complete the sentences.

1 We kindly ask that guests present their passports _throughout / towards /_ upon arrival.

2 Daniela feels a lot of anger _throughout /_ towards _/ upon_ her previous manager.

3 Araf had such a bad cold that he coughed throughout _/ towards / upon_ the interview.

4 The new manager has a strange attitude _throughout /_ towards _/ upon_ the staff.

5 When she came back into the room, she had a big smile _throughout / towards /_ upon her face.

6 She worked at weekends throughout _/ towards / upon_ her degree.

Collocations and expressions

10 Complete the sentences with these words.

| brains | brush | chance | feet | luck | shoes |

1 If you can think on your _____*feet*_____ , you can make decisions quickly when under pressure.
2 You can't paint everyone with the same _____*brush*_____ – everyone is different.
3 Do you have a minute? I'd like to pick your _____*brains*_____ about this job application.
4 Try to put yourself in the interviewer's _____*shoes*_____ and think about the questions they might ask.
5 She would jump at the _____*chance*_____ of working abroad. She'd love it!
6 Knowing my _____*luck*_____ , the train will be late and I'll be late for my new job!

Words easily confused

11 Complete the sentences with the correct form of these words. Use each word at least once.

1 | current | draught | drought | flood |

  a There's a _____*draught*_____ in here. Please close the window.
  b Strong _____*currents*_____ make swimming here very dangerous.
  c _____*Floods*_____ have become common after heavy rain.
  d _____*Drought*_____ is always a problem in areas of little rainfall.

2 | advantage | benefit | exploitation | profit |

  a You shouldn't take _____*advantage*_____ of her good nature.
  b We expect to make a large _____*profit*_____ on the deal.
  c The _____*exploitation*_____ of these workers has to stop.
  d Free life insurance is just one of the _____*benefits*_____ offered by the company.

3 | demand | inform | instruct | order |

  a I wasn't _____*informed*_____ about any change to the schedule.
  b Who _____*ordered*_____ a cheese and mushroom pizza?
  c All employees will be _____*instructed*_____ in the art of self-defence.
  d The customer _____*demanded*_____ to speak to the manager in person.
  e Whoever _____*ordered*_____ the protestors to vandalise the buildings made a terrible mistake.

4 | agenda | calendar | catalogue | directory | list |

  a Have you included Liam on the guest _____*list*_____ ?
  b Look up her telephone number in the _____*directory*_____ .
  c I'm sorry I missed the meeting – it wasn't in my _____*calendar*_____ .
  d As this item is not on the _____*agenda*_____ , we can't discuss it at this meeting.
  e If you want to see all our products, take a look at our online _____*catalogue*_____ .

18

mixed → noun

12 Use the word in capitals to form a word that fits in the gap.

1 Whose ___responsibility___ is it to book meeting rooms?   **RESPONSIBLE**

2 We stayed in all morning waiting for a ___delivery___ that never came.   **DELIVER**

3 It is a(n) ___disadvantage___ to be short if you are a basketball player.   **ADVANTAGE**

4 After working at the hospital for 30 years, Sue is looking forward to a
happy ___retirement___ .   **RETIRE**

5 I'll be happy with your decision because I trust your ___judgement___ .   **JUDGE**

6 The manager has a very good ___relationship___ with the whole team.   **RELATE**

7 My sister loves maths. She wants to be a financial ___analyst___ .   **ANALYSE**

8 She is going to have to do something about her ___laziness___ if she wants   **LAZY**
to be a success in life.

Sentence transformation

13 Complete the second sentence so that it has a similar meaning to the first sentence, using the word given. Do not change the word given. You must use between two and five words.

1 I hate travelling by boat because I can't swim.

ABLE

Not ___being able to swim___ , I hate travelling by boat.

2 We bought some more oil because we had used it all.

THE

Having ___used (up) all the oil___ , we bought some more.

3 We should employ more people to help us.

TAKE

We should ___take on more___ people to help us.

4 Will you show Luke the new building?

ROUND

Will you ___take / show Luke round___ the new building?

5 Anna is very good at making decisions under pressure.

FEET

Thinking ___on her feet___ is something that Anna is very good at.

6 As soon as you arrive at the resort, you must pay the bill.

UPON

You must pay the bill ___upon arrival at / upon arriving at___ the resort.

1 **Which of these sentences are correct (C) and incorrect (I)?**

1 Harry told that he wouldn't be back before noon. _I_

2 The head teacher told us that he had already made his decision. _C_

3 She said that she had to go to bed early that night. _C_

4 He asked me where did I live. _I_

5 I told him that he had to look for a better job. _C_

6 Mark said us that he had forgotten to book a table. _I_

7 She told him to not go out of the house. _I_

8 Sally told us that she had already paid the bill. _C_

9 He asked me to stop. _C_

10 Ian told that he didn't want me to help him. _I_

How many did you get right? ☐

Grammar

Reported speech

When we report what someone said or thought in the past, the tenses used by the speaker usually change. This process is called backshifting.

Direct speech	Reported speech
present simple	past simple
'She **enjoys** reading,' he said.	He said (that) she **enjoyed** reading.
present continuous	past continuous
'He is **studying** geography,' she said.	She said (that) he **was studying** geography.
present perfect simple	past perfect simple
'They have **failed** their exams,' he said.	He said (that) they **had failed** their exams.
present perfect continuous	past perfect continuous
'We **have been working** in the library,' he said.	He said (that) they **had been working** in the library.
past simple	past perfect simple
'He **gave** a presentation,' she said.	She said (that) he **had given** a presentation.
past continuous	past perfect continuous
'I **was researching** my project,' she said.	She said (that) she **had been researching** her project.

Other changes in verb forms are as follows.

can	could
'She **can** speak five languages,' he said.	He said (that) she **could** speak five languages.
may	might
'He **may** be early,' she said.	She said (that) he **might** be early.
must	had to
'She **must** do her homework,' he said.	He said (that) she **had to** do her homework.
will	would
'They **will** go to Spain for a week,' she said.	She said (that) they **would** go to Spain for a week.

1 We often use the verbs *say* and *tell* in reported speech. We follow *tell* with an object.
*Our teacher **said** we should revise for the test.*
*Our teacher **told us** we should revise for the test.*

2 We can leave out *that*.
*She **said (that)** she preferred chemistry to biology.*

3 Remember to change pronouns and possessive adjectives where necessary.
*'**We** are revising for the test,' he said. → He said (that) **they** were revising for the test.*

Reasons not to use backshifting

Do not use backshifting with the following tenses and words: past perfect simple, past perfect continuous, *would*, *could*, *might*, *should*, *ought to*, *used to*, and *had better*.
*'**I'd never studied** Italian before.' → She said she **had never studied** Italian before.*
*'You **should** apply to university.' → He told me I **should** apply to university.*

We use backshifting with *mustn't* and *must* when they refer to obligation, but not when *must* refers to logical deduction.
Obligation: *'You **must** hand in your projects on Friday.' → He told us we **had to** hand in our projects on Friday.*
Logical deduction: *'It **must** be fun to study abroad.' → She said it **must** be fun to study abroad.*

Do not use backshifting when the reporting verb is in a present tense, including the present perfect.
*'We **have** a trip in July.' → I've already **told** you that we **have** a trip in July. (Not: ~~We had~~)*

Don't use backshifting if you want to emphasise that you agree with a statement, and it's still true now.
*'Elsa **needs** to do her homework.' → Your teacher told me you **need** to do your homework, Elsa. (and I agree)*

Changes in time and place

When we report direct speech, there are often changes in words that show time and place, too.

Direct speech	Reported speech
now	then
today / tonight	that day / night
yesterday	the previous day / the day before
last week / month	the previous week / month
the week / month before
tomorrow	the next day / the following day
here	there

Reported questions

When we report questions, changes in tenses, pronouns, possessive adjectives, time and place are the same as in reported statements. In reported questions, the verb follows the subject as in ordinary statements and we do not use question marks.

When a direct question has a question word, we use this word in the reported question.
*'**When did you decide** to study engineering?' he asked.*
*He asked me **when I had decided** to study engineering.*

When a direct question does not have a question word, we use *if* or *whether* in the reported question.
*'**Do you speak** Mandarin?' he asked.*
*He asked **if / whether I spoke** Mandarin.*

Reported requests and orders

When we report orders, we usually use *tell* + object + (*not*) *to* + infinitive.
'Turn off the computer!'
He **told me to** turn off the computer.
'Don't forget your homework,' he said to the students.
He **told the students not to** forget their homework.

When we report a request, we usually use *ask* + object + (*not*) *to* + infinitive.
'Can you give me the login details, please?' she asked.
She **asked me to give** her the login details.
(Also: *She asked **if I could give** her the login details.*)
'Please don't talk during the test,' he said.
He **asked us not to talk** during the test.

Grammar exercises

2 **Complete the sentences with the correct form of *say* or *tell*.**

1 She didn't _____tell_____ the teacher that she would be late.

2 He _____said_____ that it was Maria's bag.

3 Tom _tells / told / has told_ so many lies that nobody believes him anymore.

4 Sam _____said_____ to me, 'I wasn't accepted by that college.'

5 He didn't _____say_____ anything before he left.

6 Did Anna _____tell_____ you about the science competition?

3 **Choose the correct reported statement (a–b).**

1 'I got a job on an oil rig,' said Steven.
   a Steven said that he has got a job on an oil rig.
   (b) Steven said that he had got a job on an oil rig.

2 'I can't afford to go out again,' Sally said to me.
   (a) Sally told me that she couldn't afford to go out again.
   b Sally said me that she couldn't afford to go out again.

3 'I must do my homework now,' said Emily.
   a Emily said that she must do her homework then.
   (b) Emily said that she had to do her homework then.

4 'You left the computer switched on all night,' said Dad.
   a Dad said that I left the computer switched on all night.
   (b) Dad said that I had left the computer switched on all night.

5 He said to me, 'You explain things very clearly.'
   (a) He told me that I explained things very clearly.
   b He told me that I had explained things very clearly.

6 She said, 'We have been looking for images for two hours.'
   (a) She said that they had been looking for images for two hours.
   b She said that they were looking for images for two hours.

19

4 Complete the sentences with one word in each gap.

1 'I want to see your presentation today,' I said to her.

I told her that I _____*wanted*_____ to see her presentation _____*that*_____ day.

2 'I've missed the train. I'll be late,' said Beth.

Beth said that she _____*had*_____ missed the train and she _____*would*_____ be late.

3 Alice said, 'My teacher made me rewrite my essay yesterday.'

Alice said that her teacher _____*had*_____ made her rewrite her essay the day _____*before*_____ .

4 Piotr said, 'I am waiting for the results of my experiment.'

Piotr told me that he _____*was*_____ waiting for the results of _____*his*_____ experiment.

5 I said to my sister, 'I would like to borrow your laptop tomorrow.'

I told my sister that I would like to borrow _____*her*_____ laptop the _____*next / following*_____ day.

6 The professor said to us, 'I've marked your tests. I did it last night.'

The professor told us that she _____*had*_____ marked our tests the _____*previous*_____ night.

7 Carol said to him, 'I need you to put the whiteboard here.'

Carol told him that she needed _____*him*_____ to put the whiteboard _____*there*_____ .

8 My mother said to my brother, 'You have to do your homework now.'

My mother told my brother that _____*he*_____ had to do his homework _____*then*_____ .

5 Rewrite the sentences in reported speech.

1 His mother said to us, 'He has been talking on the phone for an hour.'

His mother told us (that) he had been talking on the phone for an hour.

2 Ben said to Jen, 'I really don't feel ready to give my presentation tomorrow.'

Ben told Jen (that) he really didn't feel ready to give his presentation the next / following day.

3 'I am trying to concentrate on my work now,' said John.

John said (that) he was trying to concentrate on his work then.

4 'I can't find the file anywhere,' said Max.

Max said (that) he couldn't find the file anywhere.

5 Her brother said to us, 'She'll come to your house when she has finished her homework.'

Her brother told us (that) she would come to our house when she had finished her homework.

6 'I haven't spoken to Jo since last month,' said Fiona.

Fiona said (that) she hadn't spoken to Jo since the previous month / the month before.

7 Her father said to her, 'You must revise for the exam today.'

Her father told her (that) she had to revise for the exam that day.

8 'I met an old friend of mine yesterday,' said Emily.

Emily said (that) she had met an old friend of hers the previous day / the day before.

6 Complete the reported questions so that they mean the same as the direct questions.

1 'When did Mr Brown leave the club?' asked the inspector.
The inspector asked *when Mr Brown had left the club* .

2 'Where's the tablet, Freddie?' asked Jessica.
Jessica asked Freddie *where the tablet was* .

3 'What do you think happened?' enquired Zoe.
Zoe asked me *what I thought had happened* .

4 'Are you having a party on your birthday, Harry?' asked Toby.
Toby asked Harry *if he was having a party on his birthday* .

5 'Do you have a phone charger?' he asked me.
He wanted to know *if I had a phone charger* .

6 'Why do you want to study here?' asked the interviewer.
The interviewer asked me *why I wanted to study there* .

7 Rewrite the orders and requests in reported speech.

1 'Please don't mention it again,' he said to me.
He asked me not to mention it again.

2 'Don't bite your nails,' she said to him.
She told him not to bite his nails.

3 'Drink all your milk,' she said to her.
She told her to drink all her milk.

4 'Stop complaining, please,' he said to me.
He asked me to stop complaining.

5 'Don't lend Alex any money,' she said to me.
She told me not to lend Alex any money.

6 'Don't be rude to our guests,' he said to me.
He told me not to be rude to our guests.

7 'Tidy up your room, please,' she said to him.
She asked him to tidy up his room.

8 'Please follow me,' the guide said to us.
The guide asked us to follow him / her.

Vocabulary

Phrasal verbs

8 Match the phrasal verbs (1–8) with their meanings (a–h).

1 breeze through — b — a quit a course of study
2 drop out — a — b succeed easily
3 fall through — d — c get an answer or result
4 get across — e — d fail to happen
5 get through — h — e succeed in making someone understand something
6 go through — g — f check something carefully
7 read through — f — g experience something difficult or unpleasant
8 work out — c — h come successfully to the end of a difficult time

9 Complete the sentences with the correct form of the phrasal verbs from Exercise 8.

1 Maria is _____going through_____ a difficult time at the moment.
2 He is so clever that he _____breezes through_____ every exam he takes.
3 Don't forget to _____read through_____ your essay to make sure there are no mistakes.
4 Matt _____dropped out_____ of university to start his own business.
5 I've finally _____worked out_____ how this experiment works!
6 Eating and sleeping well will help you _____get through_____ your exams.
7 She's a great teacher – she _____gets_____ difficult ideas _____across_____ really clearly.
8 I'm afraid the trip to London has _____fallen through_____ because the hotel is closed that week.

Prepositions

10 Choose the correct option to complete the sentences.

1 The doctor helped the child, even though she was *from / off / over* duty.
2 We had a geography trip to an island *from / off / over* the south coast.
3 Soon, the funny video was all *from / off / over* the internet.
4 Who knows what we'll be doing five years *from / off / over* now?
5 They spoke *from / off / over* the intercom, then she let him into the school office.
6 The teacher lets us have a longer break *from / off / over* time to time.

Collocations and expressions

11 Match the sentence beginnings (1–6) with their endings (a–f) to make definitions.

1 When you say you are brain dead,   `f`   a you think about it all the time.
2 A brainwave is   `e`   b is the person who had the idea.
3 If you brainstorm something   `c`   c you all try to solve a problem or think of ideas together.
4 The brains behind something   `b`   d you think very hard.
5 If you have something on your brain,   `a`   e a sudden, unexpected idea.
6 When you rack your brains   `d`   f you mean that you are too tired to think.

Words easily confused

12 Complete the sentences with the correct form of these words. Use each word at least once.

1   **belong   own   possess**

   a Who does this bag _____belong_____ to?
   b Do you know who _____owns_____ this coat? We found it on the school field.
   c For a person who _____possesses_____ such skill, his work could be better!

2   **danger   emergency   risk   urgency**

   a According to the head teacher, it was a matter of _____urgency_____ .
   b You can only use your phone in class in a(n) _____emergency_____ .
   c Several employees are in _____danger_____ of losing their jobs.
   d Our teachers are very careful not to take _____risks_____ on school trips.

3   **bunch   bundle   collection   packet**

   a I always have a small _____bunch_____ of grapes with my lunch.
   b We saw an amazing _____collection_____ of ancient artefacts in the museum.
   c They had found the old papers tied up in a _____bundle_____ at the bottom of the drawer.
   d He threw his _____packet_____ of crisps away because they tasted strange.

4 | decrease   drop   lessen   lower |

a Please _____*lower*_____ your voice.

b Take some extra blankets in case the temperature _____*drops*_____ in the evening.

c The number of new students has _____*decreased*_____ from 270 to 240.

d Don't use too much text – it _____*lessens*_____ the impact of the image.

Word formation   mixed

13 Use the word in capitals to form a word that fits in the gap.

1 The teacher said our final _____*assessment*_____ would be based on essays and exams.   **ASSESS**

2 This is one of the _____*trickiest*_____ assignments I have ever done in my life.   **TRICK**

3 Mr Bennett suggested that Maths Club would be _____*beneficial*_____ for me.   **BENEFIT**

4 You will be asked to go home and change if you are not dressed _____*suitably*_____ .   **SUIT**

5 It's really _____*unhelpful*_____ when you shout at the children like that – it only makes things worse.   **HELP**

6 Penicillin was the most important medical _____*discovery*_____ of the 20th century.   **DISCOVER**

7 My brother has just finished university. We're going to his _____*graduation*_____ ceremony next week.   **GRADUATE**

8 Sam's mother is a famous _____*novelist*_____ .   **NOVEL**

Sentence transformation

14 Complete the second sentence so that it has a similar meaning to the first sentence, using the word given. Do not change the word given. You must use between two and five words.

1 'Please don't park here,' she said to me.

ASKED

She _____*asked me not to*_____ park there.

2 He told the children not to run.

NOT

'Do _____*not run*_____ ,' he told the children.

3 'Where do you want to go tonight?' he asked us.

THAT

He asked us where _____*we wanted to go that*_____ night.

4 Our teacher told us to listen to him.

ME

'_____*Listen to me*_____ !' our teacher told us.

5 'I can help you fix that,' she said.

ME

She told me that she _____*could help me*_____ fix that.

6 'Do you want to go to university?' the professor asked them.

IF

The professor asked _____*them if they wanted*_____ to go to university.

7 'I'm busy now,' she said.

WAS

She said she _____*was busy then*_____ .

Unit 20

Awareness

1   Which of these sentences are correct (C) and incorrect (I)?

1   Thank you for agreeing help us. __I__
2   I advise you not to spend all your money. __C__
3   She reminded me buying some tomatoes. __I__
4   He recommends to put it in the oven for 50 minutes. __I__
5   I apologise for being so thoughtless. __C__
6   The teacher accused him of copying. __C__
7   She persuaded me go with her. __I__
8   I promised taking them to the cinema. __I__
9   They demanded that I bought them ice cream. __C__
10   He was complaining about having to go to work so early. __C__

How many did you get right? ☐

Grammar

Reporting verbs

As well as the verbs *say*, *tell* and *ask*, we can use other verbs to report what someone says more accurately. Notice the different structures.

verb + *to* + infinitive	
agree	'Yes, I'll fix it for you,' he said. He **agreed to fix** it for us.
claim	'I'm good at fixing things,' he said. He **claimed to be** good at fixing things.
decide	'I think I'll fix it,' he said. He **decided to fix** it.
offer	'Shall I fix it?' he said. He **offered to fix** it.
promise	'Don't worry, I'll fix it,' he said. He **promised to fix** it.
refuse	'I won't fix it,' he said. He **refused to fix** it.
verb + object + *to* + infinitive	
advise	'If I were you, I'd revise more,' she said. She **advised me to revise** more.
encourage	'Go on, revise more and you'll get better marks,' she said. She **encouraged me to revise** more.
order	'Revise!' she said. She **ordered me to revise**.
persuade	'You should revise more – you'll feel more confident,' she said. 'You're right!' I said. She **persuaded me to revise** more.
remind	'Don't forget to revise,' she said. She **reminded me to revise**.
warn	'Revise more – don't fail your exam,' she said. She **warned me not to fail** my exam.
verb + *-ing* form	
admit	'I lost your headphones,' he said. He **admitted losing** my headphones.
deny	'I didn't lose your headphones,' he said. He **denied losing** my headphones.
recommend	'You should buy new headphones,' he said. He **recommended buying** new headphones.
suggest	'Let's buy new headphones,' he said. He **suggested buying** new headphones.
verb + preposition + *-ing* form	
apologise for	'I'm sorry I broke your laptop,' she said. She **apologised for breaking** my laptop.
complain of / about	'I broke my laptop again,' she said. She **complained about breaking** her laptop again.
insist on	'Don't be silly. I'll buy a new laptop for you,' she said. She **insisted on buying** a new laptop for me.

verb + object + preposition + -ing form	
accuse someone of	'I'm sure you copied my answers,' he said. He **accused me of copying** his answers.
congratulate someone on	'You got all the answers right! Well done!' he said. He **congratulated me on getting** all the answers right.
verb + that clause	
announce	'I'm going to do it,' she said. She **announced that** she was going to do it.
complain	'I don't have time to do it,' she said. She **complained that** she didn't have time to do it.
demand	'You do it,' she said. She **demanded that** I do it.
verb + indirect question	
enquire	'Can I present first?' he asked. He **enquired whether he could** present first.
question	'Why do we need to arrive so early?' She **questioned why they needed to arrive** so early.
wonder	'What will university be like?' he asked. He **wondered what university would be** like.

Many reporting verbs can have more than one pattern.

She admitted **copying / that she had copied**.
She claimed **to be / that she was** ...
She insisted **on / that she would** ...
She promised **to / that she would** ...
She recommended **going / that we should go** ...

She reminded me **to / that I should** ...
She suggested **taking / that we should take** ...
She threatened **to / that she would** ...
She warned me **not to / that I shouldn't** ...

Grammar exercises

2 Choose the correct option to complete the sentences.

1 The head teacher (advised) / suggested me to apply to university.
2 The boy apologised / (admitted) breaking the window.
3 He (complained) / refused that he was tired.
4 My dad (congratulated) / encouraged me on winning the competition.
5 I'm surprised that he denied / (refused) to sign the papers.
6 The teacher (persuaded) / demanded them to sit down and work quietly.
7 I (accused) / warned my classmate of copying my work.
8 My sister offered / (reminded) me to take my tennis racket.

3 Complete the sentences with the correct form of the verbs.

1 She suggested _____eating_____ (eat) at the new restaurant.
2 The man denied _____stealing_____ (steal) the laptop.
3 I was so glad that Dan agreed _____to come_____ (come) with us.
4 My tutor encouraged me _____to enter_____ (enter) the competition.
5 Liz demanded that I _____drive_____ (drive) her home.
6 I apologised for _____not remembering_____ (not / remember) my sister's birthday.

4 Complete the sentences with one word in each gap.

1 He decided _____to_____ move to Italy.
2 She advised _____me_____ not to buy it, so I didn't.
3 I don't believe he accused you _____of_____ lying.
4 What was she apologising _____for_____ ? It wasn't her fault!
5 My dad insisted _____on_____ paying the bill.
6 The teacher announced _____that_____ there was going to be a test the next day.

5 Complete the sentences in reported speech using a suitable reporting verb.

1 'You took my phone and broke it,' he said to me. *Possible answers*

He _accused me of taking his phone and breaking it_ .

2 'You should go to bed earlier,' she said.

She _advised me to go to bed earlier_

3 'Don't forget to bring the things I asked for,' she said to me.

She _reminded me to bring the things she had asked for_ .

4 'I'm so sorry I damaged the bike,' the child said.

The child _apologised for damaging the bike_ .

5 'You hit Pablo with your bag,' said the teacher to Jake.

The teacher _accused Jake of hitting Pablo with his bag_ .

6 'Leave the courtroom immediately,' the judge said to the jury.

The judge _ordered the jury to leave the courtroom immediately_ .

6 Rewrite the sentences in direct speech.

1 Adam ordered Ben to be quiet, but Ben refused.
Adam: _'Be quiet.'_   **Ben:** _'No. (I won't.)'_

2 The twins asked Sophie to help them. Sophie agreed.
Twins: _'Will you help us?'_   **Sophie:** _'Yes, OK.'_

3 Sara accused Tom of eating her sandwich. Tom denied it.
Sara: _'You ate my sandwich!'_   **Tom:** _'No, I didn't.'_

4 Mum reminded me to buy a present for Georgie. I thanked her.
Mum: _'Don't forget to buy a present for Georgie.'_   **Me:** _'Thanks. (I won't.)'_

5 The doctor advised me to drink more water, and I agreed.
Doctor: _'You should drink more water.'_   **Me:** _'I will / I know.'_

6 The police officer ordered the boy to get off his bike. The boy refused.
Police officer: _'Get off your bike!'_   **Boy:** _'No. (I won't.)'_

Vocabulary

Phrasal verbs

7 Match the phrasal verbs (1–8) with their meanings (a–h).

1	go for	b	a	say that someone has done something wrong
2	go over	c	b	try to get
3	hand in	d	c	look at again, revise
4	hand out	g	d	submit work
5	look out for	h	e	find information about
6	look up	e	f	write something so you remember it later
7	note down	f	g	distribute something among a group
8	tell off	a	h	try to notice something or somebody

8 Complete the sentences with the correct form of the phrasal verbs from Exercise 7.

1 You might find it helpful to _____note down_____ the key points.
2 _____Look out for_____ Gina when you go to the conference. She said she was going.
3 I'm training very hard because this time I am _____going for_____ the gold medal.
4 The teacher _____told_____ Mia _____off_____ for answering her phone in class.
5 If you don't know what I'm talking about, _____look_____ it _____up_____ on the website.
6 He _____went over_____ the vocabulary list one more time before doing the test.
7 Your homework will not be marked if you _____hand_____ it _____in_____ late.
8 The teacher _____handed out_____ the worksheets to everyone in the class.

Prepositions

9 Choose the correct option to complete the sentences.

1 It's (against)/ after / along the law to drive without a seatbelt on.
2 They never went on a school trip again against /(after)/ along the way they behaved.
3 What do your parents think about you having a party in their house? Mine are (against)/ after / along it.
4 The football pitch is just against / after /(along) the road from the school.
5 I knew all against / after /(along) that Stefan was not an honest person.
6 It turned out that we were going in the right direction against /(after)/ along all.

Collocations and expressions

10 Complete the sentences with *take*, *get* or *keep*.

1 Susan _____takes_____ great pleasure in editing the school magazine.
2 I _____get_____ the feeling that Theresa is going to leave her job soon – she seems very unhappy.
3 Would you like me to _____keep_____ you company on the journey home?
4 Let me _____get_____ straight to the point – I don't think you are working hard enough.
5 I didn't know the sports centre was open on Sunday, but I'll _____take_____ your word for it.
6 Dad _____kept_____ his promise to me and bought me a bicycle for my birthday.

Words easily confused

11 Complete the sentences with the correct form of these words. Use each word at least once.

1 | comment | mention | notice | refer |

   a Please don't _____mention_____ the party to Oscar – I didn't invite him.
   b He didn't _____comment_____ on your work at all.
   c I wish I hadn't _____referred_____ to my ambitions during the discussion.
   d The pickpocket was so quick that only one witness _____noticed_____ what he was wearing.

2 | only | separate | single | unique |

   a Being a(n) _____only_____ child, she had no brothers or sisters to play with.
   b It's a(n) _____unique_____ opportunity for you learn Spanish in Spain.
   c Are you married or _____single_____ ?
   d Remember to keep your school shirts _____separate_____ from the others.

3 | certificate | degree | licence | subject |

   a History was the one _____subject_____ I was never good at.
   b I seem to have lost my birth _____certificate_____ .
   c She has a _____degree_____ in architecture from Birmingham University.
   d This driving _____licence_____ is not valid in Canada.

20

4 adviser   coach   instructor   tutor

a My driving _____instructor_____ thinks I'm ready to take my driving test.
b I hadn't thought of studying law until the careers _____adviser_____ suggested it.
c The team has improved so much with the new _____coach_____ .
d Do you think a few English lessons with a private _____tutor_____ would help?

Word formation   mixed

12 **Use the word in capitals to form a word that fits in the gap.**

1 The teacher was concerned about one pupil's high rate of _____absence_____ .   **ABSENT**
2 It is not _____reasonable_____ to expect a young child to understand such complex maths.   **REASON**
3 I am writing in _____reference_____ to your recent podcast.   **REFER**
4 Everyone was surprised when our team won the _____championship_____ .   **CHAMPION**
5 I've got a test tomorrow, but I'm worried that I'll never _____memorise_____ all my notes!   **MEMORY**
6 My lecturers have given me so much support and _____encouragement_____ .   **ENCOURAGE**
7 I'm so relieved – I've got my essay back and there are only a few _____corrections_____ .   **CORRECT**
8 Greg was shocked at the _____unfriendliness_____ of the people – nobody spoke to him!   **FRIENDLY**

Sentence transformation

13 **Complete the second sentence so that it has a similar meaning to the first sentence, using the word given. Do not change the word given. You must use between two and five words.**

1 'OK, I'll give you a lift to the concert,' said Tom.
   TO
   Tom _____agreed to give_____ us a lift to the concert.

2 'Sit down!' she said to us.
   ORDERED
   She _____ordered us to sit_____ down.

3 'It's true, I forgot my homework,' Becky said.
   ADMITTED
   Becky _admitted forgetting / (that) she had forgotten_ her homework.

4 'I'm really sorry I hurt you,' he said to her.
   FOR
   He _____apologised for hurting_____ her.

5 'Well done! You won the competition,' he said to me.
   ON
   He _____congratulated me on winning_____ the competition.

6 'Tell me how you discovered my password!' she said to me.
   THAT
   She demanded _____that I tell her_____ how I discovered her password.

7 'You lied to me,' she said.
   OF
   She _____accused me of lying_____ to her.

8 'No, I won't do what you tell me,' he said to them.
   REFUSED
   He _____refused to do what_____ they told him.

B2 Practice: First

Part 1

For questions 1–8, read the text below and decide which answer (A, B, C or D) best fits each gap. There is an example at the beginning (0).

Jailbirds

Although the therapeutic **(0)** ___ of pets has been appreciated for some time, they have not been permitted in British prisons until relatively **(1)** ___ . Not long ago it occurred to the prison authorities that prisoners serving long sentences must feel **(2)** ___ by society and that was the reason why they became less cooperative. It was then suggested that they were likely to respond positively if they were **(3)** ___ to keep a budgie. Realising that long-term prisoners go through a great deal of suffering, the appropriate government department went **(4)** ___ with the idea.

After a trial period, the authorities reached the conclusion that looking after a small, helpless bird brought out a **(5)** ___ side in most prisoners. This, in turn, **(6)** ___ some prisoners and their jailers closer together. The authorities were relieved because there had been some opponents to the scheme, who had passionately warned against it. Since the scheme was set up, inmates have been able to **(7)** ___ from the boredom of prison life and see their situation from a completely different **(8)** ___ .

0	A	price	B	cost	(C)	value	D	worth
1	A	lately	(B)	recently	C	shortly	D	soon
2	(A)	abandoned	B	vanished	C	mislaid	D	left
3	(A)	allowed	B	let	C	left	D	agreed
4	A	across	(B)	along	C	down	D	up
5	(A)	sensitive	B	sensible	C	logical	D	truthful
6	A	fetched	B	took	(C)	brought	D	carried
7	A	prevent	B	avoid	C	block	(D)	escape
8	A	corner	B	edge	(C)	angle	D	opinion

Part 2

For questions 9–16, read the text below and think of the word which best fits each gap. Use only one word in each gap. There is an example at the beginning (0).

Childhood obesity

The problem of obesity, **(0)** ___which___ refers to the excessive accumulation of body fat, is affecting more and more children in Western society **(9)** ___these___ days. It is estimated that about one in ten six-year-olds is obese. Meanwhile, figures in the United States suggest that up **(10)** ___to___ 30% of US children **(11)** ___are___ overweight.

Although very few health problems **(12)** ___have___ been observed in obese children so far, it is believed that they run a greater risk of developing conditions such **(13)** ___as___ high blood pressure or heart disease later in life. Already, the number of children suffering from type-2 diabetes, a serious illness that previously mostly affected middle-aged people, has gone **(14)** ___up___ .

Experts blame this weight problem **(15)** ___on___ unhealthy eating habits. These habits combined with the sedentary lifestyle of many children, **(16)** _who / that_ spend hours in front of their computers or TVs, are responsible for most cases of obesity.

Part 3

For questions 17–24, read the text below. Use the word given in capitals at the end of some of the lines to form a word that fits in the gap in the same line. There is an example at the beginning (0).

Taking the blame

Among many other things, **(0)** ___pollution___ is a sensitive political issue in many	**POLLUTE**
countries in the world today. All parties, not just the Greens, now include	
(17) ___environmental___ policies in their election manifestos. As a result of this, one would	**ENVIRONMENT**
be forgiven for assuming that the amount of **(18)** ___industrial___ waste being released	**INDUSTRY**
is decreasing. However, the evidence suggests that this is very unlikely to be the case. In fact,	
all the research to date shows that the **(19)** ___destruction___ of our environment is not	**DESTROY**
slowing down at all. It is a truly **(20)** ___global___ issue which requires international	**GLOBE**
cooperation to combat, and it appears that we are failing.	
Many attempts have been made to **(21)** ___identify___ the reasons for this. It is easy to	**IDENTITY**
point the finger at government ministers and business people, and it does appear that many of	
them are behaving **(22)** ___irresponsibly___ . But it could be argued that putting the blame	**RESPONSIBLE**
on these people simply gives the general public licence to continue **(23)** ___greedily___	**GREEDY**
consuming the very products which are causing such devastating damage to the environment.	
If the public's **(24)** ___response___ was more positive and well-informed, perhaps the	**RESPOND**
situation would change for the better.	

Part 4

For questions 25–30, complete the second sentence so that it has a similar meaning to the first sentence, using the word given. Do not change the word given. You must use between two and five words, including the word given. Here is an example (0).

Example:

0 It isn't necessary for you to go to every lesson.

ATTEND

You _____ *needn't / don't need to attend* _____ every lesson.

25 The president found what the manager said embarrassing.

EMBARRASSED

The president _____ *was embarrassed by the manager's* _____ comments.

26 Her brother didn't have nearly as much success in the job as she did.

MORE

She did the job _____ *a lot / much more successfully than* _____ her brother.

27 A famous architect is designing a house for them.

DESIGNED

They _____ *are having / getting a / their house designed* _____ by a famous architect.

28 He started his stamp collection about 20 years ago.

COLLECTING

He _____ *has been collecting stamps for* _____ about 20 years.

29 I'd rather work here than get a job in the city.

PREFER

I _____ *prefer working here to getting* _____ a job in the city.

30 Liz often forgets to switch on the alarm.

TIME

It's not the _____ *first time Liz has forgotten* _____ to switch on the alarm.

B2 Practice: ECCE

Grammar

For questions 1–20, choose the word or phrase that best completes the sentence or conversation.

1 Julia ___ that she'd be back soon.
   A said
   B told
   C asked
   D talked

2 Mrs Smith, ___ I thought was on holiday, is here.
   A which
   B that
   C who
   D she

3 He apologised ___ being late.
   A for
   B to
   C of
   D with

4 The police officer ___ ride on the pavement.
   A told me to not
   B told me not to
   C said me not to
   D said me to not

5 The woman ___ at the moment is my mum.
   A speaking
   B speaks
   C to speak
   D speak

6 ___ being able to dance, I don't enjoy parties.
   A No
   B None
   C Not
   D Can't

7 ___ from the air, the patterns are quite beautiful.
   A Seeing
   B See
   C Saw
   D Seen

8 Not wanting ___ rude, I sat quietly until the end of the meal.
   A being
   B be
   C was
   D to be

9 Why did you insist ___ early?
   A to leave
   B on leaving
   C leaving
   D on leave

10 Did he ___ if you were OK?
    A say
    B tell
    C ask
    D talk

11 Do you know the reason ___ it happened?
    A how
    B when
    C which
    D why

12 I asked her ___ she would like to have dinner.
    A whether
    B that
    C may
    D could

13 ___ heard the music, I didn't download it.
    A Being
    B Having
    C Doing
    D Making

14 Greta decided ___ at home.
    A stay
    B staying
    C stayed
    D to stay

15 I'm furious! He accused me ___ !
    A to cheat
    B of cheating
    C cheating
    D cheat

16 Our house, ___ we bought in 2015, is for sale.
    A which
    B what
    C who
    D it

17 'Why didn't Dan want to eat anything?'
    'He said he ___ dinner.'
    A already has
    B had already
    C has already has
    D had already had

18 I recommend ___ to see this play.
    A to go
    B of going
    C going
    D go

19 That's the girl ___ dad is the new head teacher.
    A which
    B who's
    C that's
    D whose

20 This is ___ I sleep.
    A room
    B where
    C bed
    D place

Vocabulary

For questions 21–40, choose the word or phrase that most appropriately completes the sentence.

21 Could you ___ in this application form, please?
   A   put
   B   fill
   C   hold
   D   write

22 I knew who the killer was all ___ .
   A   against
   B   after
   C   along
   D   away

23 She ___ through her final exams easily.
   A   blew
   B   ran
   C   breezed
   D   whistled

24 Have you ___ out how to do it yet?
   A   stood
   B   dropped
   C   handed
   D   worked

25 Why don't you ___ the initiative and contact the company?
   A   keep
   B   make
   C   take
   D   get

26 Playing computer games ___ up too much of your time.
   A   makes
   B   takes
   C   spends
   D   holds

27 Do you think you'll still be here five years ___ now?
   A   by
   B   from
   C   out
   D   away

28 I've worked here long enough. I think it's time to ___ on.
   A   go
   B   make
   C   move
   D   leave

29 I'll pop ___ to your house this evening.
   A   after
   B   under
   C   through
   D   over

30 The sun shone ___ the weekend.
   A   in
   B   throughout
   C   out
   D   within

31 I had to think on my ___ when they asked me a question I wasn't expecting.
   A   feet
   B   shoes
   C   brains
   D   luck

32 He ___ at the chance of working from home.
   A   jumped
   B   kicked
   C   put
   D   got

33 There is litter ___ over the place!
   A   every
   B   all
   C   some
   D   around

34 Keep ___ the good work, Jerry!
   A   up
   B   down
   C   on
   D   off

35 May I ___ your brains about this project?
   A   pick
   B   rack
   C   kick
   D   pack

36 You ___ up the language very quickly.
   A   lifted
   B   got
   C   took
   D   picked

37 Look ___ for the traffic wardens around here!
   A   out
   B   up
   C   over
   D   along

38 Do you ever ___ the feeling that you're being watched?
   A   take
   B   make
   C   hold
   D   get

39 It was boring with nobody to ___ me company.
   A   give
   B   hand
   C   keep
   D   bring

40 Their plans to travel round Europe fell ___ when their van broke down.
   A   through
   B   down
   C   over
   D   off

Unit 21

Awareness

1 **Which of these sentences are correct (C) and incorrect (I)?**

1 My new phone is most expensive than yours.   I

2 The weather is too hot today.   C

3 Your test results weren't enough good.   I

4 This cartoon isn't as funny as the last one.   C

5 The higher you climb, the more you see.   C

6 You'll get there more quick if you cycle.   I

7 She gave the toy to the child who asked the most politely.   C

8 That dress is such gorgeous.   I

9 This is the worst photography exhibition I've ever seen.   C

10 The weather was so bad that we didn't leave our hotel.   C

How many did you get right? ☐

Grammar

Comparative and superlative structures

We use the comparative to compare two people or things. We usually form the comparative by adding -er to an adjective or adverb. If the adjective or adverb has two or more syllables, we use the word *more*. We often use the word *than* after the comparative.
*Taking the train is **cheaper than** flying.*
*The bus goes **more frequently than** the train.*

We use the superlative to compare one person or thing with other people or things of the same type. We usually form the superlative by adding -est to the adjective or adverb. If the adjective or adverb has two or more syllables, we use the word *most*. We usually use the word *the* before the superlative.
*What is **the longest** mountain range in the world?*
*I understood Carlos because he spoke **the most slowly** of all the people in the group.*

Spelling: hot → ho**tt**er / ho**tt**est, brave → brav**er** / brav**est**, tiny → tin**ier** / tin**iest**

Some adjectives and adverbs are irregular and form their comparative and superlative in different ways.

Adjective / Adverb	Comparative	Superlative
good / well	better	the best
bad / badly	worse	the worst
far	farther / further	the farthest / furthest

Other comparative structures

We use *as* + adjective / adverb + *as* to show that two people or things are similar in some way.
*Do you think self-catering cottages are **as comfortable as** hotels?*

We use *not as / so* + adjective / adverb + *as* to show that one person or thing has less of a quality than another.
*New York isn't **as polluted as** Los Angeles.*

We use *less / the least* + adjective / adverb to mean the opposite of *more / the most*.
*The resort is **less crowded** than it used to be. (= It's emptier.)*
*This hotel is one of **the least expensive** in the area.*

We use *the* + comparative, *the* + comparative to show that as one thing increases or decreases, another thing is affected.
***The warmer** the weather, **the higher** the number of people on the beach.*

Intensifiers

We can use *much, far, a lot* or *considerably* before a comparative to make the meaning stronger.
*The pool is **considerably hotter** than the sea.*

We can use *slightly, a bit* or *a little* before a comparative to make the meaning weaker.
*This cottage is **slightly cheaper** than the other one.*

We can use *easily, by far* or *by a long way* before or after a superlative to make the meaning stronger.
*This is **easily / by far** the best trip I've been on.*
*This is the best trip I've been on **by far / by a long way**.*

so, such, too, enough

We use *too* + adjective / adverb to show that something is more than we want or need.
*It's **too cold** to go swimming.*
*She was speaking **too quickly** for me to understand.*

We use adjective / adverb + *enough,* or *enough* + noun to show something is or isn't as much as we want / need.
*The tent wasn't **big enough**.*
*I have **enough sandwiches** for everyone.*

Structures with *too* and *enough* are often followed by *to* + infinitive.
*That hotel is **too expensive to stay** in.*
*You need to be **strong enough to carry** all your own equipment.*

We use *so* and *such* for emphasis. It is stronger than *very*.

- We use *so* + adjective / adverb. *The sea was **so warm**!*
- We use *such* + (adjective) + noun. *This is **such an amazing view**.*

We can also use *so* and *such* with a *that* clause to emphasise characteristics that lead to a result or action.
*It was **such** an amazing view **that** I took 50 photos of it!*
*I was **so** tired **that** I fell asleep on the train.*

Grammar exercises

2 **Choose the correct option to complete the sentences.**

1 The journey wasn't as *smoother* / smooth as we had hoped it would be.
2 Antonio speaks English less / *the least* well than he used to.
3 Our flight to Madrid took *the longest* / longer than we expected.
4 The Empire State Building was once *the taller* / the tallest building in the world.
5 He didn't answer the questions as quickly / *quick* as I did.
6 This is *a bit* / by far the best food I've ever eaten.
7 The sea is warm *too* / enough to swim in.
8 The food is too / *enough* cold to eat.
9 It was *so* / such terrible weather that the streets were empty.
10 The sea was so / *such* rough that the boat trip was cancelled.

3 **Complete the sentences with the comparative or superlative form of the adjectives.**

1 Last night, I went to one of the _____*best*_____ (good) concerts I have ever been to.
2 Living in the country is _____*healthier*_____ (healthy) than living in a city.
3 Business Class is ___*more comfortable*___ (comfortable) than Economy.
4 Mount Everest is the _____*highest*_____ (high) mountain in the world.
5 This is ___*the most delicious*___ (delicious) food that I've ever eaten.
6 'How are you today?' 'Well, I feel _____*worse*_____ (bad) than yesterday.'

4 Rewrite the sentences with *as ... as* or *the* + comparative, *the* + comparative.

1 Flying to New York takes more time than flying to Athens.
Flying to Athens doesn't *take as long as flying to New York* .

2 You have visited more places in Scotland than I have.
I haven't *visited as many places in Scotland as you have* .

3 Shopping centres are more convenient than small shops.
Small shops aren't *as convenient as shopping centres* .

4 James can run faster than Tim can.
Tim can't *run as fast as James can* .

5 You are more likely to have an accident when you drive fast.
The faster *you drive, the more likely you are to have an accident* .

6 If you work quickly, you'll be able to leave sooner.
The more quickly *you work, the sooner you'll be able to leave* .

7 As he went further into the forest, he became more frightened.
The further *he went into the forest, the more frightened he became* .

8 As I learned more about the place, it seemed to be more interesting.
The more *I learned / learnt about the place, the more interesting it seemed* .

5 Use the prompts to write comparative or superlative sentences.

1 I / run / much / fast / you
I run much faster than you.

2 Mo / drive / slightly / carefully / his brother
Mo drives slightly more carefully than his brother.

3 The South Pole / be / by far / cold / place / the world
The South Pole is by far the coldest place in the world.

4 This / be / easily / good / restaurant / the city
This is easily the best restaurant in the city.

5 Your hotel room / be / considerably / big / mine
Your hotel room is considerably bigger than mine.

6 This / be / bad / journey / I / have / by a long way
This is the worst journey I've had by a long way.

6 Write sentences with *too* or *enough*.

1 That car is very expensive. I can't buy it.
That car is too expensive to buy.

2 Mike isn't tall. He can't be a firefighter.
Mike isn't tall enough to be a firefighter.

3 This coffee is very sweet. I can't drink it.
This coffee is too sweet to drink.

4 Jake is very clever. He can solve the puzzle.
Jake is clever enough to solve the puzzle.

7 Complete the sentences with one word in each gap.

1 My sister doesn't cook _____as_____ well as I do. In other words, I am a much better cook _____than_____ her.
2 Finn is _____the_____ youngest boy in the class.
3 The smaller the rucksack you take, _____the_____ easier it will be to carry.
4 She walks _____so_____ slowly that people get impatient with her.
5 Yesterday was _____such_____ a beautiful day.
6 I am not tall _____enough_____ to put my bag in that locker. Can you help, please?

Vocabulary

Phrasal verbs

8 Match the phrasal verbs (1–8) with their meanings (a–h).

1	book into	a	**a**	arrange for a room in a hotel
2	check in	f	**b**	exercise
3	check out	c	**c**	pay the bill and leave a hotel
4	head back	g	**d**	drive your car off the road and into a place
5	pull in	d	**e**	sleep at someone's house for a night
6	stay over	e	**f**	arrive and register at a hotel or airport
7	stop over	h	**g**	return
8	work out	b	**h**	stay at a place on the way to somewhere else

9 Complete the sentences with the correct form of the phrasal verbs from Exercise 8.

1 The driver needed a break, so we _____pulled in_____ to a roadside café for a drink.
2 The flight to Argentina isn't direct. We have to _____stop over_____ in Madrid for three hours.
3 We always _____book into_____ a hotel close to the airport the night before we fly.
4 Ellen isn't at home tonight. She's _____staying over_____ at her friend's house.
5 Danny is _____working out_____ in the hotel gym at the moment.
6 It's getting cold, so we're going to _____head back_____ now.
7 When we got to the airport, the first thing we did was _____check in_____ .
8 We _____checked out_____ of the hotel at 1 a.m. and got a taxi to the station.

Prepositions

10 Choose the correct option to complete the sentences.

1 Uncle Jim is *in /* **on** */ within* a luxury cruise around the Bahamas at the moment.
2 Is there a doctor *in /* **on** */ within* board the ship?
3 We travelled south **in** */ on / within* search of sun, sea and sand.
4 Fortunately, there was a chemist *in / on /* **within** walking distance of our hotel.
5 Our team is *in / on /* **within** five points of winning the match.
6 I really hate having to stand **in** */ on / within* line at airports.

21

Collocations and expressions

11 Complete the sentences with these words.

| compartment   crew   excess   gate   in-flight   pass |

1 If you don't have a boarding _____ *pass* _____ , they won't let you on the plane.
2 Please put your hand luggage in the overhead _____ *compartment* _____ .
3 I don't mind long plane journeys as long as there is plenty of _____ *in-flight* _____ entertainment.
4 The cabin _____ *crew* _____ on this plane are very friendly.
5 We bought so much on holiday that we had to pay for _____ *excess* _____ baggage on the flight home.
6 Flight B34 to Berlin is ready for boarding at departure _____ *gate* _____ 18.

Words easily confused

12 Complete the sentences with the correct form of these words. Use each word at least once.

1 | last   late   latest   latter   recent |

a She's the _____ *last* _____ person I expected to see here.
b _____ *Recent* _____ research suggests that time travel might be possible.
c Ben and Dan both showed great ability, but only the _____ *latter* _____ won an Olympic medal.
d His _____ *latest* _____ film is set to become a blockbuster.
e The _____ *late* _____ Dr Evans will be missed by family and friends alike.

2 | combine   join   share   stick |

a We had better _____ *stick* _____ together, or we might get lost.
b It's far from easy for me to _____ *combine* _____ work with leisure.
c Please _____ *share* _____ the water I gave you with your cousin.
d How do I go about _____ *joining* _____ the club?

3 | crossing   cruise   expedition   passage |

a Going on a world _____ *cruise* _____ sounds like fun.
b Scott led a(n) _____ *expedition* _____ to the South Pole.
c The _____ *crossing* _____ from the mainland to the island takes two hours.
d Only the Red Cross workers were guaranteed safe _____ *passage* _____ through the dangerous area.

4 | bank   border   boundary |

a We stayed in a small town near the Mexican _____ *border* _____ .
b This wall marks the _____ *boundary* _____ between our property and theirs.
c As a teenager, he spent hours fishing from the _____ *bank* _____ of the river.

Word formation   suffixes

13 Use the word in capitals to form a word that fits in the gap.

1 _____ *Motorists* _____ are responsible for most of the road accidents in this city. **MOTOR**
2 Our flight from London was delayed, so we missed our _____ *connection* _____ in Athens. **CONNECT**
3 We took a shortcut through a _____ *muddy* _____ field. **MUD**
4 It was windy at the airport, so we had a very bumpy _____ *landing* _____ . **LAND**
5 Any painting by Da Vinci is _____ *priceless* _____ – nobody could afford one. **PRICE**
6 The journey was _____ *considerably* _____ longer than they expected. **CONSIDER**
7 My mum is a medical _____ *consultant* _____ at City Hospital. **CONSULT**
8 Our party will fight for liberty, freedom and _____ *equality* _____ for all. **EQUAL**

Sentence transformation

14 **Complete the second sentence so that it has a similar meaning to the first sentence, using the word given. Do not change the word given. You must use between two and five words.**

1 Felipe and Roberto are the same height.

TALL

Felipe _____*is as tall as*_____ Roberto.

2 Sirius is the brightest star of all.

SHINES

Sirius _____*shines more brightly than*_____ any other star.

3 She can't go away on holiday alone because she is too young.

OLD

She _____*isn't / is not old enough*_____ to go away on holiday on her own.

4 This bed is so uncomfortable.

SUCH

This _____*is such an uncomfortable*_____ bed.

5 Dubai is not nearly as far away as Tokyo.

MUCH

Tokyo is _____*much further / farther away than*_____ Dubai.

6 We could walk from the hotel to the beach.

WITHIN

The beach _____*was within walking distance*_____ of our hotel.

7 When do we have to pay the bill and leave the hotel?

CHECK

What time do we have to _____*check out of*_____ the hotel?

8 Do you exercise very often when you are on holiday?

WORK

How often _____*do you work out*_____ when you are on holiday?

Unit 22

1 **Which of these sentences are correct (C) and incorrect (I)?**

1 I'm a bit worried about missing the flight. _C_
2 It was fairly freezing yesterday. _I_
3 I am absolutely starving. _C_
4 Andy was extremely annoyed. _C_
5 It's very boiling in the sun today. _I_

6 I got up lately because my alarm didn't go off. _I_
7 Hurry up! You've hardly done anything so far. _C_
8 The sea looks beautifully today. _I_
9 Dan always seems very friendly. _C_
10 I'm afraid your goldfish is extremely dead. _I_

How many did you get right? ☐

Grammar

Gradable adjectives

Gradable adjectives can:

- vary in intensity.
*It's **hot** today, but it was **very hot** yesterday.*
- be used with grading adverbs such as *a little, extremely, fairly, hugely, immensely, intensely, rather, reasonably, slightly, unusually, very*, etc.
*The hotel was **fairly big**, but it was **reasonably cheap**.*
- have comparative and superlative forms.
*The Science Museum was **more interesting** than the art exhibition, but the Cinema Museum was **the most interesting** of all.*

Ungradable adjectives

Ungradable adjectives:

- cannot vary in intensity because they are already at their limit.
*It was **boiling** in the middle of the day.*
- are often used alone.
*It was **freezing** in the mountains.*
*I was **furious** when my passport was stolen.*
- can only be used with non-gradable adverbs such as *absolutely, utterly, completely, totally*, etc.
*We were **completely exhausted** after travelling overnight.*
*That meal was **absolutely perfect**.*

> **Note**
>
> The adverbs *really, fairly, pretty* and *quite* can often be used with gradable and non-gradable adjectives.
> *Jason is **pretty clever** for his age.*
> *The book was **pretty terrible**, wasn't it?*

Adjectives and adverbs

We usually form adverbs by adding *-ly* to an adjective.
helpful → *helpful**ly***
quick → *quick**ly***

If the adjective ends in *-le*, we change it to *-ly*.
gentle → *gent**ly***
able → *ab**ly***

If the adjective ends in *-ic*, we add *-ally*.
scientific → *scientific**ally***
dramatic → *dramatic**ally***

If the adjective already ends in *-ly*, we can't make an adverb, so we can use the structure *in a / an … way*.
lonely → ***in a** lonely **way***
silly → ***in a** silly **way***

Some words like *hard*, *early*, *late*, *straight* and *fast* can be both adjectives and adverbs.
*Max is a **hard** worker. He works very **hard**.*
*We've got an **early** flight, so we need to get up **early**.*
*I wanted to watch the **late** film, so I went to bed very **late**.*

The words *hardly* (= barely) and *lately* (= recently) are not the adverbs of *hard* and *late*.
*Max **hardly** does any work. (= he does almost none)*
***Lately**, I've been getting up very early. (= recently)*

Verbs followed by adjectives

Most verbs can be followed by adverbs, to describe how they are done (e.g. *drive slowly / carefully*). However, a few verbs are followed by adjectives, which describe the subject, not the verb:

- *be*.
*Lucy **is** friendly.*

- verbs of 'becoming'.
*Lucy **became** thirsty.*
*David **has gone** bald.*
*It's **getting** warm.*
*You're **growing** up.*
*His face **turned** pale.*

- verbs of 'seeming'.
*Lucy **seems** kind.*
*David **appears** confident.*
*The cake **looked** odd and it **smelled** unusual, but it **tasted** delicious.*
*You **sound** nervous.*
*It **feels** uncomfortable.*

Grammar exercises

2 **Choose the correct option to complete the sentences.**

1 Elena was a bit *annoyed* / *furious* when her friend was late.
2 Are you absolutely *unsure* / *certain* that we don't need to book?
3 We had a very *excellent* / *good* taxi driver in Rio de Janeiro.
4 They were *completely* / *a little* exhausted after walking around the city all day.
5 The view from the top of the mountain was *utterly* / *slightly* beautiful.
6 The restaurant is *extremely* / *totally* popular, so we should book a table.

3 Complete the sentences with the adverb that best fits each gap.

1 That dessert was _____ very _____ good. (absolutely / very)
2 Luckily, the instructions were _____ fairly _____ easy to understand. (completely / fairly)
3 Tanya was _____ utterly _____ furious with Mario. (utterly / slightly)
4 The new restaurant turned out to be _____ absolutely _____ excellent. (extremely / absolutely)
5 It's _____ virtually _____ impossible to find a room in Edinburgh at this time of the year. (virtually / very)
6 Are you totally _____ totally _____ certain that Daniel hasn't been in today? (rather / totally)
7 We'd go outside, but it's _____ extremely _____ cold today. (totally / extremely)
8 The train fair to London is _____ reasonably _____ cheap at weekends. (utterly / reasonably)

4 Complete the answers using these words.

| boiling | cold | freezing | hot | hungry | starving |

1 'What was the weather like?'
'It was absolutely _____ boiling _____ . We had to sit in the shade every lunchtime.'

2 'Shall I make you a sandwich?'
'Yes please – I'm completely _____ starving _____ .'

3 'Would you like to go for a walk?'
'Not at the moment. It's quite _____ cold _____ , and I don't have any gloves.'

4 'Are you OK? Your face is very red.'
'I'm fine, thanks – just a bit _____ hot _____ because I've been running.'

5 'What would you like for lunch?'
'I'm not very _____ hungry _____ , so a sandwich will be fine.'

6 'Why are you wearing three jumpers?'
'Because it's utterly _____ freezing _____ in here!'

5 Choose the correct option to complete the sentences.

1 You look exhausted! Have you been working (hard) / hardly?
2 Late / (Lately,) I've started getting up half an hour earlier.
3 The tour guide introduced herself friendly / (in a friendly way).
4 Do you think Alex is OK? He looks a bit (nervous) / nervously.
5 Luckily, there was hard / (hardly) any money in my purse when it was stolen.
6 I'm not going to eat this chicken sandwich. It doesn't smell (good) / well.
7 You should leave now if you don't want to arrive (late) / lately.
8 I don't want to watch that film. It sounds a bit (silly) / in a silly way.

Vocabulary

Phrasal verbs

6 Match the phrasal verbs (1–8) with their meanings (a–h).

1	let down	*h*	a	go towards a place
2	make for	*a*	b	say goodbye to someone at an airport, station, etc.
3	make out	*e*	c	start a journey
4	run into	*f*	d	arrive somewhere, sometimes unexpectedly
5	see off	*b*	e	be able to see or hear something with difficulty
6	set off	*c*	f	meet someone by chance
7	set up	*g*	g	organise and establish something
8	turn up	*d*	h	not do something that someone expects you to do

7 Complete the sentences with the correct form of the phrasal verbs from Exercise 6.

1 If you listen hard, you can just _____*make out*_____ the sound of music in the distance.
2 We _____*saw off*_____ the twins at the airport yesterday.
3 When he finished university, he _____*set up*_____ his own software company.
4 She walked out of the hotel and _____*made for*_____ the beach.
5 We _____*turned up*_____ in the city late at night with nowhere to stay.
6 What time shall we _____*set off*_____ for the station tomorrow?
7 I wasn't happy when my friend _____*let*_____ me _____*down*_____ .
8 I couldn't believe it when I _____*ran into*_____ an old friend at the bus stop in Milan.

Prepositions

8 Choose the correct option to complete the sentences.

1 We were (at)/ by / with sea for four weeks, and I was getting tired of it.
2 Two thousand miles is a long way to travel at /(by)/ with car.
3 I think there's something wrong at / by /(with)you if you don't like going to the beach.
4 That was at /(by)/ with far the best meal we have had so far this holiday.
5 He was stopped by the police driving down the motorway(at)/ by / with 120 miles per hour.
6 I went into hospital at / by /(with)food poisoning on the first day of the holiday.

Collocations and expressions

9 Complete the sentences with the correct form of these words.

get	give	have	hold	put	take

1 I'd love to _____*take*_____ a trip to Australia and New Zealand.
2 The government has _____*put*_____ limits on the number of climbers allowed on the mountain.
3 What do you think the future _____*holds*_____ for eco-tourism?
4 Can you _____*give*_____ me an idea of how many nights you'd like to stay in each place?
5 Buenos Aires and Madrid _____*have*_____ a lot of things in common.
6 Sorry we're late – we _____*got*_____ stuck in some very slow traffic.

22

Words easily confused

10 Complete the sentences with the correct form of these words. Use each word at least once.

1 | know | realise | recognise | understand |

    a Although I hadn't been there for 30 years, I ___*recognised*___ the house immediately.

    b I don't ___*know*___ what this street is called.

    c It wasn't until we arrived that I ___*realised*___ I'd been there before.

    d In order to ___*understand*___ the map, you need to be able to interpret the symbols.

2 | damp | humid | mild | wet |

    a Where have you been? You're ___*wet*___ through!

    b We'd been expecting lots of snow but it turned out to be a ___*mild*___ winter.

    c Having lived in the tropics, he's used to a ___*humid*___ climate.

    d The old cottage is ___*damp*___ inside because it has been empty for a year.

3 | alive | live | lively | living |

    a My oldest ___*living*___ relative is 88 years old.

    b The match will be shown ___*live*___ at ten o'clock.

    c When the rescue team found her, she was still ___*alive*___ .

    d Having ___*lively*___ children around the house is exhausting but fun.

4 | pollute | rot | spoil | stain |

    a They ___*spoiled / spoilt*___ the whole evening by insulting everyone they spoke to.

    b I'm afraid the drink you spilled has ___*stained*___ the carpet.

    c As the wooden window frames had ___*rotted*___ , we replaced them.

    d If we go on ___*polluting*___ the rivers, all living things in them will die.

Word formation   mixed

11 Use the word in capitals to form a word that fits in the gap.

    1 Please be careful when driving on ___*icy*___ roads.   **ICE**

    2 My travel guides are arranged ___*alphabetically*___ .   **ALPHABET**

    3 His ambition is to have a successful career in ___*journalism*___ .   **JOURNAL**

    4 What a strange ___*coincidence*___   **COINCIDE**

    5 We had a(n) ___*unusually*___ wet April this year – in fact, it was the wettest on record.   **USUAL**

    6 I think it is ___*immoral*___ to tell lies to children, so I never do it.   **MORAL**

    7 We had to ___*rewrite*___ the entire first scene because the director didn't like the first version.   **WRITE**

    8 She stared at her ___*reflection*___ in the mirror.   **REFLECT**

Sentence transformation

12 Complete the second sentence so that it has a similar meaning to the first sentence, using the word given. Do not change the word given. You must use between two and five words.

1 After walking in the mountains all day, we were extremely tired.

COMPLETELY

After walking in the mountains all day _____ *we were completely exhausted* _____ .

2 Eva wasn't just a little bit annoyed with Mark.

ABSOLUTELY

Eva was _____ *absolutely furious* _____ with Mark.

3 Sophie is a very fast runner.

EXTREMELY

Sophie runs _____ *extremely fast* _____ .

4 When I first saw the man, I thought I knew him.

FAMILIAR

When I first saw the man, he _____ *looked familiar* _____ .

5 Sanjay had been waiting nearly half an hour when Priya finally arrived.

UP

Sanjay had been waiting nearly half an hour when Priya finally _____ *turned up* _____ .

6 Let's head in the direction of the hills.

MAKE

Let's _____ *make for* _____ the hills.

7 I'd love to visit Southern Asia one day.

TAKE

I'd love to _____ *take a trip to* _____ Southern Asia one day.

8 They started the eco-travel company in 2015.

SET

They _____ *set up* _____ the eco-travel company in 2015.

1 **Which of these sentences are correct (C) and incorrect (I)?**

1 I wish I know how to speak Arabic. ⊥
2 If only you hadn't lost your address book. C
3 Are you OK? You look as you need to lie down. ⊥
4 It's about time I went home. C
5 I'd much rather to stay at home tonight. ⊥

6 Would you prefer to live in the country? C
7 I rather eat an apple than a banana. ⊥
8 I wish I could fly. C
9 She prefers junk food. C
10 If only you weren't so stubborn. C

How many did you get right?

Grammar

Wishes

We use *wish* to talk about a situation or an action we are not happy about, or to say how we would like something to be different. We use *wish* + past simple or continuous when we talk about the present or the future.
I wish I knew *how to do karate.*
I wish I were playing *football this weekend.*

We use *wish* + past perfect simple or continuous when we talk about the past.
I wish I hadn't slept *for so long this morning.*
I wish I'd been listening *when the coach explained the rules.*

We use *wish* + *would* + infinitive when we talk about other people's annoying habits or to say that we would like something to be different in the future. We use it for actions, not states. Do not use *wish* + *would* when the subjects are the same; use *wish* + *could* + infinitive instead.
I wish the school canteen **would sell** *more fruit.*
I wish the gym **would stop** *putting up their prices every year.*
I wish **I could run** *more than once a week. (not:* ~~I wish I would~~ *...)*

We can use *If only* instead of *wish* in affirmative and negative sentences when we feel especially strongly about something.
If only I didn't have *a broken arm.*
If only I hadn't lost *my tennis racket.*

as if and as though

We can use *as if* and *as though* to say what something is similar to. There is no difference in meaning between *as if* and *as though*. They are usually followed by 'normal' tenses (i.e. present to talk about the present; past to talk about the past), whether we're talking about something real / likely or unreal / unlikely.
Are you OK? You **sound as if** *you're tired.*
After running 10 km, I **felt as though** *I* **was running** *through thick mud.*

When we are talking about the unreal present, we can choose whether to use the present or the past. Both forms are equally good and mean the same.
It's too early for me – it's as if **I'm / I were** *still asleep.*

it's (about / high) time ...

We can use *it's time, it's about time* and *it's high time* + past tense to talk about something that should have already been done in the present.
It's time *you* **started** *doing more regular exercise.*
It's about time *I* **went** *to the dentist's.*
It's high time *Tim* **stopped** *eating junk food.*

would rather

We use *would rather* to show a preference in the present or future. We use *would rather* + infinitive when we are talking about ourselves.
I'd rather run *outside than in a gym.*

We use *would rather* followed by a pronoun and a past tense when we are talking about someone else in the present or future.
I'd rather we went *to a restaurant than cooked at home this evening.*

would prefer and prefer

We use *would prefer* to show preference in a particular situation (not in general). We can use:
- *would prefer* + noun.
'Would you like salad or chips with that?'
'I'd prefer salad.'
- *would prefer* + to + infinitive.
I'd prefer to stay *in tonight.*
- would *prefer* + to + infinitive + *rather than* + infinitive.
I'd prefer to go *swimming* **rather than go** *to the gym.*

We use prefer to show preference in general. We can use:
- *prefer* + noun.
I **prefer fruit juice** *(to fizzy drinks).*
- *prefer* + to + infinitive + *rather than* + infinitive.
I **prefer to eat** *potatoes* **rather than eat** *chips.*
- *prefer* + -ing + to + -ing.
I **prefer doing** *sport* **to watching** *sport.*

Grammar exercises

2 **Choose the correct option to complete the sentences.**

1 Maria wishes she *can* / could type faster.
2 I wish I spoke / *speak* French.
3 She wishes she *learned* / had learned Spanish when she was much younger.
4 I have put on a lot of weight. If only I *didn't eat* / hadn't eaten so much on holiday.
5 If only I could go / *went* on holiday next month.
6 I wish I *bought* / had bought that car a year ago.
7 James wishes he *didn't sleep* / hadn't slept on the beach. Now he's sunburned.
8 I wish Mary *doesn't drive* / didn't drive so fast.
9 They wish I *came* / had come home earlier last night.
10 If only I could come / *came* with you tomorrow.

3 **Complete the sentences with one word in each gap.**

1 I _____*wish*_____ I knew how to dance.
2 If _____*only*_____ I had tried this years ago.
3 He looks as _____*though / if*_____ he needs some water.
4 It's about _____*time*_____ you learned how to cook.
5 I'd _____*rather*_____ cook pasta than boil rice.
6 I prefer to relax at home rather _____*than*_____ do tiring sports.

4 Complete the sentences with *prefer* or *rather*.

1 Do you _____ *prefer* _____ swimming in a pool or in the sea?
2 I'd _____ *prefer* _____ a smaller portion, please. I'm not very hungry.
3 I'd _____ *rather* _____ we went to the rugby match than the football match.
4 You'd _____ *rather* _____ play basketball than volleyball, wouldn't you?
5 Would you _____ *prefer* _____ to play tennis tomorrow or on Thursday?
6 To be honest, I'd _____ *rather* _____ not play with you if you are going to cheat.

5 Complete the sentences with the correct form of the verbs.

1 If only I _____ *had* _____ (have) more money. I'd like to buy that surfboard.
2 She wishes she _____ *had studied* _____ (study) medicine when she had the chance.
3 My father loves sailing. He wishes he _____ *lived* _____ (live) nearer the sea.
4 I wish I _____ *could study* _____ (study). I can't concentrate.
5 I wish you _____ *would come* _____ (come) to yoga classes with me.
6 Amelie wishes I _____ *hadn't told* _____ (not / tell) everybody about the party.
7 Jack wishes he _____ *hadn't eaten* _____ (not / eat) so much. Now he feels awful.
8 If only our neighbours _____ *would turn* _____ (turn) the volume down a little. I can't sleep.

6 Complete the sentences with these verbs and *It's time*.

buy	cut	go	grow	have	wash

1 'My car is very dirty.'
'*It's time you washed* _____ it.'

2 'The grass is really long in our garden.'
'*It's time you cut* _____ it.'

3 'My computer is eight years old.'
'*It's time you bought* _____ a new one.'

4 'I've been working too hard recently.'
'*It's time you went* _____ on holiday.'

5 'My hair is too long.'
'*It's time you had* _____ it cut.'

6 'John is acting like a child.'
'*It's time he grew* _____ up.'

7 Correct the sentences where necessary. Tick those which do not need correcting.

1 I'd prefer eat in tonight.
I'd prefer to eat in tonight.

2 Do you prefer swimming or surfing?
✓

3 I prefer healthy food than fast food.
I prefer healthy food to fast food.

4 He'd prefer to sleep in a tent rather sleep on a sofa.
He'd prefer to sleep in a tent rather than sleep on a sofa.

5 I prefer dancing to sing.
I prefer dancing to singing.

6 Would you prefer to go alone?
✓

Vocabulary

Phrasal verbs

8 Match the phrasal verbs (1–8) with their meanings (a–h).

1	bring up	*d*	**a**	get an illness
2	care for	*f*	**b**	vomit
3	clear up	*g*	**c**	become conscious again
4	come down with	*a*	**d**	begin to talk about a particular subject
5	come round	*c*	**e**	(of a vehicle) stop by the roadside temporarily
6	pull up	*e*	**f**	look after someone who is sick or can't look after themselves
7	stand up for	*h*	**g**	make tidy
8	throw up	*b*	**h**	defend something or somebody from attack

9 Complete the sentences with the correct form of the phrasal verbs from Exercise 8.

1 I didn't feel well on the boat because the sea was rough. I almost _____*threw up*_____ .

2 A car _____*pulled up*_____ next to me while I was waiting for a bus – it was my uncle.

3 Don't forget to _____*bring up*_____ the subject of the lunch menu at the next meeting.

4 I _____*came down with*_____ the flu on the first day of the summer holidays.

5 When he _____*came round*_____ , he was lying on the pavement surrounded by people.

6 His big sister always _____*stood up for*_____ him in the playground, so he never got bullied.

7 Can you _____*clear up*_____ this mess before I cook dinner, please?

8 I was very grateful to the nurses who _____*cared for*_____ me in hospital.

Prepositions

10 Choose the correct option to complete the sentences.

1 By the time I saw the dentist I was *in* / under / up agony.

2 You ought to take up a sport, because you are *in* / under / up really bad shape at the moment.

3 After three weeks in bed, my grandmother was finally in / under / *up* and about.

4 If you're feeling in / *under* / up the weather, why not take the day off?

5 Children are in / *under* / up a lot of pressure to succeed at school these days.

6 Someone was riding a motorbike in / under / *up* and down the street late last night.

Collocations and expressions

11 Complete the sentences with the correct form of these verbs.

apply   catch   hold   lose   skip   take

1 If you _____*catch*_____ a cold, you should rest and drink lots of water.

2 Take this cream and _____*apply*_____ it to your cut.

3 I was late, so I _____*skipped*_____ breakfast and went straight to school.

4 Lie down and I'll _____*take*_____ your temperature.

5 How long can you _____*hold*_____ your breath under water?

6 Nick can't give his presentation today – he has _____*lost*_____ his voice.

23

Words easily confused

12 Complete the sentences with the correct form of these words. Use each word at least once.

1 contest event game match

a I'm not in the mood for a(n) _____game_____ of cards.

b After winning a talent _____contest_____ , she appeared on national television.

c The charity cricket match is the village's most popular annual _____event_____ .

d Several football _____matches_____ had to be postponed due to heavy snow.

2 crest lid peak top

a There was a crow's nest at the _____top_____ of the tree.

b The surfer stayed on the _____crest_____ of a wave for a few seconds before falling into the water.

c At the _____peak_____ of her career, she earned vast sums of money.

d He couldn't get the _____lid_____ off the biscuit tin.

3 direct immediate instant straight

a There are no _____direct_____ flights to Washington from this airport.

b She was so tired that she went _____straight_____ to bed.

c The residents cut off by the floods are in no _____immediate_____ danger.

d I haven't got enough _____instant_____ coffee to make us all a cup.

4 chop grate peel slice

a Could you _____grate_____ some cheese to put on the spaghetti, please?

b I can never _____peel_____ a potato without wasting half of it.

c _____Chop_____ the parsley on this board, will you?

d They'll _____slice_____ the ham for you at the supermarket.

Word formation noun → adjective

13 Use the word in capitals to form a word that fits in the gap.

1 You look _____ridiculous_____ in that pirate costume. **RIDICULE**

2 We cycle more than we drive because it is more _____ecological_____ . **ECOLOGY**

3 That film has a very _____dramatic_____ ending. **DRAMA**

4 I have never had such a _____painful_____ toothache in my life! **PAIN**

5 We found a _____rusty_____ old bike at the bottom of the garden. **RUST**

6 He didn't expect his business to be very _____profitable_____ , but it was. **PROFIT**

7 It is not a good idea to set up a factory in a _____residential_____ area. **RESIDENT**

8 You don't have to study a language here – it's _____optional_____ . **OPTION**

Sentence transformation

14 Complete the second sentence so that it has a similar meaning to the first sentence, using the word given. Do not change the word given. You must use between two and five words.

1 Your bedroom really needs to be painted.

HIGH

It's _____ *high time your bedroom* _____ was painted.

2 I'm not going to the beach this weekend, but I would like to.

WAS

I wish _____ *I was going to* _____ the beach this weekend.

3 Going to the park would be better than doing homework.

RATHER

I _____ *'d / would rather go* _____ to the park than do homework.

4 Sue thinks it's better to ride than to walk.

PREFERS

Sue _____ *prefers riding to* _____ walking.

5 Greg is always protected by his best friend.

STANDS

Greg's best friend _____ *always stands up for* _____ him.

6 I caught a cold on my first day of school.

DOWN

I _____ *came down with a cold* _____ on my first day of school.

7 Mum is finally able to get out of bed again.

ABOUT

Mum is finally _____ *up and about* _____ again.

8 You are always tired because of your poor physical condition.

SHAPE

You are _____ *in bad shape / out of shape* _____ , which is why you are always tired.

Awareness

1 **Which of these sentences are correct (C) and incorrect (I)?**

1 Not only did he win, but he also broke the record. **C**

2 Never she had seen such a boring film. **I**

3 Under no circumstances are you allowed in here. **C**

4 Seldom you see a bear in a suit. **I**

5 Not once anyone came to help me. **I**

6 Little did he know the police were waiting for him. **C**

7 No sooner we had got home than the electricity went off. **I**

8 Only then did he realise his mistake. **C**

9 Not since I was a child I've ridden a horse. **I**

10 Rarely does she swim in the sea. **C**

How many did you get right? ☐

Grammar

Negative inversion

We can use certain negative words and expressions at the beginning of a sentence for emphasis. When we do this, the word order changes. The auxiliary verb comes before the subject. This is called inversion. If there is no auxiliary verb (i.e. we are using the present or past simple), we use *do / does / did*, in exactly the same way as when we're making questions.

*I've **never seen** such a beautiful forest.*
***Never have I seen** such a beautiful forest!*

*Jake **not only fixes** computers, he makes them.*
***Not only does** Jake **fix** computers, but he also makes them.*

*You **are not allowed** to take photos here **under any circumstances**.*
***Under no circumstances are you allowed** to take photos here.*

***We had no idea** that the restaurant would be so busy.*
***Little did we know** that the restaurant would be so busy.*

*You **rarely / seldom see** children playing outside.*
***Rarely / Seldom do you see** children playing outside.*

*The **instructor didn't help** me once with the routine.*
***Not once did the instructor help** me with the routine.*

*I **didn't realise** I'd left my goggles at the pool before I got home.*
*I got home. **Only then did I realise** that I'd left my goggles at the pool.*

*It started to rain **when we got into the boat**.*
***No sooner / Hardly had we got into the boat** when it started to rain.*

*I **haven't done** gymnastics **since** I was at school.*
***Not since** I was at school **have I done** gymnastics.*

Grammar exercises

2 **Choose the correct option to complete the sentences.**

1 Little *they knew* / *did they know* that it would rain all day.
2 Rarely do *I have* / *have I* eggs for breakfast.
3 Under no circumstances *are children* / *children are* allowed here without an adult.
4 Never *she had* / *had she* run so quickly.
5 Not since *they were* / *were they* on holiday had they been surfing.
6 Hardly *they had* / *had they* started cooking when the guests arrived.
7 Only then *he realised* / *did he realise* he hadn't brought his wallet.
8 Not once *did I manage* / *I managed* to hit the ball over the net.
9 Not only *she plays* / *does she play* basketball, she's also a fast runner.
10 Seldom *does he go* / *he goes* into the office these days.

3 **Write sentences with Not only ... , but also ... .**

1 They spent a month in Bali. They also spent a month in the Bahamas.
   Not only did they spend a month in Bali, but they also spent a month in the Bahamas.

2 She owns a large flat in the city. She has a villa in the country, too.
   Not only does she own a large flat in the city, but she also has a villa in the country.

3 She had been spying on the diplomat. She had also given him false information.
   Not only had she been spying on the diplomat, but she had also given him false information.

4 The car is very fast. It is safe, too.
   Not only is the car very fast, but it is also very safe.

5 It was very cold. There was also a strong wind.
   Not only was it very cold, but there was also a strong wind.

6 He's a great guitarist. He's a brilliant songwriter, too.
   Not only is he a great guitarist, but he is also a brilliant songwriter.

4 **Choose the correct beginning (a–c) to complete the sentences.**

1 ___ has Barry won a race.
   a Never   **b** Little   **c** Not only

2 ___ had we sat down to eat than the baby started to cry.
   a Only then   **b** Hardly   **c** Had

3 ___ are dogs allowed in the shop.
   a No sooner   **b** Little   **c** Under no circumstances

4 ___ did I know they had made me a birthday cake.
   a Not only   **b** Little   **c** No sooner

5 ___ he been informed, he would have acted differently.
   a Seldom   **b** Only   **c** Had

6 ___ did anyone ask why I was there.
   a Not only   **b** Not once   **c** Little

5 Rewrite the sentences using inversion.

1 I have never had such a great time.
Never *have I had such a great time*.

2 You may not, under any circumstances, leave the room while the exam is in progress.
Under no *circumstances may you leave the room while the exam is in progress*.

3 She had no idea that there was a surprise party waiting for her when she got home.
Little *did she know (that) there was a surprise party waiting for her when she got home*.

4 You rarely see a police officer on a bicycle these days.
Rarely *do you see a police officer on a bicycle these days*.

5 She did not stop once for a rest.
Not once *did she stop for a rest*.

6 As soon as I shut the door, I realised my keys were still inside.
No sooner *had I shut the door than I realised my keys were still inside*.

7 If she had remembered her umbrella, she would have stayed dry.
Had *she remembered her umbrella, she would have stayed dry*.

6 Complete the sentences with one word in each gap.

1 *Under* no circumstances is anyone allowed into this room.
2 Not *only* does he play football, but he also plays tennis.
3 Little *did* we know that our tour guide was actually a professor.
4 Only *then* did I realise I'd forgotten my swimming costume.
5 *Had* you asked for permission first, nobody would have objected.
6 No *sooner* had they unpacked the picnic than it started to rain.

Vocabulary

Phrasal verbs

7 Match the phrasal verbs (1–8) with their meanings (a–h).

1 burn out — e — a remove something
2 cut off — h — b recover from an illness or upsetting situation
3 fight off — g — c lose consciousness
4 get over — b — d slowly stop having an effect
5 pass on — f — e become too ill or tired to do any more work
6 pass out — c — f tell someone something that another person has told you
7 take away — a — g resist
8 wear off — d — h make isolated

8 Complete the sentences with the correct form of the phrasal verbs from Exercise 7.

1 The flood waters rose so high that our whole village was *cut off* from the surrounding villages.
2 When you tell Maria the news, you can be sure she'll *pass* it *on*!
3 It took a few months for Ben to *get over* his broken leg.
4 It was so hot that day that many of the spectators *passed out* and had to be taken to hospital.
5 You need to take some time off soon, or you might *burn out*.
6 There are many different drugs you can take to *fight off* the flu these days.
7 As the effects of the painkillers *wore off*, I became more and more uncomfortable.
8 My parents *took away* my tablet as punishment for failing all of my exams.

Prepositions

9 Choose the correct option to complete the sentences.

1 Are you allergic *for* / *from* / *to* dairy products?
2 Perhaps he will benefit *of* / *from* / *to* a course of vitamin tablets.
3 If you have had all your vaccinations, you should be immune *for* / *from* / *to* all the major childhood diseases.
4 It didn't take long for Rosie to get sick *of* / *from* / *to* the hospital food.
5 Fortunately, I don't suffer *for* / *from* / *to* any allergies.
6 A lack *of* / *from* / *to* vitamin C is one reason why your teeth bleed when you brush them.

Collocations and expressions

10 Complete the sentences with these words.

| birth breath good shape stomach what |

1 I try to keep in _____*shape*_____ by cycling to work and running twice a week.
2 Do you think a walk in the forest would do you _____*good*_____ ?
3 Kate has an upset _____*stomach*_____ , so she doesn't feel like eating.
4 Alex is out of _____*breath*_____ because he's just been running.
5 Laura gave _____*birth*_____ to a baby boy at four o'clock this morning.
6 As the saying goes: you are _____*what*_____ you eat!

Words easily confused

11 Complete the sentences with the correct form of these words. Use each word at least once.

1 | base bed bottom end |

a Apparently, there is a lot of treasure lying on the sea _____*bed*_____ .
b There must be several unknown species living at the _____*bottom*_____ of the ocean.
c The statue stands on a marble _____*base*_____ .
d Many people have predicted the _____*end*_____ of the world.

2 | cure heal recover treat |

a He was taken to Walton Hospital, where he was _____*treated*_____ for shock.
b It'll take time for her to _____*recover*_____ from her injuries.
c The wound _____*healed / has healed*_____ more quickly than I anticipated.
d If this stuff doesn't _____*cure*_____ you, I don't know what will.

3 | close draw shut turn off |

a Talks are going smoothly and we hope to _____*close*_____ the deal this evening.
b _____*Turn off*_____ the radio for a moment.
c Please _____*shut*_____ the door on the way out.
d When it gets dark, _____*draw*_____ the curtains.

4 | complete total whole |

a It took three _____*whole*_____ weeks to repair the robot.
b They won't stop until the work is _____*complete*_____ .
c The _____*total*_____ number of students present is 91.
d I'll give you £50 for the _____*whole*_____ lot.
e These volumes contain the _____*complete*_____ works of Shakespeare.
f You must tell the _____*whole*_____ truth.

24

Word formation   mixed

12 **Complete the sentences with a form of the word in capitals**

1   What a _____ colourful _____ dress you're wearing tonight!   **COLOUR**

2   Anna's _____ disability _____ has never prevented her doing the things she really   **DISABLE**
    wants to do.

3   The children complained _____ continuously _____ throughout the entire car journey.   **CONTINUE**

4   Tragically, there were no _____ survivors _____ of the accident.   **SURVIVE**

5   I couldn't get rid of the horrible feeling of _____ sickness _____ I had since I'd woken up.   **SICK**

6   Germs enter your blood _____ invisibly _____ , and that is how you catch the disease.   **VISIBLE**

7   Some people have a dangerous _____ reaction _____ to nuts.   **REACT**

8   He is an imaginative child, but he sometimes has difficulty in distinguishing
    _____ reality _____ from fantasy.   **REAL**

Sentence transformation

13 **Complete the second sentence so that it has a similar meaning to the first sentence, using the word given. Do not change the word given. You must use between two and five words.**

1   It only hurts when I laugh.
    DOES
    Only _____ when I laugh does it _____ hurt.

2   You seldom see three-wheeled cars these days.
    DO
    Seldom _____ do you see _____ three-wheeled cars these days.

3   Animals are never allowed in the hotel rooms.
    CIRCUMSTANCES
    Under _____ no circumstances are animals _____ allowed in the hotel rooms.

4   As soon as we switched off the lights, the music started.
    SOONER
    No _____ sooner had we switched off _____ the lights than the music started.

5   He's an excellent cook, and he eats really healthily.
    ONLY
    Not _____ only is he _____ an excellent cook, he also eats really healthily.

6   It was so hot in the stadium that I thought I would become unconscious.
    OUT
    It was so hot in the stadium that I thought I _____ 'd / would pass out _____ .

7   As time passes, the effects of the drug will become weaker.
    WEAR
    The effects of the drug _____ will wear off _____ as time passes.

8   These pills will do you good.
    BENEFIT
    You _____ 'll / will benefit from _____ these pills.

Part 1

For questions 1–8, read the text below and decide which answer (A, B, C or D) best fits each gap. There is an example at the beginning (0).

Modern tourism

Tourism has (0) ___ in for a lot of criticism recently. One common fault found with it is that (1) ___ no longer broadens the mind. But why should it? Surely, the holidaymakers who choose to go on a package tour know just what such a holiday (2) ___ . This is what (3) ___ to them, so why shouldn't they go on this type of holiday? Travel writers generally (4) ___ down on them because of their lack of adventure – 'all they want is a room with a sea view!' But what if they don't want broader minds? Maybe they choose these holiday (5) ___ because their minds can't get any broader!

Another criticism levelled at tourism concerns the changes (6) ___ at holiday destinations: the local culture changes, land is developed and (7) ___ roads are built. The tourist is provided with a copy of the place he or she has just left, plus service. So why should there be any criticism? The world is changing rapidly and neither you nor I have the (8) ___ to stop it. Or do we … ?

0	(A) come	B	gone	C	stayed	D	been
1	A journey	B	voyage	(C)	travel	D	expedition
2	(A) involves	B	forms	C	consists	D	holds
3	A draws	B	pleases	C	attracts	(D)	appeals
4	A see	(B)	look	C	let	D	keep
5	(A) resorts	B	ports	C	places	D	shores
6	A watched	B	viewed	(C)	observed	D	glanced
7	A principal	B	significant	(C)	main	D	chief
8	(A) ability	B	qualification	C	skill	D	talent

Part 2

For questions 9–16, read the text below and think of the word which best fits each gap. Use only one word in each gap. There is an example at the beginning (0).

The other point of view

Very often a disagreement (0) _between_ two friends, neighbours or colleagues can lead to problems. In order to avoid falling (9) _out_ with a friend, neighbour or workmate, it is always an excellent idea to try to see the other person's point of view. If you carefully consider how (10) _someone / somebody_ else thinks, your own thinking might improve, so write down the views your friend, neighbour or colleague is likely to have. Not only will their thoughts surprise you, but you may (11) _also_ find a solution to the problem.

Recently a friend of mine bought a new printer. The dealer in the shop had recommended it, but she was let (12) _down_ when she found out it was no better than her old one. Before taking it back, she had a thought. She realised that if the dealer was criticised, he (13) _would / might / could_ be offended. So, instead of complaining, she said that she had (14) _made_ a mistake by not asking for the right printer. The dealer changed it free of charge. If my friend (15) _had_ not handled the problem in this way, the dealer would not have provided her (16) _with_ a free replacement.

Part 3

For questions 17–24, read the text below. Use the word given in capitals at the end of some of the lines to form a word that fits in the gap in the same line. There is an example at the beginning (0).

A stressful time

Life is stressful for all of us sometimes. However, most of us would agree that the most

(0) _confusing_ time in a person's life is adolescence. It is a time when   **CONFUSE**

(17) _choices_ that will affect a person's future have to be made. Perhaps this is   **CHOOSE**

unfortunate, because it is also the time when teenagers are so distracted by other things that they

may not be capable of making such decisions. (18) _Independence_ comes at a time when   **DEPEND**

it is most difficult to handle.

These two factors, together with the pressure to be academically (19) _successful_ , can   **SUCCESS**

mean that sometimes teenagers behave badly when they are subject to (20) _criticism_ .   **CRITIC**

All too often adults regard those in their teens as being (21) _thoughtless_ , and make   **THINK**

continuous (22) _complaints_ about their attitude towards older people. Yet, if an adult   **COMPLAIN**

under stress behaves unnaturally at any time, things are different. (23) _Rudeness_ from   **RUDE**

an adult, for example, may be excused because they are under pressure. Why is this? People tend

to lose (24) _sight_ of the fact that adolescents are also under great pressure when   **SEE**

going through this difficult time of their lives.

Part 4

For questions 25–30, complete the second sentence so that it has a similar meaning to the first sentence, using the word given. Do not change the word given. You must use between two and five words, including the word given. Here is an example (0).

Example:

 0 Adam plays hockey. He is also a great dancer.
   ONLY
   Not _____ *only does Adam play hockey* _____ , he's also a great dancer.

25 Many people think that scientists have received signals from other life forms.
   THOUGHT
   Scientists _____ *are thought to have received* _____ signals from other life forms.

26 Taking care of four young children is difficult.
   LOOK
   It isn't _____ *easy to look after* _____ four young children.

27 We enjoyed ourselves at the beach.
   TIME
   We _____ *had a good / great / fun / an enjoyable time* _____ at the beach.

28 What they need to do is form a new committee.
   OUGHT
   They really _____ *ought to set* _____ up a new committee.

29 Be very quiet and you can watch me repair the clock.
   LONG
   You can watch me repair the clock _____ *as long as you are* _____ very quiet.

30 He drew cartoons before he began making films.
   WORKED
   He _____ *worked as a cartoonist* _____ before he began making films.

B2 Practice: ECCE

Grammar

For questions 1–20, choose the word or phrase that best completes the sentence or conversation.

1 I'm not as sporty ___ you.
   - (A) as
   - B like
   - C than
   - D for

2 The hotter the weather, the ___ it is at the beach.
   - A busy
   - (B) busier
   - C busiest
   - D busily

3 Never ___ such a friendly person.
   - A I've met
   - (B) have I met
   - C I'm meeting
   - D am I meeting

4 If only he ___ about the new rules.
   - A knows
   - B is knowing
   - (C) had known
   - D have known

5 The further he ran, the ___ he became.
   - (A) more tired
   - B tireder
   - C most tired
   - D tiredest

6 I'm not ___ to join the club, it's just for adults.
   - A enough old
   - B too old
   - (C) old enough
   - D old too

7 I'm sorry, you're ___ to watch this film.
   - A young enough
   - B enough young
   - C young too
   - (D) too young

8 That photograph is ___ beautiful.
   - A such
   - (B) so
   - C enough
   - D much

9 The film was ___ good.
   - A absolutely
   - B totally
   - C utterly
   - (D) extremely

10 I need some fresh air – it's ___ boiling in here!
   - A a little
   - B fairly
   - C hugely
   - (D) absolutely

11 Rarely ___ abroad on holiday.
   - A we do go
   - B go we
   - (C) do we go
   - D we go

12 He's the ___ man I know.
   - A braver
   - (B) bravest
   - C most brave
   - D more brave

13 It's ___ time you learned to swim!
   - (A) high
   - B low
   - C tall
   - D around

14 I prefer ___ rather than take public transport.
   - A driving
   - B drive
   - C driven
   - (D) to drive

15 That was ___ ride ever!
   - A the excitingest
   - B the more exciting
   - C the exciting
   - (D) the most exciting

16 ___ there been such a celebration in this house!
   - A There never
   - B Has ever
   - (C) Never has
   - D Has never

17 'Shall we go out?'
   '___ stay in.'
   - (A) I'd rather
   - B I've rather
   - C I'm rather
   - D I'll rather

18 You're ___ baby!
   - (A) such a
   - B so
   - C such
   - D so a

19 Not ___ do they misbehave, but they won't eat!
   - A just
   - B solely
   - C alone
   - (D) only

20 We arrived later ___ anyone.
   - A as
   - B like
   - (C) than
   - D for

Vocabulary

For questions 21–40, choose the word or phrase that most appropriately completes the sentence.

21 I like to ___ out in the gym three times a week.
   A check
   B work
   C pull
   D figure

22 You shouldn't ___ breakfast – it's important.
   A jump
   B skip
   C leap
   D hop

23 What time do we have to check ___ when we leave?
   A up
   B down
   C in
   D out

24 Why do we always have to stand in ___ for ages in this place?
   A line
   B queue
   C row
   D wait

25 Rosie always stands ___ for her sister at school.
   A in
   B out
   C up
   D down

26 I'm already sick ___ boiled eggs for breakfast.
   A from
   B to
   C of
   D about

27 She's exhausted – she's just ___ birth.
   A given
   B taken
   C kept
   D had

28 I've had a(n) ___ stomach, so I'll just have toast.
   A anxious
   B sad
   C tired
   D upset

29 When the sun came out, they made ___ the beach.
   A out
   B for
   C off
   D away

30 I couldn't ___ what the words said.
   A make out
   B make off
   C make up
   D make over

31 How long were you ___ sea for?
   A on
   B in
   C by
   D at

32 She passed ___ in fright at the sight of the shark.
   A out
   B off
   C under
   D up

33 He ___ up this company at the age of 20.
   A made
   B did
   C put
   D set

34 I hope you've booked us ___ a nice hotel.
   A up
   B into
   C over
   D in

35 When did you come ___ with this cold?
   A down
   B up
   C over
   D across

36 It's a long way to walk, but it's ___ cycling distance.
   A in
   B with
   C within
   D on

37 Oh no! We've ___ stuck behind a tractor!
   A given
   B got
   C put
   D taken

38 Call a doctor. I'm ___ agony!
   A under
   B with
   C in
   D on

39 Dan will call you later – he's ___ his voice!
   A lost
   B missed
   C held
   D taken

40 I'm trying to ___ off the flu at the moment, but I'm not succeeding.
   A push
   B battle
   C box
   D fight

Irregular verbs

Infinitive	Past simple	Past participle
be	was / were	been
beat	beat	beaten
become	became	become
begin	began	begun
bite	bit	bitten
blow	blew	blown
break	broke	broken
bring	brought	brought
broadcast	broadcast	broadcast
build	built	built
burn	burned / burnt	burned / burnt
buy	bought	bought
can	could	–
catch	caught	caught
choose	chose	chosen
come	came	come
cost	cost	cost
cut	cut	cut
deal	dealt	dealt
do	did	done
draw	drew	drawn
dream	dreamed / dreamt	dreamed / dreamt
drink	drank	drunk
drive	drove	driven
eat	ate	eaten
fall	fell	fallen
feed	fed	fed
feel	felt	felt
fight	fought	fought
find	found	found
fly	flew	flown
forbid	forbade	forbidden
forget	forgot	forgotten
freeze	froze	frozen
get	got	got
give	gave	given
go	went	gone
grow	grew	grown
hang	hung	hung
have	had	had
hear	heard	heard
hide	hid	hidden
hit	hit	hit
hold	held	held
hurt	hurt	hurt
keep	kept	kept
know	knew	known
learn	learned / learnt	learned / learnt
leave	left	left
lend	lent	lent
let	let	let

Infinitive	Past simple	Past participle
lie	lay	lain
light	lit	lit
lose	lost	lost
make	made	made
mean	meant	meant
meet	met	met
mow	mowed	mowed / mown
pay	paid	paid
prove	proved	proven
put	put	put
read	read (pronounced /red/)	read (pronounced /red/)
ride	rode	ridden
ring	rang	rung
run	ran	run
say	said	said
see	saw	seen
sell	sold	sold
send	sent	sent
set	set	set
shake	shook	shaken
shine	shone	shone
shoot	shot	shot
show	showed	shown
shut	shut	shut
sing	sang	sung
sit	sat	sat
sleep	slept	slept
slide	slid	slid
smell	smelt	smelt
speak	spoke	spoken
spend	spent	spent
spoil	spoiled / spoilt	spoiled / spoilt
spread	spread	spread
stand	stood	stood
steal	stole	stolen
stick	stuck	stuck
stink	stank	stunk
swim	swam	swum
take	took	taken
teach	taught	taught
tear	tore	torn
tell	told	told
think	thought	thought
throw	threw	thrown
understand	understood	understood
wake	woke	woken
wear	wore	worn
win	won	won
write	wrote	written

Phrasal verbs

act as	=	do a job for a short time	(U17)
add to	=	increase the size, number or amount of something	(U15)
back up	=	make a spare copy of something on a computer	(U9)
be taken in	=	be fooled or cheated by someone	(U10)
believe in	=	be sure that something is right	(U12)
block out	=	stop light or noise passing through	(U15)
blow over	=	(of a storm or argument) end without causing harm	(U15)
blow up	=	destroy with a bomb	(U15)
book into	=	arrange for a room in a hotel	(U21)
bottle up	=	hide strong emotions	(U2)
break down	=	suddenly stop working	(U9)
breeze through	=	succeed easily	(U19)
bring up	=	begin to talk about a particular subject	(U23)
burn down	=	destroy something (usually a building) with fire	(U13)
burn out	=	become too ill or tired to do any more work	(U2), (U24)
burst out	=	begin doing something suddenly	(U12)
call (sb) back	=	telephone somebody again	(U3)
call for	=	require or demand	(U4)
call off	=	cancel an event	(U3)
call on	=	ask	(U4)
call round	=	visit somebody's house	(U3)
calm down	=	become less excited	(U2)
care for	=	look after someone who is sick or can't look after themselves	(U23)
catch on	=	become popular	(U5)
catch up on	=	find out what's been happening	(U5)
check in	=	arrive and register at a hotel or airport	(U21)
check out	=	pay the bill and leave a hotel	(U21)
cheer up / cheer (sb) up	=	feel happier, or make someone feel happier	(U1)
chicken out	=	become too afraid to do something	(U2)
chill out	=	relax	(U1)
clear up	=	make tidy	(U23)
come across	=	discover by accident	(U3)
come along	=	go somewhere with somebody	(U3)
come down with	=	get an illness	(U23)
come in for	=	receive (criticism or praise)	(U5)
come out	=	become available to buy	(U3)
come round	=	become conscious again	(U23)
come to	=	the total, when added together	(U4)
come up	=	be mentioned in a conversation	(U4)
come up	=	appear on a screen	(U9)
come up with	=	suggest an idea or plan	(U5)
cut down	=	make something fall by using a sharp tool at its base	(U15)
cut down on	=	reduce the number or amount of something	(U12), (U17)
cut off	=	make isolated	(U24)
date back	=	exist since a particular time in the past	(U3)
do away with	=	kill or get rid of	(U13)

do up	=	fix or decorate something, so that it looks good	(U13)
drop out	=	quit a course of study	(U19)
fall for	=	quickly become attracted to somebody	(U2)
fall out	=	have an argument and stop being friends	(U1)
fall through	=	fail to happen	(U19)
feel up to	=	be well or confident enough to do something	(U11)
fight off	=	resist	(U24)
fill in	=	complete a form	(U17)
finish with	=	end a relationship	(U2)
freak out	=	suddenly become very afraid or upset	(U2)
freeze over	=	(the surface of water) turn to ice	(U16)
get (sb) down	=	make someone sad	(U1)
get across	=	succeed in making someone understand something	(U8), (U19)
get at	=	be able to reach something	(U8)
get away	=	to go on holiday or a break	(U7)
get away with	=	not be punished for doing something wrong	(U5), (U13)
get down to	=	start doing something properly	(U17)
get hold of	=	find	(U10)
get in	=	be chosen or accepted into an institution	(U8)
get on	=	have a good relationship with	(U8)
get out of	=	avoid doing something which you don't want to do	(U8)
get over	=	recover from an illness or an upsetting situation	(U2), (U24)
get round to	=	finally do something which you meant to do	(U8)
get through	=	succeed in a competition or exam	(U8)
get through	=	come successfully to the end of a difficult time	(U19)
get together	=	meet with socially	(U11)
get up	=	stand up	(U8)
give away	=	give something to someone for free	(U13)
give up	=	stop doing or trying to do something	(U11)
give yourself up	=	surrender to the police	(U13)
go ahead	=	start to do something	(U4)
go around	=	circulate or spread	(U5)
go by	=	(of time) pass	(U5)
go for	=	try to get	(U20)
go off (sth / sb)	=	stop liking	(U1)
go off	=	make a sudden loud noise	(U14)
go over	=	look at again, revise	(U20)
go through	=	experience something difficult or unpleasant	(U19)
hack into	=	illegally enter another computer system	(U9)
hand in	=	submit work	(U20)
hand out	=	distribute something among a group	(U20)
hang on	=	wait for a short while	(U7)
hang out	=	spend time with somebody socially	(U7)
hang up	=	stop a telephone conversation	(U7)
head back	=	return	(U21)
hit it off	=	be friendly with someone	(U1)

Phrasal verbs

hold down	=	keep a job	(U17)
hold up	=	rob	(U13)
identify with	=	understand, feel the same as	(U4)
keep to	=	stick with a plan	(U17)
keep up	=	continue	(U17)
keep up with	=	move at the same speed as someone / something	(U12)
key in	=	type information into a computer or other machine	(U10)
knock over	=	hit someone / thing and make them / it fall to the ground (including with a vehicle)	(U11)
let down	=	not do something that someone expects you to do	(U22)
live for	=	have something or someone as the most important thing in your life	(U6)
live on	=	mainly eat a particular kind of food	(U6)
live up to	=	be as good as	(U5)
log in	=	join a computer network	(U10)
log out	=	disconnect from a computer network	(U10)
look back at	=	remember, think about the past	(U3)
look down on	=	think you are better than someone else	(U6)
look into	=	investigate or examine	(U6)
look out for	=	try to notice something or somebody	(U20)
look up	=	find something in a list of things	(U20)
look up to	=	respect and admire	(U6)
make for	=	go towards a place	(U22)
make out	=	be able to see or hear something with difficulty	(U22)
make up for	=	when something good replaces something bad	(U6)
miss out on	=	not have the opportunity to enjoy something	(U6)
move in	=	to start living in a place	(U7)
move on	=	to change the subject you are talking about	(U7)
move on	=	start something new	(U18)
move out	=	to leave the place you live in	(U7)
note down	=	write something so you remember it later	(U20)
own up	=	admit to doing something wrong	(U14)
pass away	=	die	(U13)
pass on	=	tell someone something that another person has told you	(U24)
pass out	=	lose consciousness	(U24)
pick up	=	learn	(U18)
plug in	=	connect a machine to an electricity supply	(U9)
pull in	=	drive your car off the road and into a place	(U21)
pull up	=	(of a vehicle) stop by the road side temporarily	(U23)
put away	=	put somebody in prison	(U14)
put down	=	write someone's name on a document	(U14)
put off	=	make someone dislike something	(U14)
put up with	=	tolerate	(U1), (U16)
read through	=	check something carefully	(U19)
run away	=	leave or escape suddenly	(U14)
run into	=	meet someone by chance	(U11), (U22)
run out	=	use up or finish a supply of something	(U16)
see off	=	say goodbye to someone at an airport, station, etc.	(U22)

see through	=	realise someone is trying to trick you	(U14)
see to	=	deal with something that needs attention	(U14)
set off	=	start a journey	(U22)
set up	=	organise and establish something	(U22)
settle down	=	to start feeling comfortable in a place	(U7)
show around	=	show someone a place	(U11)
show off	=	try to impress other people	(U11)
show up	=	arrive somewhere, usually unexpectedly	(U11)
shut down	=	turn off a computer	(U9)
sleep in	=	get out of bed later than usual	(U12)
slow down	=	go or make something go less quickly	(U15)
soak up	=	take in and hold water	(U16)
speak up	=	talk more loudly	(U9)
spread out over	=	happening over a long period of time	(U4)
stand (sb) up	=	not meet someone you've arranged to meet	(U1)
stand back	=	move a short distance from something	(U12)
stand out	=	be easy to see or notice	(U18)
stand up for	=	defend something or somebody from attack	(U23)
start out	=	begin	(U6)
stay over	=	plan to sleep at someone's house for a night	(U21)
stop over	=	stay at a place on the way to somewhere else	(U21)
switch on	=	turn on a computer, light, etc.	(U9)
take away	=	remove something	(U24)
take off	=	become successful or popular very quickly	(U12)
take off	=	have a short holiday	(U18)
take on	=	employ	(U18)
take out	=	remove money from your bank account	(U18)
take over	=	take control	(U16)
take round	=	walk around a place with somebody to show it to them	(U18)
take up	=	fill an amount of time or space	(U18)
talk (sb) into	=	persuade somebody to do something	(U4)
talk into	=	persuade someone to do something	(U15)
tell off	=	say that someone has done something wrong	(U20)
throw up	=	vomit	(U23)
turn down	=	to make the volume or heat lower	(U10)
turn down	=	reject an invitation	(U12)
turn up	=	to make the volume or heat higher	(U10)
turn up	=	arrive somewhere, sometimes unexpectedly	(U22)
use up	=	take all of something so there is nothing left	(U15)
watch out for	=	pay close attention to something to avoid anything bad happening	(U10)
wear away	=	make smaller or smoother over time	(U16)
wear off	=	slowly stop having an effect	(U24)
wear out	=	make somebody feel very tired	(U16)
wipe out	=	cause to become extinct	(U16)
work on	=	develop and improve	(U17)
work out	=	get an answer or result	(U19)
work out	=	exercise	(U21)

Prepositions

(be / make) aware **of**	(U15)	**by** far	(U3), (U22)	**on** sb's behalf	(U6)
(be) accused **of**	(U14)	**by** heart	(U3)	**on** the phone	(U9)
(be) **against** sth	(U20)	concentrate **on**	(U2)	pop **over**	(U17)
(be) **against** the law	(U13), (U20)	confess **to**	(U13)	protection **from**	(U15)
(be) ashamed **of**	(U1)	cope **with**	(U15)	rely **on**	(U16)
(be) **at** a loose end	(U11)	day **by** day	(U4)	respond **to**	(U2)
(be) **at** sea	(U22)	deep **down**	(U1)	result **in**	(U9), (U16)
(be) **at** the airport	(U1)	discourage **from**	(U15)	ride **up** and **down**	(U23)
(be) bad **for** sth	(U9)	do **without**	(U10)	sentence sb **to** sth	(U13)
(be) banned **from** sth	(U14)	drive **at** (speed)	(U22)	speak **over** the intercom	(U19)
(be) exposed **to**	(U16)	equipped **with**	(U10)	stand **in** line	(U21)
(be) **in** agony	(U23)	experiment **with** sth	(U10)	suffer **from**	(U9)
(be) responsible **for**	(U2)	feel anger **towards** sb	(U18)	suspect sb **of** sth	(U24)
(be) satisfied **with**	(U15)	feel **under** the weather	(U23)	threat **of**	(U14)
(be) **under** arrest	(U13)	find sb guilty **of** sth	(U13)	**throughout** an event	(U15)
(be) **under** attack	(U17)	focus **on**	(U2)	**to** sb's astonishment	(U18)
(be) **under** control	(U17)	follow **in** sb's footsteps	(U5)	travel **by** car	(U6)
(be) **under** pressure	(U23)	**for** a change	(U8)	**under** control	(U22)
(be) **under** suspicion	(U13)	**for** real	(U12)	**under** pressure	(U6)
(be) **up** and **about**	(U23)	**for** the moment	(U8), (U12)	**under** the impression	(U6)
(be) **within**	(U21)	**from** time **to** time	(U19)	**upon** arrival	(U1)
(be) wrong **with** sb	(U12), (U22)	get **on** sb's nerves	(U1)	win **at** all costs	(U18)
a combination **of**	(U12)	get sick **of**	(U24)	with reference **to**	(U3)
a smile **upon** sb's face	(U18)	glance **through**	(U17)	**within** budget	(U12)
a steep rise **in**	(U16)	go **to** hospital **with**	(U22)	**within** the next few days	(U10)
advantage **of** sth	(U7)	hide **from** sight	(U14)	**without** a doubt	(U10)
after all	(U20)	immune **to**	(U24)	**without** delay	(U6)
after sth	(U20)	**in** connection **with**	(U3)	years **from** now	(U10)
all **over**	(U17), (U19)	**in** favour **of**	(U4)		(U19)
allergic **to**	(U24)	**in** general	(U3)		
along the road	(U20)	**in** other words	(U4)		
among other things	(U7)	**in** private	(U5)		
among the most …	(U7)	**in** public	(U5)		
appeal **to** sb	(U11)	**in** search **of**	(U21)		
arrange **for**	(U9)	**in** secret	(U8)		
arrest sb **for** sth	(U14)	**in** writing	(U8)		
as a matter **of** fact	(U8)	increase **by**	(U4)		
as a result **of**	(U7)	just **for** sth	(U12)		
as far **as**	(U8)	know all **along**	(U20)		
at a price	(U5)	lack **of**	(U24)		
at fault	(U4)	lead **to**	(U2)		
at risk **of**	(U4), (U9)	let sb **through**	(U17)		
at sb's disposal	(U3)	move **on**	(U11)		
attitude **towards** sb	(U18)	object **to**	(U16)		
behind the scenes	(U5)	**off** the coast	(U19)		
benefit **from**	(U24)	**on** a daily basis	(U7)		
break a leg **in** two places	(U1)	**on** account **of**	(U6)		
burst **into** tears	(U2)	**on** condition that	(U7)		
by all accounts	(U5)	**on** second thoughts	(U11)		

Collocations and expressions

(be / get) stuck in traffic	(U22)	get straight to the point	(U20)	put an end to sth	(U15)
(be) a bad influence on	(U1)	get the feeling	(U20)	put limits on sth	(U22)
(be) brain dead	(U19)	get under sb's skin	(U2)	put one's life at risk	(U12)
(be) held	(U4)	ghost town	(U7)	put oneself in sb's shoes	(U18)
(be) in agony	(U2)	give a speech	(U4)	rack one's brains	(U19)
(be) lost for words	(U2)	give birth	(U24)	resist the temptation	(U8)
(be) none of one's business	(U10)	give sb an idea	(U22)	save space	(U4)
(be) on good terms with each		give sb the sack	(U17)	see the funny side	(U5)
other	(U2)	give sth a go	(U13)	seize the chance	(U5)
(be) on the edge of one's seat	(U2)	go bungee jumping	(U11)	set an example	(U5)
(be) on the increase	(U8)	go climbing	(U11)	sewing machine	(U9)
(be) out of breath	(U24)	go on strike	(U17)	skip breakfast	(U23)
(be) widely known	(U4)	go to town on sth	(U7)	tackle a problem	(U15)
all over the place	(U7)	have no choice	(U13)	take a trip	(U22)
answering machine	(U9)	have roots in sth	(U3)	take action	(U15)
apply cream	(U23)	have sth in common	(U22)	take into consideration	(U7), (U10)
as busy as a bee	(U16)	have sth on one's brain	(U19)	take oneself too seriously	(U12)
at one's convenience	(U10)	hold a place in one's heart	(U12)	take pleasure in	
best of both worlds	(U7)	hold one's breath	(U23)	something	(U20)
beyond one's control	(U10)	household name	(U6)	take responsibility	(U13)
boarding pass	(U21)	in-flight entertainment	(U21)	take sb's temperature	(U23)
brainstorm	(U19)	jump at the chance	(U18)	take sb's word for	
brainwave	(U19)	keep an eye on sth	(U14)	something	(U20)
break sb's heart	(U1)	keep in shape	(U24)	take the initiative	(U17)
break the law	(U13)	keep one's promise	(U20)	talk of the town	(U7)
build a good relationship	(U4)	keep sb company	(U20)	the brains behind sth	(U19)
build a reputation	(U3)	know better than to do sth	(U1)	the secret of sb's success	(U6)
build an empire	(U3)	knowing one's luck	(U18)	think on one's feet	(U18)
cabin crew	(U21)	lead the way	(U5)	time machine	(U9)
cash machine	(U9)	let the cat out of the bag	(U16)	upset stomach	(U24)
catch a cold	(U23)	life sentence	(U14)	urban jungle	(U8)
catch sb's attention	(U10)	live life in the fast lane	(U8)	use without permission	(U3)
change one's ways	(U14)	lose one's passion	(U5)	vending machine	(U9)
claim to fame	(U6)	lose one's voice	(U23)	walk of life	(U8)
come close to	(U12)	lose track of time	(U14)	washing machine	(U9)
come out of nowhere	(U6)	make a difference	(U12)	what the future holds	(U22)
community service	(U14)	make a fool of oneself	(U1), (U13)	with regret	(U2)
convey apologies to sb	(U1)	make no difference	(U10)	without fail	(U8)
couldn't care less	(U13)	make sb redundant	(U17)	wolf in sheep's clothing	(U16)
cry crocodile tears	(U16)	miss the deadline	(U17)	worm the information	
departure gate	(U21)	never get anywhere	(U6)	out of sb	(U16)
do damage to	(U3)	not know the first thing		You are what you eat!	(U24)
do justice	(U14)	about sth	(U12)		
do karate	(U11)	open doors for sb	(U6)		
do one's bit	(U15)	overhead compartment	(U21)		
do sb good	(U24)	paint everyone with the			
do yoga	(U11)	same brush	(U18)		
draw attention to oneself	(U5)	pick sb's brains	(U18)		
drop litter	(U15)	play a part	(U15)		
excess baggage	(U21)	play a role	(U3)		
face doing sth	(U1)	play by ear	(U4)		
fish for compliments	(U16)	play chess	(U11)		
get a promotion	(U17)	play volleyball	(U11)		

Word formation

Adjective → adjective

TINY	TINIEST	U10

Adjective → noun

ABSENT	ABSENCE	U20
ANXIOUS	ANXIETY	U2
BRAVE	BRAVERY	U9
DIFFERENT	DIFFERENCE	U2
DISTANT	DISTANCE	U2
EQUAL	EQUALITY	U21
FESTIVE	FESTIVITIES	U3
FIT	FITNESS	U2
FRIENDLY	UNFRIENDLINESS	U20
HONEST	DISHONESTY	U12
KIND	KINDNESS	U10
LAZY	LAZINESS	U18
MAD	MADNESS	U2
ORIGINAL	ORIGINS	U3
POPULAR	POPULARITY	U2
REAL	REALITY	U10, U24
RESPONSIBLE	RESPONSIBILITY	U18
SAFE	SAFETY	U2
SICK	SICKNESS	U24
STRONG	STRENGTH	U2
TENSE	TENSION	U2
TRADITIONAL	TRADITIONS	U3
TRUE	TRUTH	U2
WEAK	WEAKNESS	U11

Adjective → opposite adjective

ATTRACTIVE	UNATTRACTIVE	U7
FORMAL	INFORMAL	U7
HONEST	DISHONEST	U7
LEGAL	ILLEGAL	U7, U13
LIKELY	UNLIKELY	U7
MORAL	IMMORAL	U22
ORDINARY	EXTRAORDINARY	U7
ORGANISED	DISORGANISED	U7
POLITE	IMPOLITE	U7
POSSIBLE	IMPOSSIBLE	U12
REGULAR	IRREGULAR	U7
RESPONSIBLE	IRRESPONSIBLE	U7

Adjective → verb

SPECIAL	SPECIALISE	U11

Adverbs

ACCIDENT	ACCIDENTALLY	U10
ALPHABET	ALPHABETICALLY	U22
ATTRACTIVE	UNATTRACTIVELY	U16
AUTOMATIC	AUTOMATICALLY	U8
CARE	CARELESSLY	U8
COMFORT	COMFORTABLY	U8
CONSCIOUS	UNCONSCIOUSLY	U8
CONSIDER	CONSIDERABLY	U21
CONTINUE	CONTINUOUSLY	U24
CONTROVERSY	CONTROVERSIALLY	U16
DANGER	DANGEROUSLY	U8
EXTRAORDINARY	EXTRAORDINARILY	U8
FOOL	FOOLISHLY	U16
FURY	FURIOUSLY	U16
GENERAL	GENERALLY	U8
GUILT	GUILTILY	U16
IRRITATE	IRRITATINGLY	U16
MEMORY	MEMORABLY	U16
OFFEND	OFFENSIVELY	U8
REPEAT	REPEATEDLY	U8
SKILL	SKILFULLY	U16
STEADY	STEADILY	U8
SUIT	SUITABLY	U19
THOUGHT	THOUGHTFULLY	U12
TRUE	TRULY	U10
USUAL	UNUSUALLY	U22
VIRTUAL	VIRTUALLY	U10
VISIBLE	INVISIBLY	U24

Noun → adjective		
AMAZEMENT	AMAZED	U1
COLOUR	COLOURFUL	U24
CONFIDENCE	CONFIDENT	U1
DANGER	ENDANGERED	U15
DESPAIR	DESPERATE	U1
DRAMA	DRAMATIC	U15, U23
ECOLOGY	ECOLOGICAL	U15, U23
EMBARRASSMENT	EMBARRASSED	U1
END	ENDLESS	U12
FRUSTRATION	FRUSTRATED	U1
GUILT	GUILTY	U1
ICE	ICY	U22
JOY	OVERJOYED	U1
LUCK	LUCKY	U9
MASS	MASSIVE	U15
MEMORY	MEMORABLE	U11
MUD	MUDDY	U21
OPTION	OPTIONAL	U23
PAIN	PAINFUL	U23
POWER	POWERFUL	U9
PRICE	PRICELESS	U21
PROFIT	PROFITABLE	U23
REASON	REASONABLE	U20
RELIEF	RELIEVED	U1
RESIDENT	RESIDENTIAL	U23
RIDICULE	RIDICULOUS	U23
RUST	RUSTY	U23
SENSE	SENSITIVE	U1
SYMPATHY	SYMPATHETIC	U1
TRICK	TRICKIEST	U19
WIRE	WIRELESS	U9

Noun → noun		
ACT	ACTION	U6
BAKER	BAKERY	U6
BLOG	BLOGGERS	U6
BURGLAR	BURGLARY	U13
CHAMPION	CHAMPIONSHOP	U20
CHARACTER	CHARACTERISTIC	U6
CRIME	CRIMINAL	U13
CRITIC	CRITICISM	U6
ECONOMY	ECONOMIST	U12
EXAM	EXAMINER	U6
FRIEND	FRIENDSHIP	U6
JOURNAL	JOURNALISM	U22
MEMBER	MEMBERSHIP	U11
MOTOR	MOTORISTS	U21
NATION	NATIONALITY	U6
NOVEL	NOVELIST	U19
PARTNER	PARTNERSHIP	U9
PRESENT	PRESENCE	U12
SCIENCE	SCIENTISTS	U6
SPONSOR	SPONSORSHIP	U6
TERROR	TERRORISM	U13

Noun → verb		
APOLOGY	APOLOGISE	U4
CLASS	CLASSIFY	U4
COURAGE	ENCOURAGE	U4
CRITIC	CRITICISE	U4
MEMORY	MEMORISE	U20
PROOF	PROVE	U4
RELIEF	RELIEVE	U4
SUCCESS	SUCCEED	U4
TERROR	TERRORISE	U4

Prefixes		
ADVANTAGE	DISADVANTAGE	U18
AGREE	DISAGREE	U12
APPEAR	DISAPPEAR	U17
APPROVE	DISAPPROVAL	U17
BUILD	REBUILD	U17
CREDIBLE	INCREDIBLE	U17
EMPLOY	UNEMPLOYED	U17
LIKE	DISLIKE	U11
PATIENT	IMPATIENT	U17
PAY	REPAY	U17
UNDERSTAND	MISUNDERSTANDING	U17
WRITE	REWRITE	U22

Verb → noun		
AMAZE	AMAZEMENT	U11
ANALYSE	ANALYST	U18
ASSESS	ASSESSMENT	U19
ATTACH	ATTACHMENT	U9
COINCIDE	COINCIDENCE	U22
CONCLUDE	CONCLUSION	U14
CONNECT	CONNECTION	U21
CONSULT	CONSULTANT	U21
CORRECT	CORRECTIONS	U20
DECIDE	DECISION	U14
DELIVER	DELIVERY	U18
DETERMINE	DETERMINATION	U5
DISABLE	DISABILITY	U24
DISCOVER	DISCOVERY	U19
ENCOURAGE	ENCOURAGEMENT	U5, U20
FAIL	FAILURE	U5
GOVERN	GOVERNMENT	U9
GRADUATE	GRADUATION	U19
INFLUENCE	INFLUENCE	U5
INSPIRE	INSPIRATION	U5
JUDGE	JUDGEMENT	U18
LAND	LANDING	U21
OCCUPY	OCCUPATION	U14
OFFEND	OFFENCE	U13
OFFEND	OFFENDER	U14
OPERATE	OPERATION	U14
PERFORM	PERFORMERS	U10
PHOTOGRAPH	PHOTOGRAPHER	U14
PREFER	PREFERENCE	U12
PROVE	PROOF	U14
PUNISH	PUNISHMENT	U13
REACT	REACTION	U24
REALISE	REALITY	U5
RECEIVE	RECEPTION	U3
REFER	REFERENCE	U20
REFLECT	REFLECTION	U22
RELATE	RELATIONSHIP	U18
RETIRE	RETIREMENT	U18
ROB	ROBBERY	U13
SIGNIFY	SIGNIFICANCE	U14
SPECTATE	SPECTACLE	U3
SPONSOR	SPONSOR	U5
SUCCEED	SUCCESS	U5
SURVIVE	SURVIVORS	U24

Verb → adjective		
ACCEPT	UNACCEPTABLE	U15
AMAZE	AMAZING	U9
BENEFIT	BENEFICIAL	U19
COMPETE	COMPETITIVE	U11
EDUCATE	EDUCATIONAL	U15
HELP	UNHELPFUL	U19
LIVE	ALIVE	U10
RENEW	RENEWABLE	U15
SIGNIFY	SIGNIFICANT	U3
SUIT	SUITABLE	U3
SUSPECT	SUSPICIOUS	U11, U13
USE	USELESS	U15
VARY	VARIOUS	U3

National Geographic Learning,
a Cengage Company

New Close-up English in Use B2 Teacher's Book,
Second Edition
Author: David McKeegan

Additional material: Helen Kidd

Program Director: Sharon Jervis
Editorial Manager: Claire Merchant
Project Manager: Adele Moss
Head of Strategic Marketing: Charlotte Ellis
Head of Production and Design: Celia Jones
Content Project Manager: Nick Lowe
Manufacturing Manager: Eyvett Davis
Cover Design: Geoff Ward
Compositors: Jonathan Bargus, Elisabeth Heissler,
  and Geoff Ward

Teacher's Edition:
ISBN: 978-1-473-78637-0

National Geographic Learning
Cheriton House, North Way,
Andover, Hampshire, SP10 5BE
United Kingdom

Locate your local office at **international.cengage.com/region**

Visit National Geographic Learning online at **ELTNGL.com**
Visit our corporate website at **www.cengage.com**

CREDITS

Photos: 10 © Westend61/Getty Images; **16** © SpeedKingz/Shutterstock; **43** © monkeybusinessimages/iStockphoto; **49** © fizkes/iStockphoto; **50** © your personal camera obscura/Moment/Getty Images; **51** © CoffeeAndMilk/E+/Getty Images; **61** © anyaivanova/Shutterstock; **67** © peshkov/iStockphoto; **68** © narvikk/iStockphoto; **73** © IM_photo/Shutterstock; **79** © shannonstent/iStockphoto; **80** © imagenavi/Getty Images; **101** © anatoliy_gleb/Shutterstock; **106** balipadma/Shutterstock; **110** © amenic181/iStockphoto; **126** © Africa Studio/Shutterstock; **129** © Panther Media GmbH/Alamy Stock Photo; **149** © Ashraf Salah Eldin/Eyeem/Getty Images; **150** © Ghulam Hussain/iStockphoto; **155** © simonkr//iStockphoto; **157** © Johan Swanepoel/Alamy Stock Photo; **161** © Tashi-Delek/iStockphoto; **162** © FatCamera/iStockphoto.

ON THE COVER

The cover image shows the ceiling of the lobby in the Burj Al Arab hotel in Dubai. It is one of the world's tallest and most luxurious hotels. Guests can choose from seventeen different pillows for the perfect night's sleep!
© Nick Fewings/Unsplash

Printed in Greece by Bakis, SA
Print Number: 01   Print Year: 2022